MODERN HUMANITIES RESEARCH ASSOCIATION
TEXTS AND DISSERTATIONS
VOLUME 88

NARRATIVE AND NATIONAL ALLEGORY IN
RÓMULO GALLEGOS'S VENEZUELA

MODERN HUMANITIES RESEARCH ASSOCIATION
TEXTS AND DISSERTATIONS

Established in 1970, the series promotes important work by younger scholars by making the most accomplished doctoral research available to a wider readership. Titles are selected and edited by a Board of distinguished experts from across the modern Humanities.

Editorial Board

English: Professor Catherine Maxwell, Queen Mary, University of London
French: Professor William Brooks, University of Bath
Germanic: Professor Ritchie Robertson, University of Oxford
Hispanic: Professor Derek Flitter, University of Exeter
Italian: Professor Brian Richardson, University of Leeds
Latin American: Professor Catherine Davies, University of Nottingham
Portuguese: Professor Thomas Earle, University of Oxford
Slavonic: Professor David Gillespie, University of Bath

Managing Editor: Dr Graham Nelson

Narrative and National Allegory in Rómulo Gallegos's Venezuela

by
Jenni M. Lehtinen

Modern Humanities Research Association
2013

Published by

The Modern Humanities Research Association
1 Carlton House Terrace
London SW1Y 5AF
United Kingdom

© Modern Humanities Research Association 2013

Jenni M. Lehtinen has asserted her right under the Copyright, Designs and Patents Act 1988 to be identified as the author of this work. Parts of this work may be reproduced as permitted under legal provisions for fair dealing (or fair use) for the purposes of research, private study, criticism, or review, or when a relevant collective licensing agreement is in place. All other reproduction requires the written permission of the copyright holder who may be contacted at rights@mhra.org.uk.

Copy-Editor: Nigel Hope

First published 2013

ISBN 978-1-907322-79-2 (hardback)
ISBN 978-1-907322-80-8 (paperback)
ISSN (MHRA Texts and Dissertations) 0957–0322

CONTENTS

	Acknowledgements	vii
	Note on the Texts	viii
	Introduction	1
1	*Canaima*: A Plunge into Pessimism	33
2	Alternative Paths to Progress in *Pobre negro*	75
3	*Sobre la misma tierra*: A New Socio-Political Agenda?	117
	Conclusion	164
	Bibliography	169
	Index	179

TO MY PARENTS

ACKNOWLEDGEMENTS

I would like to thank Wolfson College Oxford, the Arts and Humanities Research Council, and the Abbey-Santander Travel Grant for a research trip to Venezuela, for funding the doctoral research on which this book is based.

I feel fortunate in having been surrounded by very kind and supportive people throughout my doctoral studies. I have received invaluable assistance from numerous members of the Spanish Sub-faculty of the University of Oxford. For his unfaltering guidance, trust, and encouragement my first and foremost thanks go to my supervisor, Robin Fiddian. I am also deeply grateful for the very useful advice given to me by my Internal Examiners Edwin Williamson and Clive Griffin at crucial stages of my postgraduate career. A further, very special expression of gratitude goes to my friend and colleague Tyler Fisher who selflessly and with meticulous care proofread the final version of my thesis. In addition to my Oxford colleagues, I would like to thank my External Examiner Philip Swanson for urging me to get my thesis published.

This book would have not been the same without my research trip to Venezuela and Trinidad. I shall always remember with warmth the people who brought me closer to the world of Rómulo Gallegos during my trip. Most notably, I would like to thank Lancelot Cowie, who not only opened his home to me, but also put me in touch with various Venezuelan Gallegos specialists and helped me to acquire indispensable primary material in Caracas. I am extremely grateful to Rafael Tomás Caldera as well for sharing his insightful ideas about Gallegos and for giving me fruitful feedback on my chapter on *Pobre negro*. The management of the Centro de Estudios Latinoamericanos Rómulo Gallegos also deserves a special mention for allowing me access to the Gallegos museum even though it had been officially closed down by the time of my visit.

Lastly, but not least, I would like to thank all those extraordinary people who provided me moral support over the years I was working on this research project. I will always be grateful to my parents, Maijaliisa and Harri Lehtinen, and to my grandmother, Aino Vienonen, for their encouragement and love and for being there through thick and thin.

J. L., August 2012

NOTE ON THE TEXTS

Doña Bárbara, *Canaima*, *Pobre negro*, and *Sobre la misma tierra* are cited from individual editions. The publication details of those fictional works by Gallegos that are merely referred to in passing in the main text are provided in the bibliography. I have consulted these supplementary works in the 1958 edition of *Obras completas*. Throughout this book I use the one-volume, Ediciones del Gobierno del Estado Miranda 1985 edition of *Una posición en la vida*.

INTRODUCTION

∼

> No soy un escritor de novelas ni para solazarme en humanas miserias, ni para evadirme de la realidad; sino antes bien para captar y fijar en obra estimuladora de algún interés, los rasgos característicos de la [vida] cotidiana sobre los cuales debemos poner atención; pero tampoco [soy] un realista, de posición asumida dentro de un encasillamiento exclusivamente artístico, que se limite a copiar y a exponer lo que observó y comprobó [...] aspiro a que mi mundo de ficción le retribuya al de la realidad sus préstamos con algo edificante.
>
> RÓMULO GALLEGOS, 'La pura mujer sobre la tierra'[1]

In this enlightening passage the Venezuelan author, politician, and statesman Rómulo Gallegos sums up the intrinsic connection that exists between his fiction and socio-political reality. Far from being escapist, his novels address a set of socio-political issues that demand to be taken into account. As Gallegos further points out, the overall purpose of his fiction, in his view, is no other than to return something worthwhile to the socio-political milieu that has provided the subject matter for his novels. Gallegos's novelistic production, as the critic Carlos Pacheco notes, can accordingly be best described as 'un intento por conocer y comprender a Venezuela, analizando las causas de sus males, y proponiendo soluciones'.[2] Building on Gallegos's pre-eminent concern for the fate of his country, I will suggest that his novels should be read primarily as allegories of the Venezuelan nation. Yet unlike existing studies on the socio-political aspect of Gallegos's novels, this work will focus specifically on the previously neglected developments that take place in Gallegos's later Venezuelan novels, *Canaima* (1935), *Pobre negro* (1937), and *Sobre la misma tierra* (1943).[3] One of the main purposes of this work is in fact to illustrate how Gallegos's conception of the Venezuelan nation, and particularly its relationship with socio-political progress, changes over the course of these three novels. I will suggest that in his later Venezuelan novels Gallegos experiments with a number of innovative yet realistic national projects of improvement, projects on which he also touches, though more lightly, in his socio-political essays. In addition to looking at national allegory as a concept, I will consider how allegory operates on the structural and temporal levels of Gallegos's novels. I will argue that Gallegos's disillusionment with his previously idealistic vision of the Venezuelan nation, and his consequent abandonment of the relatively uncomplicated interpretation of progress, is mirrored by the increasingly complex manipulations of structural and temporal factors in his novels. As my analyses of *Canaima*, *Pobre negro*, and *Sobre la misma tierra* will demonstrate, this particular type of reading based around the concept of national allegory opens up new, previously ignored dimensions in Gallegos's novels.

A Position in Socio-Political Life

I

Born in 1884, Gallegos's formative years, as well as his years of political and literary activity, span a historical period which is not only marked by the shadow of successive dictatorships but also by profound socio-political change. The rise to power of the *caudillo andino* Cipriano Castro in 1899 did not end the bloodshed and social instability that had characterized life in late nineteenth-century Venezuela; on the contrary, it gave rise to what has been termed yet another 'huracán de violencia y anarquía'.[4] In fact, the armed conflicts known as the Revolución Libertadora, which between 1901 and 1903 strove to put an end to the Castro government, were the most extensive conflicts that Venezuela had witnessed since the Wars of Independence.[5] All in all, Castro's nine-year-long dictatorship is remembered mainly for these violent disputes, rather than for any effective social, political, or economic reforms. As the historian Judith Ewell has pointed out, Castro 'did not envisage an industrialized national economy', but showed instead an evident preference for the old-fashioned and corrupt tradition of granting the monopoly of various industries to his friends and supporters.[6] Indeed, he was openly hostile towards any kind of change: he blockaded foreign investment, showed no concern for the demands for public services, and opposed directly the development of the nation's intellectual life by closing down the universities on several occasions. In late 1908 Castro was succeeded by the notorious Juan Vicente Gómez, another *caudillo andino*, who was to rule Venezuela for the next twenty-seven years. Yet unlike the Castro years, Gómez's time in power was characterized by a period of economic improvements and of revival of international trade, both of which were by-products of the emergent oil industry that changed Venezuelan society for good. As Venezuela became the world's greatest exporter of petroleum, wealth flooded into the country — the Venezuelan government's income rose between 1922 and 1941 from 70,927 to 345,683 *bolívares*.[7] With increasing amounts of money at his disposal Gómez was able to implement a number of socio-economic changes. For instance, as early as 1928 he established the Banco Agrícola y Pecuario with the specific purpose of offering some help to hard-pressed smallholders in the form of mortgages. Also, Venezuela's infrastructure was subjected to significant alterations during this period. Most notably, there were attempts to improve the nation's road network, the construction of the

Transandean Highway being undoubtedly the most ambitious undertaking along these lines. However, many of these socio-economic improvements had little effect on the lives of the Venezuelan masses, as almost no money was spent on public health and education. Besides, throughout the Gómez years, economic and political power remained in the hands of a chosen few while the activities of intellectuals continued to be limited by harsh laws of censorship. Famous for his innate shrewdness, Gómez was aware of the fact that, if it was important to keep one's friends close, it was necessary to keep one's enemies even closer. Consequently, when Gómez learned that Gallegos had been attacking his regime in his 1929 novel *Doña Bárbara*, he tried to incorporate the author into his own political clan by making him the Senator for the Apure State, which Gallegos had described so well in his novel. Because he was unwilling to compromise his political integrity through association with the corrupt politics of the Gómez government, this clever offer of conciliation by Gómez triggered Gallegos's self-imposed exile in the United States and Spain, which lasted from 1931 until the dictator's death in December 1935.

It was only in 1936 that Venezuela opened up to genuine socio-political change.[8] While Gómez's successor, General Eleazar López Contreras, did not dismantle totally the remaining vestiges of autocracy, it was, nevertheless, during his five-year-long presidency that new left-wing parties, such as Rómulo Gallegos's Acción Democrática, started to emerge. Moreover, in the April 1941 elections López Contreras went as far as to allow Acción Democrática (then still known as the Partido Democrático Nacional, or more commonly PDN) to participate by putting forward Gallegos as its presidential candidate.[9] Although Gallegos did not win these elections, the successful candidate, Isaías Medina Angarita, ensured the further expansion of political freedoms. His time in power saw the organization of various opposition parties, which were allowed to express their respective views and agendas openly thanks to the abolition of press censorship. Even though Medina Angarita's open-minded attitude towards politics gained him broad support, making him 'perhaps the most popular Venezuelan President since Simón Bolívar', disagreements arose in 1945 when the time arrived for him to choose a successor.[10] Civilian political parties, such as Acción Democrática, alongside sections of the military rebuffed Medina Angarita's suggestion that the Minister of Agriculture, Ángel Biaggini, should fill his shoes as the President of Venezuela. Out of fear that the progressive thinking that had steered all social, political, and economic interactions of the Medina Angarita period was about to be replaced by a conservative, *gomecista* outlook, the progressive sectors of the military staged a *golpe de estado*, which wrested power from the hands of the Medina government and placed it in those of Acción Democrática. With the guidance of the provisional President Rómulo Betancourt, the new Acción Democrática government embarked on a further modernization programme, which aimed to secularize education and to distribute land more evenly among the peasants.[11] The most important accomplishment of the Acción Democrática programme was, nonetheless, the significant stride made towards genuine democratic organization; in the spring of 1946 suffrage was extended to all Venezuelan citizens, regardless of gender, education, or wealth. And, by the end of the following year, Gallegos had become Venezuela's first democratically elected President. However, Gallegos did not have the chance to enjoy his newly gained political role for long, as he was overthrown in November 1948, after only seven months in office, by a military conspiracy led by Marcos Pérez Jiménez. Following this event, Gallegos was forced to leave Venezuela and spent the next ten years in exile, living in Cuba and Mexico, where he pursued a vehement campaign against the military dictatorship. He was able to return to Venezuela only after Pérez Jiménez's dictatorship collapsed in early 1958 as the result of yet another revolution. Although Gallegos remained concerned about the socio-political fate of his country until his death in 1969, his return from this second period of exile marked the end of his active struggles in the field of politics.

II

Interestingly, Gallegos formulates the key ideas concerning the character and ills of the Venezuelan nation — which he will develop further both in his fiction and through political actions — already in a set of essays that were mainly published in 1909.[12] These essays, which apart from the slightly later 'Necesidad de valores culturales' (1912) originally appeared in *La Alborada*, provide an excellent insight into Gallegos's views regarding the problems and potential of the Venezuelan nation.[13] In them Gallegos addresses specifically the inherent fragility of the very notion of a Venezuelan nation, while also exploring a set of shortcomings, which he deems to be characteristic of the *alma nacional*. Yet in general, Gallegos's tone remains strikingly optimistic throughout these early essays — he does not give the impression that Venezuela's socio-political ills are insurmountable, but rather goes so far as to propose a set of cures for these ills.

'Las causas' (1909) is probably the essay that captures most lucidly the two main factors that stand in the way of, and threaten, national unity. Gallegos identifies *mestizaje* as the necessary precondition for accomplishing anything close to a solid and stable nation, and explains that the mixing of races has not yet effectively borne fruit on Venezuelan soil. As he sees it,

> El carácter de nuestra raza no ha cristalizado todavía en una forma netamente definida; nuestra alma nacional es algo abigarrado y complejo, sin colorido especial ni determinada fisonomía, con todos los matices de las sangres confundidas y todas las condiciones de las razas originarias.[14]

Gallegos suggests rather vehemently that the Venezuelan race has still not established its defining contours, and further draws our attention to the fact that the Venezuelan 'alma nacional' remains a confusing medley of different races and their corresponding socio-cultural conditions.[15] After having identified Venezuela's racial and cultural heterogeneity as a significant factor that complicates the articulation of a national identity, he goes on to illustrate how the 'diversidad de pueblos' poses another important threat to national unity (19). As he explains, because of Venezuela's vast geographical landscape, the nation is strewn with 'pueblos' that are not only 'extraños unos a otros', but actually exist at the very periphery of national life (19). The diversity of regions, as well as the general lack of firm connections to the nation's legislative centre, provokes an extreme form of regionalism, which generally finds expression in the unquestioning adherence to an autocratic regional *caudillo*. As Gallegos concludes, the fact that '[c]ada ciudad, cada uno de los más míseros villorios tiene su caudillo', is extremely detrimental to national life, because a *caudillo* is in essence a figure who stands between 'la ciudadanía y la Patria', that is to say, he is an individual who is capable of gradually breaking up the nation (19–20).

Indeed, as Gallegos insists in almost all of his essays of 1909, each of the deficiencies of the *alma nacional* can be traced back in one way or another to the Venezuelan people's fondness for *caudillo* figures. Venezuelans, as he explains repeatedly, show little interest in organized political enterprises such as political parties or doctrines, they are instead blindly seduced by the personal charms of any autocratic leader who crosses their path. In the essay 'El verdadero triunfo' (49–52), Gallegos further points out that this lack of regard for organized politics has its roots in Venezuelan people's impatient disposition:

> Nuestro temperamento se aviene mal con todo aquello que exija un empeño paciente y prolongado: nuestra obra ha de ser de hoy para hoy mismo, necesitamos apreciar sus resultados inmediatos, ver con nuestros propios ojos el coronamiento final, o de lo contrario no se mueven nuestras energías para el primer esfuerzo. (49)

In other words, Venezuelans find it incredibly difficult to make any long-term plans, and they therefore most often solve their problems through violent and spontaneous actions. As Gallegos notes in 'Las causas', this is why Venezuelans have over and over again opted for war as the way out of their most pressing troubles (16). Meanwhile, the obtuse and militaristic *caudillos* have always been the ones to promote that type of violent solution. Admiration for *caudillo*-figures and an inclination to spontaneous action are not exclusive characteristics of the uneducated masses, but they even determine the nature of politics in Venezuela. Illustratively, Gallegos argues in 'Los poderes' (36–39) that the Venezuelan governmental institutions seem to favour 'más la audacia del aventurero, que los méritos y aptitudes de quien acrisoló su destreza en el estudio y su conciencia en el deber' (37). A similar point of view is put forward in 'Por los partidos' (31–35), where Gallegos complains about how the existing political parties are built 'en torno a guerreros' and show little concern for '[e]l elemento intelectual' (33). As he further specifies in 'Los congresos' (53–57) — which expounds the benefits of giving political power to the people — even the most prominent political leaders, such as Castro and Gómez, are nothing but ignorant *caudillos*. What is more, in the lengthy essay 'El factor educación' (58–81), Gallegos draws attention to the fact that the Venezuelan education system is to a large extent to be blamed for the political phlegmatism of the Venezuelan people.[16] According to Gallegos, rather than aiding the moral and intellectual development of the individual, the system simply corrupts Venezuelans by fostering social, moral, and religious vices and prejudices. The harsh punishments that form part of the conventional Venezuelan educational ideology, he argues, teach the Venezuelans nothing about self-discipline and moral obligations, but make them simultaneously both submissive and rebellious. In Gallegos's words, by the time the Venezuelan student leaves the school gates behind, he already carries within himself 'aquel odio cobarde, que le hará rebelde a toda ley, deber o autoridad, y esclavo de toda fuerza, instrumento de toda tiranía' (75). The Venezuelan education system as it stands thus assures the continuation of *caudillismo* by reproducing individuals with limited willpower and initiative, that is, individuals who can be easily mobilized by *caudillos*.

Yet while the education system in its current form is to be blamed for the persistence of the ills inherent in the *alma nacional*, Gallegos emphasizes repeatedly in his essays that a correct type of education can help to purge these very ills. As he notes in 'El factor educación', education has the power to alter permanently the mindset of the Venezuelan people, 'creando hábitos, que fijados luego por la herencia, vengan a ser instintos, hasta formar un nuevo carácter de raza' (76). Although Gallegos acknowledges that the transformation of the Venezuelan mindset will not take place in the blink of an eye, he seems in his early essays rather confident that it is possible to teach the Venezuelans to respect law and order. As he suggests in 'El verdadero triunfo' (49–52), over time Venezuelans will learn how to exchange their violent solutions for systematic projects of socio-political improvement. Education can thus be regarded, alongside *mestizaje*, as the quintessential foundation for national unity and prosperity. Furthermore, in essays such as 'Por los partidos' and 'Necesidad de valores culturales', Gallegos anticipates the birth of a new type of politicized intellectual, who will help to educate the masses and guide them through the projects of socio-political improvement. This said, some of the responsibility for the successful implementation of projects of national renewal also rests on the shoulders of the masses themselves, as is explained in 'Hombres y principios' (5–14):

A esta obra cada quien debe aportar su entero valor, sus energías todas, toda la decisión y buena fe que pide labor tan alta y todo el desinterés que necesita para la realización de un ideal elevado. Y, no redunda decirlo, ninguno otro más alto y noble que éste: la patria. (6)

As Gallegos points out, the Venezuelans will need to learn to compromise their individual privileges for the collective good of the nation: national well-being can be obtained if, and only if, everyone contributes selflessly towards this higher aim. By overlooking their differences while cooperating in wider-scale projects, the Venezuelans will further lay out the foundations for a democratic society. In a spirit reminiscent of his other early essays, Gallegos does not suggest in 'Hombres y principios' that the Venezuelan nation and its inhabitants are unredeemable; on the contrary, he acknowledges that both have plenty of untapped potential, which only needs to be channelled in the right direction.

Gallegos explores this unreleased potential in depth in 'Necesidad de valores culturales' (82–109). Here he draws specific attention to how Venezuela (and by extension Latin America) can be regarded both as a land of relentless barbarism and as a '[t]ierra de promisión', that is, the cradle of a new heterogeneous race, as well as that of a genuinely democratic society (84–85). Although Gallegos admits that the age-old European cultural traditions can act as useful models, he is clearly convinced that it is the unrefined character of Latin American countries, such as Venezuela, which holds within it the seeds of vigorous cultural and political alternatives. In Gallegos's eyes, even the outright barbarism that characterizes Venezuelan national life has potential, because 'si bien se mira barbarie [...] quiere decir juventud, y juventud es fuerza, promesa y esperanza' (84). On the whole, statements like this capture well the wavering attitude towards barbarism which will haunt much of Gallegos's subsequent fiction; even though Gallegos identifies barbarism as an obstacle that stands in the way of socio-political progress, he nevertheless admits that barbarism is the actual life-force of Venezuela.[17] As my readings of Gallegos's later novels will illustrate, Gallegos is constantly looking for ways to accommodate the inherently Venezuelan traditions and ways of life, which he associates with barbarism, within a progressive agenda which aims to transform Venezuela into a modern and democratic nation.

III

'Necesidad de valores culturales', which was published in 1912 in *El Cojo Ilustrado*, turned out to be the last significant socio-political essay that Gallegos would write in almost twenty years. In point of fact, *La Alborada*, which had functioned as the main outlet for his socio-political ideas, had already been closed down much earlier on, after only three months of existence, because of its opposition to *gomecismo*. However, as the Italian critic Antonio Scocozza has pointed out in his discussion of Gallegos's early writings, as *gomecismo* tightened its grip, Gallegos the essay writer retreated, giving way to Gallegos the storyteller.[18] Over the next ten years or so, Gallegos put forward his socio-political thoughts in a series of short stories that paved the way for his first two novels, *El último Solar* (1920) and *La trepadora* (1925), as well as for his masterpiece, *Doña Bárbara* (1929).[19] Generally speaking, Gallegos remained relatively inactive as an *ensayista* until 1931, when he openly declared his hostility towards the Gómez regime by renouncing his post as Senator for the Apure State. Yet even so, it was the early 1940s that saw his effective comeback as a writer of non-fiction, as he returned to Venezuela from self-imposed exile. Overall, the socio-political pieces written in the 1930s and the 1940s differ from Gallegos's earlier essays not only in terms of subject matter, but also with regard to purpose and tone. While the early essays tend to lace their investigations of the defining traits of the Venezuelan nation and its inhabitants with a fair dose of idealism, most of the later non-fiction approaches specific social, political, and economic issues from a far more critical perspective. Formulated mainly as direct attacks against *gomecismo* or as campaign speeches, the socio-political writings of this period reveal an increasingly politicized Gallegos, who practises what he preaches. Moreover, by recording the shifts in Gallegos's attitude towards socio-political change, which results in him gradually formulating more realistic agendas of modernization, these non-fictional pieces illustrate the same trajectory of development as novels such as *Canaima*, *Pobre negro*, and *Sobre la misma tierra*. Throughout my study of these three novels, I will in fact be paying particular attention to the characteristics that they share with the socio-political pieces, which were written roughly around same time.

Two pieces of socio-political writing, which date back to 1931, reveal a surprisingly pessimistic and resigned Gallegos, who seems to have accepted the inevitability of *caudillismo*. Strictly not an essay, the first of these pieces of 1931 is Gallegos's formal resignation from his post as the Senator for the Apure State. Written in New York, 'Una renuncia' (110–11) presents Venezuelan politicians, and particularly the Head of State, in the worst possible light. According to Gallegos, the political leaders have not only violated the most basic principles of democracy, but they have further compromised the dignity of the Venezuelan nation by presenting it to the whole world as 'una colectividad que no entiende ni quiere ser gobernada sino con los recursos extremos de las autoridades absolutas, como una colectividad rudimentaria que no puede vivir sino a la sombra del jefe' (110). Gallegos closes his letter of resignation by angrily declaring that the main reason why he wishes to give up his post as Senator is because he does not want to have his name associated in any way with this kind of authoritarian, backward, and corrupt politics. However, in 'Las tierras de Dios' (112–44) — the second socio-political piece that was written in 1931 — Gallegos seems to have reached a point where he questions his most fundamental ideas concerning socio-political organizations. Starting out as a rather conventional discussion of the still unreleased primitive potential of the Venezuelan environment, as well as a satirical attack on Castro and Gómez, 'Las tierras de Dios' surprises the reader by gradually turning into a celebration of *individualismo*. In so doing, the essay, which was originally delivered as a lecture in New York, strikes a discordant note with the earlier declarations, where Gallegos specifically argued that individuals should always put the collective good of the *Patria* first. Disillusioned with the Venezuelan people's inability to adjust to political organizations, Gallegos tries to find in 'Las tierras de Dios' at least something positive to say about these very people's stubborn resistance to laws and institutions. Indeed, at one point in his essay he goes as far as to claim that '[la] fuerza', 'virtud', and 'esperanza' of the Venezuelan people lies in *individualismo*, which in his words, makes Venezuela distinctively different from Europe and the United States (127).[20] Curiously, Gallegos does not even try to deny that *caudillismo* — which is built around the cult of the individual — has close ties with *individualismo*. On the contrary, he draws attention to the connection that exists between the two by pointing out that a genuine 'individualista [...] no sabe tolerarse sino a sí mismo y no está tranquilo mientras no haya moldeado el mundo a imagen y semejanza suyas' (134). After providing this definition — which could be used just as well to capture the essence of any self-obsessed and autocratic *caudillo* — Gallegos goes on to explain, using Simón Bolívar as an example, that while on the political level *individualismo* has been generally associated with despotism, not all *individualista* leaders are destructive. In fact, according to Gallegos, good *individualista* leaders are what he terms 'hombres-organizaciones': that is, individual men who, with the efficiency of political organizations, are able to mobilize the masses in socio-political enterprises (138). Gallegos concludes 'Las tierras de Dios' by noting that, considering the willingness with which Venezuelans subject themselves to the authority of any given *caudillo*-figure, Venezuela's socio-political problems could be solved simply by the emergence of one benevolent and effective *caudillo*. Though hopeful in terms that he is confident that such a leader will eventually emerge, Gallegos's acceptance of the continuation of the traditional *caudillo* system is a far cry from the exaltation of democracy, which underlies his earlier essays. As I will explain in Chapter 1, the resigned attitude expressed in Gallegos's 1931 writings also finds its way into his 1935 novel, *Canaima*, which fails to replicate the overly idealistic vision of *Doña Bárbara*, and registers instead a sudden plunge into pessimism.

However, in the socio-political writings produced during Gallegos's increased political activity in the late 1930s and the early 1940s, the disillusionment regarding Venezuela's democratic potential already appears a thing of the past. Written originally as political speeches, the overarching purpose of the writings of this period is to convince the Venezuelan citizens of the benefits of democratic principles. In the 1937 speech 'Soy un hombre que desea el orden' (145–52), Gallegos argues that the political chaos which has followed the fall of Gómez's regime is a necessary stage of political transition; as he puts it, 'era imposible [...] que el país pasara de aquel régimen [dictatorial] a éste, iniciado bajo una amplia promesa democrática, sin que sobreviniera un período de convulsión de la opinión pública' (150).[21] As Gallegos declares repeatedly in this speech, the unrestrained circulation of ideas fostered by democracy does not in itself encourage disorder and disunity. Again, in 'Había aquí una lección por dar' (182–99) — which is one of many speeches that constitute Gallegos's symbolical 1941 presidential campaign — he appeals more specifically to the democratic responsibility of each and every Venezuelan citizen.[22] After pointing out that Venezuelans were very lucky that someone like López Contreras took charge of the nation's politics upon Gómez's death, Gallegos goes on to note that they should nonetheless stop putting their fate in the hands of any single man. According to Gallegos, the time has come for Venezuelans to 'decidir su propia suerte por sí mismo[s]', to which effect suffrage should be extended to everyone, including women (188). Apart from enumerating the various benefits of a democratic system, this campaign speech reveals Gallegos's increasing interest in the role that women should play in Venezuela's socio-political future, an interest which is further teased out in *Pobre negro* and *Sobre la misma tierra*. Yet even though Gallegos's 1941 campaign speeches focus primarily on the need to establish a less hierarchical, more democratic society, speeches such as 'Ante su juicio, yo concluyo y espero' (200–17) and 'Constancia puesta en empeño de iluminación' (218–37) also put forward specific economic agendas. In both instances, Gallegos attacks Venezuela's reliance on the foreign-owned oil industry, while further encouraging the revival of agricultural enterprises and other traditional trades. Although Gallegos does not overlook the wealth that can be derived from oil, he nevertheless believes that the key to national prosperity lies in appreciating the more conventional products of the Venezuelan soil. What is more, in 'Constancia puesta en empeño de iluminación' — a speech delivered to the inhabitants of the State of Zulia, Venezuela's principal oil-production centre — Gallegos expresses a new, approving attitude towards regionalism. Rather unexpectedly, he maintains that the type of regionalism professed by the *zulianos*, which consists of loving one's land vehemently, does not have to be seen as a threat to nationalism; on the contrary, it can be regarded as the most basic type of patriotism (219–20). While this idea is not developed any further in the speech in question, Gallegos does go on to explore the potentially fruitful relationship between regionalism and nationalism in more detail in *Sobre la misma tierra*. As I will illustrate in Chapter 3, Gallegos draws specific attention throughout that novel to the way in which limited regional projects of social improvement can contribute to a more general national well-being and prosperity.

Narrating the Nation

I

Gallegos's concern for finding ways in which to bring Venezuelans together despite their racial, cultural, and regional differences, as well as his emphasis on the need to celebrate autochthonous traditions, suggests that the existence of a Venezuelan nation should not be taken for granted. In point of fact, the concept of a nation has been repeatedly identified as a highly precarious socio-political construction by historians, philosophers, literary critics, and sociologists alike. The French philosopher Ernest Renan argued as early as 1882 that a nation is above all a 'spiritual principle', while the twentieth-century literary critic Timothy Brennan has more recently dismissed the idea of nationhood as a pure 'myth'.[23] Moreover, in the 1980s the sociologist Benedict Anderson famously coined his now clichéd term 'imagined communities' to reflect specifically upon the fictional nature of nations.[24] The concept of a nation, as all these writers agree, is not rooted in geography or in shared values, such as religion, or even in a common linguistic tradition; it is rather the product of collective imagination, a sense of imagined solidarity between all the members of a nation, who in Anderson's words 'will never know most of their fellow-members, meet them, or even hear of them, yet in the minds of each lives the image of their communion'.[25] As Renan in his turn explains, this powerful feeling of belonging together generally has its roots in 'the possession [...] of a rich legacy of memories [and] the desire to live together, the will to perpetuate the value of the heritage that one has received in an undivided form'.[26] He further identifies forgetting as a crucial step in accomplishing this type of nationwide unity, because as he puts it, '[u]nity is always effected by means of brutality', that is, by the violent repression of those who do not agree with the doctrines and ideas of the nation's dominant group.[27] Indeed, in the light of the consensus that national solidarity is nothing more than a collective fiction, every nation is in constant danger of falling back into its numerous subdivisions — the imagined solidarity can be maintained only as long as the majority of citizens place greater importance on their national affiliation than on their racial, cultural, regional, religious, or linguistic differences.

The issue of nationhood appears all the more complex in the Latin American context — as I have already shown in my discussion of Gallegos's socio-political writings — thanks to a combination of factors, including the continent's vast and varied geography, its colonial past, and its multiracial heritage. With the early nineteenth-century wars for independence, which brought an end to Spain's hegemony in Latin America, nation-building became the key word on the lips of the *libertadores*, the military and political leaders of the newly liberated continent. The shared colonial past, however, did not provide enough fuel for the whole continent to be able to imagine itself as a nation, thus leaving Simón Bolívar's dream of a pan-American union in ruins.[28] Yet uniting the whole continent under the auspices of nationhood was not the most significant long-term dilemma faced by the original nation-builders to start with. From early on, the Latin American nation-builders became acutely aware of the need of finding a formula for consolidating the different, often mutually hostile, racial, regional, and social groups which existed within the boundaries of each individual nation. Most importantly, the nation-builders had to invent a fiction which would help to make the discriminated indigenous and coloured peoples forget the past (and present) exploitation, carefully turning them into willing perpetuators of the myth of nationwide solidarity. Writing became an invaluable tool in this process, which aimed to forge fictional national consciousnesses.

II

Numerous intellectuals have expressed an interest in the ways in which writing can help to shape national identities. Although Anderson's discussion of how the emergence of print culture aided the formation of 'imagined communities' focuses mainly on newspapers, he does not completely overlook the role that fiction plays in this process. At one point he specifically admits that 'the novel', just like the 'newspaper', 'provided the technical means for "re-presenting" the kind of imagined community that is the nation'.[29] What is more, slightly later on in his argument, Anderson acknowledges that the novel can act as an effective tool of social criticism and further hints at the potential, wider socio-political implications of fiction by noting that 'fiction seeps quietly and continuously into reality'.[30] Other intellectuals, such as Brennan, have on the other hand suggested that it is possible to perceive a direct analogy between the process of nation-building and the emergence of the novelistic form. Drawing on Mikhail Bakhtin's notions of heteroglossia and dialogism, Brennan argues that 'the *novel* historically accompanied the rise of nations by objectifying the "one, yet many" of national life, and by mimicking the structure of the nation, a clearly bordered jumble of languages and styles'.[31] The novel accordingly became the ideal means for capturing the rich yet often problematic plurality that exists within each nation. Fredric Jameson has addressed the connection between nation-building and fiction from a different theoretical perspective, that is, the even more specific angle of post-colonial discourse. In his widely contested essay, 'Third-World Literature in the Era of Multinational Capitalism', Jameson argues that:

> Third-world texts, even those which are seemingly private [...] necessarily project a political dimension in the form of national allegory: *the story of the private individual destiny is always an allegory of the embattled situation of the public third-world culture and society*.[32]

Jameson's argument that all Third-World literary works should be read as national allegories has attracted a great deal of negative critical attention, owing to its homogenizing and generalizing drive. The most famous attack on Jameson's interpretation of national allegory has undoubtedly been voiced by Aijaz Ahmad in his article 'Jameson's Rhetoric of Otherness and the "National Allegory"', which was published only a year after Jameson's original essay.[33] Throughout his article, Ahmad criticizes the way in which Jameson naively takes it for granted that all Third-World countries must be identical simply because of their shared 'experience of colonialism and imperialism'.[34] He also dismisses Jameson's assumption that this shared experience somehow preconditions so-called Third-World writers to focus on the problems of nationhood.

Even though I find Ahmad's criticisms valid, I think that dismissing Jameson's theory of national allegory as completely absurd is taking things slightly too far. In fact, some literary critics have made half-hearted attempts to rescue Jameson's argument. An important attempt along these lines is made by Imre Szeman in his relatively recent article 'Who's Afraid of National Allegory?'.[35] While Szeman does not overlook the deficiencies of Jameson's argument, he nevertheless identifies Jameson's essay as a 'sophisticated attempt to make sense of the relationship of literature to politics in the decolonizing world'.[36] According to Szeman's interpretation, the underlying purpose of Jameson's theory of national allegory is to illustrate how culture can work as a bridge between the individual and the wider socio-political experience, as well as between theory and practice, in formerly colonial countries that are still in the process of establishing their independent (national) identities.[37] One need only consider the way in which politics and fiction are interwoven in the Latin American context to realize that in this sense Jameson's argument certainly retains some authority: as Luis Navarrete Orta has pointed out, the Latin American intellectual is often known for 'su triple función de pensador social, de luchador político y de escritor'.[38] Not only does Latin American fiction often put forward a distinct socio-political message, but over the years authors such as Rómulo Gallegos, Gabriel García Márquez, and Mario Vargas Llosa have crossed the boundary between fiction and politics, becoming active participants in the political lives of their respective countries. Fiction has more than once provided these writers with a safe ground on which to explore those very same socio-political ideals that they have wanted to be seen put into practice. As already indicated by the opening quotation of this Introduction, Gallegos has personally gone as far as to encourage his readers to interpret his literary production through the prism of national allegory.

Romantic Resolutions

I

Doris Sommer's seminal book *Foundational Fictions: The National Romances of Latin America* (1991) has provided a valuable starting point for my exploration of the central role that national allegory plays in Gallegos's novels.[39] Sommer's ambitious enquiry into the link that exists in Latin America between politics, fiction, and nation-building does not limit itself to the type of generalizations made by Jameson, but presents the reader with a wide range of convincing case studies. Sommer argues that various canonical Latin American novels from the nineteenth century use the framework of heterosexual romance to organize narrative events, and above all, to articulate desirable national projects.[40] She thus labels these nineteenth-century novels 'national romances', the word 'romance' in this instance referring to what Sommer identifies as 'a cross between our contemporary use of the word as a love story and a nineteenth-century use that distinguished the genre as more boldly allegorical than the novel' (5). The main protagonists of national romances are, as a rule, star-crossed lovers representing the nation's competing and contradictory social, political, racial, or regional interests, which through their discord threaten the development of the particular Latin American nation. The union of the lovers accordingly becomes an allegory for the peaceful consolidation of the nation during the post-independence era — with the antagonist being pacified through mutual love rather than violence — as well as the foundation for further socio-political progress.

Yet for Sommer, who draws specifically on Walter Benjamin's theories regarding allegories, an allegory is 'a narrative structure in which one line is a trace of the other, [and] in which each helps to write the other' (42).[41] Consequently, she regards the relationship between the heterosexual liaisons and the socio-political issues in the Latin American romances as 'interlocking' rather than 'parallel'. In Sommer's words:

> Erotic interest in these novels owes its intensity to the very prohibitions against the lovers' union across racial or regional lines. And political conciliations, or deals, are transparently urgent because the lovers 'naturally' desire the kind of state that would unite them. (47)

In other words, heterosexual love and socio-political issues are not two separate affairs in these nineteenth-century novels, but are in fact tightly interwoven: erotic desire is directly stimulated by a specific set of socio-political issues, while the developments in the wider field of politics are presented as immediate outcomes of this very desire. The story of the lovers' longing and quest for an ideal state in which their love would be legitimized becomes a critical summary of existing social restrictions, these restrictions pinpointing the socio-political shortcomings, problems, and contradictions of the society the lovers inhabit.

However, despite their apparent enthusiasm for an ideal state, the polities that are projected in the Latin American national romances are generally 'ideal' only for the more elite of the two socio-political groups being symbolically united through love. As Sommer observes, the socio-political projects that these novels put forward are inherently hegemonic, and correspondingly the societies for which the heterosexual romances form the basis remain profoundly hierarchical. Though the passion of the often feminized heroes and energetic heroines seems to cross and problematize conventional social boundaries, the novels nevertheless re-establish order in the end by holding up the traditional patriarchal family unit as an ideal model for the nation-family. And as the different and often opposing backgrounds of the main couple illustrate, everyone is welcomed into the nation-family regardless of their race, class, political affiliation, or native region, as long as they know and accept their predetermined place within this socio-political construction.

While Sommer's focus is on canonical Latin American novels from the nineteenth century, she nonetheless acknowledges that the end of the nineteenth century did not mark the end of the affair with the framework of heterosexual romance. Instead romance continued to haunt twentieth-century Latin American writers, who despite pretending to reject the framework would in actuality keep on exploiting and manipulating it to meet their own ends.[42] All in all, Sommer argues that transformations in the framework of heterosexual romance can mimic and thus reveal changes in the ways in which nationhood and socio-historical development are conceived. In my subsequent readings of *Canaima*, *Pobre negro*, and *Sobre la misma tierra* I will in fact be building on this theory, as I explore how the romantic frameworks of these novels record Gallegos's changing ideas concerning the Venezuelan nation and its relationship with progress. Yet already in the chapter 'Love of Country' (257–89) Sommer provides a succulent appetizer and blueprint of the way in which the framework of romance can be adapted in response to an altered socio-political situation. In the chapter's key discussion of how the rise of populist ideologies made early twentieth-century authors revise their presentation of the Latin American national romances, Sommer uses Gallegos's earlier landmark novel, *Doña Bárbara* (1929), as one of her two main case studies.

According to Sommer, the pivotal difference between the original nineteenth-century national romances and the twentieth-century populist versions lies in the fact that these later novels mark a movement towards 'a more proprietary and less conciliatory kind of patriotism' (257). Sommer sees Latin American populism mainly as a response to North American imperialism, which posed a growing threat to the political, cultural, and economic independence of the

Southern nations. Populism thus offered Latin American nations a vehicle for counter-attack and self-assertion, often in the form of the celebration of the beloved homeland with its autochthonous traditions — *la novela de la tierra* being the literary response to this passionate 'love *of* country'.[43] In populist novels such as *Doña Bárbara*, love is therefore partly (re)directed towards the land itself, which becomes the female 'other' that needs to be courted, possessed, controlled, and finally, incorporated into the nation's scheme of socio-historical progress. As Sommer points out, it is no coincidence that the novel's eponymous female heroine, the notorious *mestiza*, Doña Bárbara, is the very '"personification" of the seductive land', while her daughter Marisela is also closely associated with the untamed nature of the *llanos* (276–77). Yet the possessive impulse of the populist enterprise undermines even the possibility of a seemingly balanced marriage between projects of development and the autochthonous traits that characterize a particular land. Incorporation into a national project of development implies above all 'absorption', which means that the very autochthonous traits that the populist novels chose to celebrate must lose their explicitly subversive elements. Henceforth, the virginal Marisela, whose domestication is constantly compared to that of the terrain which Santos Luzardo — the novel's civilizer — is trying to rein in with the *cerca*, appears as a far more suitable bride than Doña Bárbara, who can no longer be turned into a productive wife. The novel ends befittingly with the collapse of Doña Bárbara's destabilizing rule, as Santos Luzardo reasserts his patriarchal authority by firmly enclosing both Marisela and the wayward land of the *llanos* within his constraining but progressive embrace.

II

Throughout the chapter 'Love *of* Country', Sommer insists that the centrality of 'the land' in novels such as *Doña Bárbara* significantly alters the way in which the framework of national romance is employed. However, I think that despite all her emphasis on this 'new' trait, Sommer's analysis of *Doña Bárbara* reveals at points an underlying framework of romance, which is even more neatly patched together than that of many nineteenth-century Latin American romances. Indeed, as Sommer herself acknowledges, at the centre of the progressive agenda of *Doña Bárbara* lies the successful, interracial (and interregional) romance between Santos and Doña Bárbara's daughter Marisela. What is more, as she explains in a later chapter, the romance between Santos and Marisela follows an extremely conventional fairy-tale formula; in *Doña Bárbara*, Gallegos transports the story of 'la Bella Durmiente' into a Venezuelan context.[44] Yet, as I already hinted above, what makes the socio-political message of this romance essentially conservative is that its ultimate aim is to incorporate the autochthonous elements into an intrinsically hegemonic national project through 'absorption'. The lack of socio-political change epitomized by the novel's framework of heterosexual romance is further underlined by the patriarchal order, which is re-established at the end of the novel; Santos's rule as the *cacique* of the Arauca region merely promises to reassert systematically traditional (often oppressive) social, racial, and gender hierarchies.

Apart from this somewhat laboured demonstration of how the framework of romance can be altered to mirror a new socio-historical situation, Sommer's general argument seems rather tenuous in a number of other respects. To begin with, even though Sommer's thesis centres on the assumption that heterosexual romance works as the organizing principle, as well as the driving force, of the narratives of a number of canonical Latin American novels, she overlooks structural analysis almost entirely. And on top of this, she does not provide anywhere in her work a coherent explanation of precisely why the framework of romance persists in the twentieth-century novels, whose main concern is no longer national consolidation; the reader is left with the impression that the framework of romance is simply an anachronistic leftover from the earlier foundational fictions. However, the various limitations of Sommer's theory regarding Latin American national allegories do not render her thesis any less engaging; on the contrary, these crevices in her argument leave ground for further exploration. For instance, anthropologist Joanne Rappaport's article 'Fictive Foundations: National Romances and Subaltern Ethnicity in Latin America' demonstrates that the language of romance is not an exclusive property of the hegemonic foundational novels but has been also employed 'in the creation of [the] alternative nationalist dreams' of the continent's indigenous inhabitants.[45] She points out, for example, that during the Caste Wars of the late nineteenth century, the Maya of Mexico tried 'to bridge hostile ethnic relations' by writing love letters to their Yucatán enemies.[46] Incorporating an anthropological perspective, Rappaport's article makes it clear that, not only is the framework of romance susceptible to radical appropriation, but Sommer's theories can be further used as scaffolding for more innovative studies on the socio-political properties of romantic love.

Although I am not convinced by Sommer's argument that *Doña Bárbara* revises radically the traditional framework of heterosexual romance, I believe that Sommer's model remains pertinent and useful to the study of Gallegos's later novels, which express a far less solid trust in heterosexual love as a socio-political solution. In fact, I believe that *Doña Bárbara* can be regarded as a basic yardstick against which Gallegos's later, more complex novels can be measured, and I will therefore treat it as such throughout my study of *Canaima*, *Pobre negro*, and *Sobre la misma tierra*. I will demonstrate that these three novels are particularly susceptible to a reading based around the notion of national romance, at the same time as they reveal increasing challenges to, and crevices in, this traditional narrative framework. My intention is to illustrate how the lines of development within Gallegos's ideas about the Venezuelan nation's relationship with socio-political progress determine the way in which the framework of romance is exploited in his novels.

To this end I will pay particular attention to how the structural and organizational revisions are accompanied on the thematic level by the collapse of the patriarchal family structure, which, as I already mentioned, is still held up in *Doña Bárbara* as a model for the wider nation-family. Finally, I will consider in detail why the framework of romance persists in Gallegos's later Venezuelan novels, which at points directly denounce heterosexual love as an inappropriate solution to Venezuela's diverse social, racial, and political problems. Overall, I will suggest that the longevity of this outdated framework is explicable in part by the fact that Gallegos is not completely confident or convinced by the innovative socio-political programmes which he sketches in his later novels. As I will suggest, it is possible to discern behind Gallegos's sometimes vehement rejection of traditional narrative and socio-political models an overwhelming nostalgia for an old-fashioned social order built around the concepts of conciliatory romance and patriarchy.

III

The main value of the present study resides in that it offers a new and coherent appreciation of three Gallegos novels that have been previously eclipsed by the extensive critical attention devoted to *Doña Bárbara*. More specifically, this work supports its discussion of national allegory with detailed analyses of the structural properties of the chosen novels, the importance of structure having been previously disregarded not only by Sommer, but also by other critics who have explored Gallegos's literary works through the prism of national allegory. Besides, many of the critics who have addressed Gallegos's ideas concerning the inherently problematic nature of the Venezuelan nation have merely glossed over the role that allegory plays within the bounds of these socially conscious novels. Others have focused on allegory, making only fleeting references to theories of nationhood. On top of this, as with Gallegos criticism in general, the majority of the critics who have concentrated either on allegory or on issues of nationhood have constructed their arguments exclusively around *Doña Bárbara*.

An exception in this latter sense is made by Doug Yarrington in 'Populist Anxiety: Race and Social Change in the Thought of Rómulo Gallegos', an article that focuses on *Reinaldo Solar*, *La trepadora*, and *Pobre negro*.[47] Yarrington builds his argument around the assumption that these less famous Gallegos novels also offer allegories of 'national development', and he further points out, following Sommer, that both *La trepadora* and *Pobre negro* can be labelled as national romances.⁴⁸ Yet Yarrington, whose main interest lies in 'the issue of race in [Gallegos's] vision of the nation's destiny', merely explores interracial love on the thematic level, viewing it as a representative figure, and prerequisite, of *mestizaje*; nowhere in his argument does he address heterosexual romance as a narrative framework, which can be modified and challenged in accordance with the socio-political message of the literary work. Meanwhile, Mónica Marinone's *Escribir novelas, fundar naciones*, in spite of its promising title, makes no direct reference to allegory and again completely overlooks the structural developments that take place in Gallegos's later novels: Marinone, for instance, claims that '[e]l orden narrativo [de *Pobre negro*] es el de las novelas más conocidas, relativamente ágil y progresivo [...] fracturado sólo cuando la descripción pasa a primer plano'.⁴⁹ Although Marinone demonstrates how Gallegos brings together through his writing the different social, racial, and cultural elements of Venezuela, her handling of theories of nationhood to support her argument is far from persuasive. Most notably, she proceeds on the assumption that Gallegos has been influenced by Ernest Renan's definition of the nation, but then offers no proof that Gallegos had actually read Renan.⁵⁰ Julie Skurski's article, 'The Ambiguities of Authenticity in Latin America: *Doña Bárbara* and the Construction of National Identity', shows even fewer signs of innovation.⁵¹ On the whole, Skurski's argument strains under the weight of generalizations, as she tries to delineate how the concern for national integration that pervades *Doña Bárbara* also stands for a wider-scale search for a 'Latin American identity'. Skurski's discussion of the role played by national allegory in *Doña Bárbara* is further undermined by the fact that it is entirely indebted to Sommer; she even prefaces her repetitive analysis of Marisela and Santos Luzardo's relationship with a long quotation from *Foundational Fictions*.⁵² Carlos J. Alonso, on the other hand, provides a significantly more productive reading of Gallegos's most famous novel in his seminal article, '"Otra sería mi historia": Allegorical Exhaustion in *Doña Bárbara*'.⁵³ Throughout the article, Alonso artfully dissects the very structure of allegory, laying open the multiple levels on which the struggle between civilization and barbarism is played out in *Doña Bárbara*. However, even though Alonso notes that *Doña Bárbara* promotes what can be best termed as 'a Manichean conception of Venezuelan [...] reality', his scrupulous examination of the workings of allegory is achieved at the cost of any references to theories of nationhood.⁵⁴ While Alonso acknowledges the organizational power of allegory, potentially to the point of exaggeration, he does not venture as far as to explore how allegory pervades also the formal — temporal and structural — aspects of the novel.⁵⁵

Paradigms of Stability and Paradigms of Change

I

Ulrich Leo is the only critic who has come anywhere close to providing a formal analysis of Gallegos's novels. Throughout *Estudio sobre el arte de novelar* — which refreshingly covers some of Gallegos's less famous novels — Leo pays particular attention to questions of narrative style, chronology, and characterization, as well as to the use of descriptive devices and dialogue.[56] Yet even Leo fails to acknowledge exactly how the manipulation of these formal and stylistic devices affects the articulation of Gallegos's ideas concerning nationhood and socio-political progress. In addition, the highly personal tone in which Leo comments on some aspects of Gallegos's style makes his 1954 study appear somewhat lax in the eyes of the twenty-first-century critic. At various points in his study, Leo directly speculates what Gallegos should have done in order to improve the quality of his novels; for instance, when discussing *Pobre negro*, Leo observes that *Pobre negro* would have been a far better novel had the character of Pedro Miguel died at the end.[57] Furthermore, Leo jumps to the conclusion that the change in narrative style that occurs in *Pobre negro* and *Sobre la misma tierra* should be regarded as mere sloppiness, resulting from the fact that by this stage Gallegos had become more concerned about the socio-political message than the literary quality of his novels.[58]

Leo's views regarding the stylistic inferiority of Gallegos's later novels have been echoed by other leading Gallegos specialists, including Lowell Dunham and Antonio Scocozza.[59] However, these critics have not based their dismissive comments concerning narrative style on any detailed exploration of the more formal aspects of Gallegos's novels. In fact, the meaning behind the formal experimentation that begins as early as in *Canaima*, which is still regarded one of Gallegos's *obras mayores*, has been completely overlooked by the existing criticism. Consequently, in addition to Sommer's paradigm of heterosexual romance, I turn to other sources to illuminate the relationship between national allegory and narrative structure in *Canaima*, *Pobre negro*, and *Sobre la misma tierra*, drawing for this purpose on Mikhail Bakhtin's and Frank Kermode's ideas on the representative function of narrative structure and time. Looking at the more specific features of narrative paradigms that have been delineated by these two theoreticians will allow me to identify the experimental impulses that complicate and sometimes even go against the grain of the traditional framework of heterosexual romance in Gallegos's novels. This said, I will not use Bakhtin's and Kermode's ideas regarding narrative paradigms as a checklist; I will rather turn them into an analytical tool that will allow me to add an important structural and temporal dimension to my close readings.

II

In *The Sense of an Ending* (1966), Kermode provides a far more subtle insight into the dynamics of narrative than Sommer does anywhere in her discussion of heterosexual romances.[60] Kermode not only offers an answer to the question of why narrative frameworks change in response to new socio-historical situations, but he further considers the reasons why some anachronistic frameworks persist even when they no longer reflect our conception of reality. In addressing the revisions and reformulations to which narrative frameworks have been subjected over time, Kermode relies heavily on the allegory of the Apocalypse. As he puts it, human beings are by their very nature fond of 'coherent patterns which, by the provision of an end, make possible a satisfying consonance with the origins and the middle'; thus, people yearn constantly for 'fictions of the end' (17). Knowing when the Apocalypse will take place helps us to 'locate' ourselves in the present, to the same extent that the awareness that the novel is prone to have an illuminating ending allows a reader to make sense of the rest of the novel. In fact, one could say that the national allegories on which I am focusing here work according to this very same principle. The inherent attraction of national allegories lies in the way in which at the time of their writing (and original publication), they offer a sense of the direction in which the nation is going, by promoting desirable ends or solutions to national problems and conflicts. Yet as I have already noted on various occasions, the understanding of what can be considered as a desirable end is likely to change over time. For instance, in Latin American national allegories the desire for national consolidation has in the twentieth century given way to a new set of more specific socio-political aims. Indeed, as Kermode observes, even though we are fond of familiar paradigms this does not mean that we are blindly seduced by them; on the contrary, because we are conscious of what is likely to happen in reality, 'there is a recurring need for adjustments in the interest of reality' (17). A sophisticated, twentieth- (or twenty-first-) century reader is therefore no longer satisfied with a straightforward, fully predictable plot-line, climaxing in what Henry James once so wittily described as 'a distribution [...] of prizes, pensions, husbands, wives, babies, millions, appended paragraphs, and cheerful remarks' (22).[61] Authors, as Kermode explains, subject traditional paradigms to surprising changes with the specific purpose of falsifying the reader's expectations concerning the course that the narrative is about to take; readers can always rest assured that the ending will eventually come, but they cannot be confident about what kind of ending this will be, or what path they will have to follow in order to reach this concluding point. I think that Kermode's references to the author's intentionally deceptive strategies, as well as to the preconceptions that the reader holds with regard to any given literary work, can help to explain why critics have regarded Gallegos's later novels as disappointing. Blinkered by the misguided assumption that Gallegos is a traditionalist rather than an experimental writer, critics have expected the later Venezuelan novels to replicate the naive predictability of the storylines and endings of Gallegos's earlier novels, such as *La trepadora* and *Doña Bárbara*. Instead of being thrilled by Gallegos's unexpected ability to surprise his readership, these critics have criticized Gallegos for not delivering his standard literary package. They have thus failed to adapt to Gallegos's altered sense of socio-historical reality, which is so markedly reflected in his increasingly complex manipulations of familiar narrative paradigms.

This said, the breach in the communication between Gallegos and his readership cannot be blamed entirely on the closed-mindedness of the critics, but almost certainly has at least something to do with the fact that the traditional framework of heterosexual romance acts as the backdrop to Gallegos's structural and thematic experimentations. On the whole, the misleading persistence of the traditional framework openly invites comparisons to Gallegos's earlier novels. Yet as Kermode also observes, abandoning the traditional paradigms altogether is close to impossible: while our understanding of socio-historical reality (and more specifically, of relevant 'end fictions') is in constant flux, '[the] old paradigms continue in some way to affect the way we make sense of the world' (28). Later, Kermode provides a lucid example of what exactly he means by this statement, as he draws our attention to the fact that the most elementary paradigm of reality, that is, the general understanding of time, is not only shared by people who belong to different cultural groups, but has existed for centuries (44). In other words, without these types of familiar paradigms we as readers (and as human beings) would lose our bearings. Taking all this into account, the residues of the framework of romance which can be found in Gallegos's later Venezuelan novels should be regarded on at least one level as a useful orientating device. These residues remind us of the original act of national consolidation — which functions as the necessary basis for more complex socio-political projects — and thus help us to plough our way through the unfamiliar material, including the formal and thematic experimentations. However, as Kermode also explains, in experimental novels form often fails to keep up with the thematic innovations: accordingly there can exist a discernible disparity between the form and message of a particular novel. In fact, throughout my study of *Canaima*, *Pobre negro*, and *Sobre la misma tierra* I will not only be on a constant lookout for inconsistencies of this type, but my intention is also to identify the wider implications of any possible disparities between theme and form.

According to Kermode, the most basic reason why disparity arises between the formal aspects and the message of a novel is because a novel is always

INTRODUCTION 23

constrained by temporality. In order for a novel to be comprehensible it requires some sort of organizing temporal pattern; that is to say, it needs a beginning, a middle, and an end, which are joined together (146).[62] As a matter of fact, as Kermode emphasizes at various points in his discussion of novelistic paradigms, he regards the novel as an inherently temporal form of art and consequently views spatial approaches to the novel as purely bogus. Even though I agree that time rather than space is the dominant organizing principle in most literary works, I find that Kermode's exploration of the role that space plays in the novel is cursory; for instance, he quotes 'the size of the book' as an example of novelistic space (178).[63] Indeed, Kermode does not acknowledge anywhere in his discussion the ways in which chapters, sections, and paragraphs allow narrative material to be organized meaningfully on the pages of the book. He accordingly overlooks entirely the spatial dimension of narrative structure. Furthermore, he fails to identify how the inherently spatial organizational categories constantly interact with narrative time. It is in the light of these weaknesses of Kermode's analysis of narrative paradigms that Bakhtin's chronotope essay, with its emphasis on the inherent connection between narrative time and space, provides an invaluable, additional analytical tool.

III

As Bakhtin points out already on the opening page of his essay, 'Forms of Time and of the Chronotope in the Novel' (1938), the term 'chronotope' (which literally means time-space), refers to 'the intrinsic connectedness of temporal and spatial relationships that are artistically expressed in literature'.[64] Although he goes on to identify time as the 'primary category in the chronotope' (85), he nevertheless acknowledges the importance of the interaction that takes place between novelistic time and space from the very start. In Bakhtin's words, in a literary chronotope '[t]ime, as it were, thickens, takes on flesh, becomes artistically visible', while 'space becomes charged and responsive to the movements of time, plot and history' (84). Yet these promising preliminary remarks concerning the intrinsic connection between novelistic time and space are not followed by a systematic definition of the term chronotope, making this theoretical device initially less accessible to the literary critic than Kermode's theories about the 'sense of an ending'. Disappointingly, an acquaintance with secondary literature that explores Bakhtin's ideas about the chronotope casts little light on this complicated theoretical device. For instance, Toni Dorca's use of the chronotope theory in his book *Volverás a la región: el cronotopo idílico en la novela española del siglo XIX* smacks of a checklist approach: his main concern appears to be to show how it is possible to discern in his chosen novels a set of temporal and spatial attributes that according to Bakhtin's definition characterize the Idyllic Chronotope.[65] Besides, throughout his book

Dorca seems to assume, incorrectly, that the term chronotope can be used loosely as a synonym for setting.[66] Though relatively more informative, even Gary Saul Morson and Caryl Emerson's chapter devoted to 'understanding' Bakhtin's chronotope offers little help.[67] While Morson and Emerson provide a fine general summary of Bakhtin's essay, they nonetheless end up rephrasing Bakhtin's ideas without really coming any closer to a working definition of the term chronotope. Nevertheless, these two leading Bakhtin specialists do capture the problematic and elusive nature of the chronotope essay when they note that after the initial comments about the intrinsic connection between literary time and space, Bakhtin 'repeatedly alternates concrete examples with further generalizations'.[68] In fact, as I will now proceed to demonstrate, I believe that the key to understanding Bakhtin's chronotope essay lies in being able to connect his generalizations about the chronotope with the individual examples that he provides throughout his essay. It is only after familiarizing oneself with the method that Bakhtin employs in the literary analyses that support his argument that the chronotope theory gains momentum and turns into a useful theoretical tool, which digs far deeper into the structural and temporal specificities of narrative paradigms than the corresponding devices offered by Kermode. This said, the following discussion of the chronotope ought not to be regarded as an attempt to provide an authoritative reading of Bakhtin's multifaceted essay; I will be focusing exclusively on those aspects of the chronotope theory that are directly relevant to the structural analyses I will carry out on Gallegos's later Venezuelan novels.

Rather curiously, the most helpful general observations regarding the nature of the chronotope can be found in the 'Concluding Remarks' (243–58), which Bakhtin added to his essay in 1973. Read prior to the main body of the essay, these 'Concluding Remarks' can significantly facilitate the overall understanding of this otherwise complex piece of theoretical writing. In his 'Concluding Remarks', Bakhtin recognizes that the chronotope is the organizing centre of the novel; that is to say, he identifies the chronotope as the temporal-spatial matrix which determines how the novel's content, including its various events, descriptions, motifs, images, and ideas, are presented to us. Also, in this final section of his chronotope essay Bakhtin reveals more explicitly than elsewhere what he understands by novelistic time and space. Hence, the 'Concluding Remarks' help the reader to decipher Bakhtin's much earlier intriguing comments concerning how time within the chronotope 'becomes artistically visible [while] space becomes [...] responsive to the movements of time, plot and history' (84).

In essence Bakhtin's understanding of both novelistic time and space is two-dimensional. By claiming that time becomes 'artistically visible', Bakhtin on one hand refers to how the movement of time in the novel can be sensed through rhythm and duration. Yet on the other hand, this very same statement captures the way in which it is often possible to find in novels temporal markers that point to a specific historical period or to a certain type of understanding of time. Similarly, Bakhtin regards both the physical segmentation of the novel into chapters and sections, and the geographical location, where the novel's action develops, as examples of novelistic space. It is, however, the constant dialogue between the more formal aspects of novelistic space and time, that is, the interaction between narrative time and the segmentation of the novel, which make a literary work come 'alive', as Bakhtin puts it, '[w]e are represented with a text occupying a certain specific place in space [...] our creation of it, our acquaintance with it occurs through time' (252). In other words, narrative time introduces the movement necessary for the unfolding of the plot as it connects the various events, motifs, and ideas which are imprinted in a distinct order on the pages of the novel. Meanwhile, the more obviously representative time and space epitomized by the temporal markers and geographical locations allow the reader to gain a further insight into the temporal-spatial universe of a particular novel. Indeed, as Bakhtin repeatedly reminds us, time and space in a novel are never abstract time and space, but they always have a representative function, which links them with the content and aim of the novel, as well as with the socio-historical reality which the novel is trying to mirror. While the wider temporal-spatial matrix profoundly influences the meaning and message of the novel, by presenting the narrative material in a fixed order, the deliberate speculations regarding the nature of time and space often reveal significant facts about how socio-historical reality is conceived in the novel. Furthermore, as Bakhtin shows with the help of a wide range of examples, there is a direct link between certain types of representative space and time. Specific representative spaces evoke a set of temporal expectations: if a story is set in an agricultural village, for example, we are likely to assume that time in this village will rotate on an inherently cyclical axis, thus mimicking the cycles of nature. However, what complicates the understanding of novelistic time and space is that not only are the novel's events likely to be set in various locations, which are all associated with different notions of time, but there is usually more than one organizing temporal-spatial matrix to be found in any given novel. As Bakhtin points out in his 'Concluding Remarks', each [major] chronotope can include within it an unlimited number of minor chronotopes' (252). What is more, the various different temporal-spatial organizational units of the novel interact with each other in highly complex ways: they can be tightly 'interwoven with [each other]', or they can 'replace or oppose one another', or even directly 'contradict one another' (252).

While Bakhtin has been criticized by Emerson and Morson on the grounds that he chooses his examples of literary chronotopes from a set of older genres such as the ancient Greek Romance and the early modern Rabelaisian Novel, in my opinion this particular choice of examples helps to explain effectively why different temporal-spatial matrices can coexist within the same novel.[69] Notably, Bakhtin spells out already on the opening pages of his essay that his main concern is to demonstrate how (and why) the chronotopes that were worked out in older genres still persist in the modern European novel, which he regards as the highest form of literature. Much like Kermode, Bakhtin notes that even though chronotopes at first reflect certain types of socio-historical reality, they are often 'reinforced by tradition [and continue] stubbornly to exist, up to and beyond the point at which they have lost any meaning that [is] productive in actuality or adequate to later historical situations' (85). However, Bakhtin goes on to illustrate, in far more detail than Kermode, that while the residues of anachronistic temporal-spatial matrices persist in the new literary genres, they undergo significant alterations over the years. For instance, Bakhtin pays attention in his essay to how the Greek Romance, the Adventure Novel of Everyday Life, and the Chivalric Romance all offer variations of what he labels 'adventure-time'. And even more strikingly, Bakhtin shows how the entire temporal-spatial matrix originally associated with literary works portraying the idyllic country-life of the pre-industrial period was picked up in the nineteenth century by the Provincial Novel, where its cyclicality was employed to emphasize the stagnancy of everyday existence (229-30). As a matter of fact, as this last example proves, traditional temporal-spatial matrices can be effectively manipulated to reflect on a new socio-historical situation; in other words, outmoded matrices sometimes acquire an alternative meaning when introduced into a new literary and social context.

On the whole, I have found Bakhtin's examples regarding traditional matrices that have over time acquired new meanings, as well as his comments concerning the coexistence of different temporal-spatial matrices, extremely useful when developing my own method of structural analysis. To begin with, his examples of narrative frameworks that have undergone changes over time have helped me to identify the various different ways in which the traditional framework of heterosexual romance has been altered in Gallegos's later Venezuelan novels to reflect new socio-historical situations. Besides, Bakhtin's comments about the plurality of temporal-spatial matrices have encouraged me to think about the relationship that the central, organizing framework of romance may hold with regard to the novel's other organizational units. For instance, I have felt obliged to ask myself if it is possible to distinguish, within the chosen novels, smaller antagonistic temporal-spatial matrices, which in effect undermine the dominant paradigm of heterosexual romance. Moreover, while I found Kermode's theory of 'the sense of an ending' productive in terms that it captures the dynamics of narrative paradigms, Bakhtin's almost microscopic view of the different temporal and spatial components of the novel has taught me important lessons about both the novel's architecture and its ability to mimic reality.

Throughout my study of Gallegos's later Venezuelan novels I will in fact be drawing on the method that Bakhtin employs when surveying the temporal and spatial characteristics of the older genres. When analysing each of my selected novels, I will accordingly first and foremost consider how time and space function within the parameters of the given novel. While I will generally interpret novelistic space as the formal structure of the novel, I will not completely overlook the importance of the locations where the novel's action takes place. Secondly, I will examine how the temporal-spatial organization, as well as the way in which time and space are represented in the novel, reflects the novel's actual content and aims. And thirdly, I will explore how the novel's heroes or heroines relate to the representative, temporal-spatial world which they inhabit; that is to say, I will endeavour to determine if the main characters are in harmony with their surroundings. By looking at these formal elements of the novel, I will demonstrate that Gallegos paid far more attention to form, time, and structure in his later Venezuelan novels than has been traditionally acknowledged. My subsequent analyses of *Canaima*, *Pobre negro*, and *Sobre la misma tierra* reveal that during this stage of his literary career, Gallegos constructed the narrative paradigms and the temporal-spatial universes of his novels no less carefully than he composed the socio-political messages of his fictional works.

Notes to the Introduction

1. Rómulo Gallegos, 'La pura mujer sobre la tierra', in *Una posición en la vida*, ed. by Lowell Dunham (Los Teques: Ediciones del Gobierno del Estado Miranda, 1985), pp. 396-425 (p. 416).

2. Carlos Pacheco, 'Pensamiento sociopolítico en la novela galleguiana', in *Rómulo Gallegos: multivisión*, ed. by Isaac J. Pardo and Oscar Sambrano Urdaneta (Caracas: Ediciones de la Presidencia de la República, 1986), pp. 113-34 (p. 122).

3. Although *El forastero* was published in 1942, I do not categorize this work as one of Gallegos's later Venezuelan novels, because it is widely known that Gallegos had originally drafted the novel as early as 1922. For a good general overview of the socio-political aspects of Gallegos's novels, see Pacheco, pp. 113-34; and Antonio Scocozza, 'Rómulo Gallegos, labor literaria y compromiso político', in *Literatura y política en América Latina*, ed. by Rafael di Prisco and Antonio Scocozza (Caracas: La Casa de Bello, 1995), pp. 153-238.

4. Manuel Alfredo Rodríguez, 'La política en Venezuela (1884-1984)', in *Rómulo Gallegos: multivisión*, pp. 15-42 (p. 17). The story of late nineteenth-century Venezuela is that of autocratic *caudillos*, such as Antonio Guzmán Blanco and José Manuel Hernández, and of a series of armed revolts, which either aimed to overthrow the current *caudillo* or tried to bring a new one into power.

5. Judith Ewell, *Venezuela: A Century of Change* (Stanford: Stanford University Press, 1984), p. 46. Ewell specifies that during the Revolución Libertadora 'Over 12,000 were killed in over 210 armed encounters' (p. 46).

6. Ibid., p. 43.
7. Ibid., p. 71.
8. For a more detailed analysis of the politics of the immediate post-Gómez period, see Daniel H. Levine, *Conflict and Political Change in Venezuela* (Princeton: Princeton University Press, 1973), pp. 27–61.
9. PDN changed its name to Acción Democrática in September 1941 at the same time as it was officially legalized.
10. Ewell, p. 94.
11. The years between 1945 and 1948, during which Acción Democrática controlled the Venezuelan government, are often referred to as the *trienio*. For a discussion of this period, see Ewell, pp. 97–107.
12. My aim is to provide here an overview of Gallegos's socio-political ideas as expressed in his essays. I will be referring to more specific aspects of the author's socio-political thought in the chapters devoted to *Canaima*, *Pobre negro*, and *Sobre la misma tierra*.
13. 'Necesidad de valores culturales' was originally published in the magazine *El Cojo Ilustrado*. Gallegos's socio-political writings have been collected by the critic Lowell Dunham in a volume entitled *Una posición en la vida*, which was published for the first time in 1954.
14. Gallegos, 'Las causas', in *Una posición en la vida*, pp. 15–22 (p. 18). Subsequent page references to Gallegos's socio-political writings appear in parentheses in the text.
15. In his 1912 essay, 'Necesidad de valores culturales' (82–109), Gallegos notes that this ethnic and cultural heterogeneity has also complicated the formation of a specifically Venezuelan cultural identity.
16. For a more detailed study of Gallegos's educational principles, see Gustavo Adolfo Ruiz, 'Ideas educativas', in *Rómulo Gallegos: multivisión*, pp. 97–112. Something to bear in mind is that Gallegos was a schoolmaster by profession; he acted as the Director of various prestigious institutions, such as Liceo Caracas, where he influenced the formation of the new generation of Venezuelan intellectuals and politicians. His students included Rómulo Betancourt, who during the *trienio* acted as Venezuela's president before Gallegos himself was democratically elected in 1947.
17. Gallegos's shifting attitude towards barbarism recalls that of Domingo Faustino Sarmiento in *Facundo, o civilización y barbarie* (1845). While Sarmiento criticizes the barbaric lifestyle of the *gauchos*, he is, however, simultaneously fascinated by their courage and physical strength, as well as by their traditions, which capture a genuinely Argentine culture.
18. Sococza, pp. 153–74.
19. *El último Solar* was retitled as *Reinaldo Solar* in all the subsequent editions.
20. Gallegos claims that the Venezuelan spirit is characterized by 'una imaginación inflamable y una fiera propensión al individualismo', while the European and North American one is characterized by 'inteligencia reflexiva y sentido' (123).
21. In this speech Gallegos addresses the deputies of the Venezuelan Congress.
22. As Sococza explains, Gallegos's 1941 candidatura era simplemente simbólica ya que el sistema indirecto de elecciones dejaba pocas posibilidades a un candidato no oficial de ocupar la primera magistratura del Estado' (209).
23. Ernest Renan, 'What is a Nation?', trans. by Martin Thom, in *Nation and Narration*, ed. by Homi K. Bhabha (London: Routledge, 1990), pp. 8–22 (p. 19); Timothy Brennan, 'The National Longing for Form', ibid., pp. 44–70 (p. 44).
24. Benedict Anderson, *Imagined Communities: Reflections on the Origin and Spread of Nationalism*, rev. edn (London: Verso, 2006).
25. Ibid., p. 6.

26. Renan, p. 19.
27. Ibid., p. 11.
28. Anderson identifies the isolation of the different parts of this immense continent as one of the main reasons why a Latin-American-wide 'imagined community' failed to materialize in the nineteenth century (63). For a succinct general discussion of the failure of Simón Bolívar's dream of a pan-American union, see Edwin Williamson, 'Reform, Crisis and Independence', in *The Penguin History of Latin America* (London: Penguin, 1992), pp. 195–232 (pp. 231–32).
29. Anderson, p. 25.
30. Ibid., p. 36.
31. Brennan, p. 49. Emphasis in original.
32. Fredric Jameson, 'Third-World Literature in the Era of Multinational Capitalism', *Social Text*, 15 (1986), 65–88 (p. 69). Emphasis in original.
33. Aijaz Ahmad, 'Jameson's Rhetoric of Otherness and the "National Allegory"', *Social Text*, 17 (1987), 3–25. The reliability of Ahmad's thesis is somewhat undermined by his vehement Marxist bias. Throughout his essay Ahmad becomes fixated on the fact that Jameson does not seem to believe that the 'Third World' could join the 'Second World' personified by Communist Russia, but instead claims that formerly colonial countries must choose between their own nationalisms and a globalizing North American postmodernist culture. For Ahmad the solution to all socio-political problems lies in left-wing ideology — he insists that 'the only nationalisms in the so-called third world which have been able to resist US cultural pressure and have actually produced any alternatives are the ones which are already articulated to and assimilated within the much larger field of socialist political practice' (8).
34. Ibid., p. 5. Quoted by Ahmad from Jameson, 'Third-World Literature'.
35. Imre Szeman, 'Who's Afraid of National Allegory? Jameson, Literary Criticism, Globalization', *The South Atlantic Quarterly*, 100.3 (2001), 803–27. In endnote 3 of his article Szeman provides a list of other critics who have expressed their appreciation for Jameson's 'attempt to offer an abstract, general model of literary production in the colonial and postcolonial world' (822).
36. Ibid., p. 804.
37. Ibid., pp. 808–10.
38. Luis Navarrete Orta, 'El escritor ante el poder político en América Latina', in *Literatura y política en América Latina*, pp. 33–47 (p. 34).
39. Doris Sommer, *Foundational Fictions: The National Romances of Latin America* (Berkeley: University of California Press, 1991). Page references appear in parentheses in the text.
40. Sommer's case studies include the Argentine José Mármol's *Amalia* (1851), the Cuban Gertrudis Gómez de Avellaneda's *Sab* (1841), and the Colombian Jorge Isaac's *María* (1867).
41. See Walter Benjamin, 'Allegory and Trauerspiel', in *The Origin of German Tragic Drama*, trans. by John Osborne (London: NLB, 1977), pp. 159–235. In a detailed discussion of the characteristics which he associates with allegory, Benjamin illustratively notes, with reference to Shakespeare's works, that '[e]very elemental utterance [...] acquires significance from its allegorical existence, and everything allegorical acquires emphasis from the elemental aspect of the world of the senses' (228).
42. In her introduction Sommer goes as far as to assert that not even the Boom novels have been completely able to free themselves from the traditional framework of national romance. As she puts it, '[t]he Boom's parodies, its fine ironies and playfulness, are the kind of endless denial that is bound to produce the opposite effect of admission [...] the

more national romance must be resisted, the more it seems irresistible' (3).
43. In *The Spanish American Regional Novel: Modernity and Autochthony* (Cambridge: Cambridge University Press, 1990), pp. 49–55, Carlos J. Alonso has argued that *la novela de la tierra* was born out of the Spanish American need to affirm a specifically Spanish American identity in the face of the threat of being swallowed up by the North American cult of Pan-Americanism.
44. Sommer makes this observation regarding the underlying fairy-tale formula in the chapter '"It's Wrong to Be Right": *Mamá Blanca* on Fatherly Foundations' (290–321), where she compares briefly Gallegos's *Doña Bárbara* with Teresa de la Parra's 1929 novel *Las memorias de Mamá Blanca* (308). Gallegos was very open about the fact that *Doña Bárbara* was at least to some extent a rewriting of the famous fairy-tale, as can be seen from the way in which he specifically named the eleventh chapter of 'Primera Parte' of the novel 'La bella durmiente'. Elsewhere, André S. Michalski has explored in substantial detail the fairy-tale elements of *Doña Bárbara* in his article '*Doña Bárbara*: un cuento de hadas', *PMLA*, 85.5 (1970), 1015–22. As Michalski notes, in *Doña Bárbara*, 'el príncipe Rubio' (Santos Luzardo) marries 'la Bella Durmiente' (Marisela) despite the evil tricks of '[la] mala bruja' (Doña Bárbara) (1016).
45. Joanne Rappaport, 'Fictive Foundations: National Romances and Subaltern Ethnicity in Latin America', *History Workshop*, 34 (1992), 119–31 (p. 122).
46. Ibid., p. 123.
47. Doug Yarrington, 'Populist Anxiety: Race and Social Change in the Thought of Rómulo Gallegos', *The Americas*, 56.1 (1999), 65–90.
48. Ibid., p. 66.
49. Mónica Marinone, *Escribir novelas, fundar naciones: Rómulo Gallegos y la experiencia venezolana* (Mérida: Libro de Arena, 1999), p. 123.
50. Ibid., p. 121.
51. Julie Skurski, 'The Ambiguities of Authenticity in Latin America: *Doña Bárbara* and the Construction of National Identity', *Poetics Today*, 15.4 (1994), 605–42.
52. Ibid., p. 607. Skurski repeats Sommer's explanation regarding how heterosexual romance is employed in a 'new' way in the populist novels of the twentieth century.
53. Carlos J. Alonso, '"Otra sería mi historia": Allegorical Exhaustion in *Doña Bárbara*', *Modern Language Notes*, 2 (1989), 418–38. An extended version of the article was published as Chapter 3 of Alonso's book *The Spanish American Regional Novel*. In the book version, Alonso ties his reading of *Doña Bárbara* to a wider discussion of the *novela de la tierra*.
54. Ibid., p. 425.
55. Instead of revealing anything completely new about *Doña Bárbara*, Alonso's article ends up providing an insight into how allegory is constructed. In fact, the eagerness with which Alonso wants to prove his theory about the organizational power of allegory makes his reading of *Doña Bárbara* somewhat forced.
56. Ulrich Leo, *Rómulo Gallegos: Estudio sobre el arte de novelar* (Caracas: Biblioteca Popular Venezolana, 1954). Leo pays particular attention to *Pobre negro* in 'La invención en la novela' (99–181) — the third part of his study — and devotes the entire fourth part (183–267) to *Sobre la misma tierra*.
57. Ibid., p. 134.
58. Ibid., pp. 131, 215. Leo argues that the socio-political message plays such a dominant role in *Pobre negro* that Gallegos would have done better, had he written '[un] ensayo psicológico-histórico' (131). Regarding *Sobre la misma tierra*, Leo notes that '[la] simplificación estilística' originates from Gallegos's desire to focus wholeheartedly on 'los problemas indígena y petrolero en la vida pública venezolana' (215).

59. Lowell Dunham, 'Las últimas novelas', in *Rómulo Gallegos: vida y obra*, trans. by Gónzalo Barrios and Ricardo Montilla (Mexico City: Ediciones Andrea, 1957), pp. 253-87 (p. 277); and Scocozza, pp. 191-92.
60. Frank Kermode, *The Sense of an Ending: Studies in the Theory of Fiction*, rev. edn (Oxford: Oxford University Press, 2000). Page references appear in parentheses in the text.
61. Quoted by Kermode. This observation originally appeared in the preface to Henry James's *Roderick Hudson* (1875).
62. As Kermode explains, some rather unsuccessful attempts to abolish temporality were made by the avant-garde writer William Burroughs, who 'tried to defeat our codes of continuity, cultural and temporal, by shuffling his prose into random order' (117). However, when discussing the disparity that can exist between the form and the message of a novel, Kermode relies almost entirely on Jean-Paul Sartre's *La nausée* (1938). Kermode argues that

> evidently, Sartre knew about the fallacy of imitative form: his book, though it surrounds the hero with images of formlessness, inhumanity, nausea, must not itself be formless or viscous [sic] or inhuman, any more than it may repeat the formal presumptuousness of the nineteenth-century novel. (146)

63. Kermode's rejection of a spatial approach to literary analysis is formulated as an attack on Joseph Frank's essay 'Spatial Form in Modern Literature', published in his book *The Widening Gyre* (New Brunswick: Rutgers University Press, 1963). For a more elaborate discussion of space in the novel, see Joseph A. Kestner, *The Spatiality of the Novel* (Detroit: Wayne State University Press, 1978). While part of Kestner's analysis of the spatial aspects of the novel borders on the mathematical, he makes some valid observations about the architecture of the novel by pointing out the important role played by chapters and paragraphs in conveying meaning.
64. Mikhail Bakhtin, 'Forms of Time and of the Chronotope in the Novel', in *The Dialogic Imagination: Four Essays by M. M. Bakhtin*, ed. by Michael Holquist, trans. by Caryl Emerson and Michael Holquist (Austin: University of Texas Press, 1981), pp. 84-258 (p. 84). Subsequent page references appear in parentheses in the text.
65. Toni Dorca, *Volverás a la región: el cronotopo idílico en la novela española del siglo XIX* (Madrid: Iberoamericana, 2004). In his book Dorca addresses a number of Spanish *costumbrista* classics, such as Fernán Caballero's *Un verano en Bornos* (1855), Juan Valera's *Pepita Jiménez* (1874), and Benito Pérez Galdós's *Doña Perfecta* (1876). Dorca prefaces his analyses of these novels with Bakhtin's definition of the Idyllic Chronotope. As Dorca notes, according to Bakhtin there are three basic features that characterize life in an idyll: firstly, life in the idyll always takes place in a highly limited microuniverse; secondly, the existence of the people inhabiting the idyll is limited to the fundamental realities of everyday life; and thirdly, time in the idyll is inherently cyclical, with the human life following the same rhythm as nature (13). For Bakhtin's original discussion of the Idyllic Chronotope, see 'Forms of Time and of the Chronotope', pp. 224-42.
66. As I will illustrate below, unlike a 'setting', which is composed of a specific time and space binary, the chronotope additionally captures motion. Moreover, as I will also explain, rather than dealing exclusively with representative time and space, as the setting does, the chronotope functions as the organizing centre of the narrative material.
67. Gary Saul Morson and Caryl Emerson, 'The Chronotope', in *Mikhail Bakhtin: Creation of a Prosaics* (Stanford: Stanford University Press, 1990), pp. 366-432.
68. Ibid., pp. 366-67.

69. Morson and Emerson complain that

> although Bakhtin's main impulse is evidently to celebrate the novel since the eighteenth century, he focuses almost entirely on much earlier literary works. We learn what the novel is by examining works that contrast with it or are deficient in comparison with it. (373)

CHAPTER 1

Canaima:
A Plunge into Pessimism

I

In many respects, *Canaima* (1935) builds on the attack on the Gómez regime begun by Gallegos already in *Doña Bárbara* (1929). Yet the socio-political context in which Gallegos wrote *Canaima* differs significantly from the one in which he composed his earlier masterpiece. In summer 1931 Gallegos directly denounced *gomecismo* when he resigned his post as the Senator for the Apure State, a post with which Gómez had rewarded him after developing a peculiar liking for *Doña Bárbara*, despite the novel's evident criticism of his dictatorship. Gallegos's letter of resignation, written from self-imposed exile in New York, specifically clarified that the reason behind his decision to disassociate himself from Venezuelan politics lay in the fact that he did not want to contribute in any way to a political system which forced its subjects to live in the constant 'sombra del jefe'.[1] Although the early and mid-1930s — a period which coincides with the author's absence from his native country — mark a relatively unproductive phase in terms of Gallegos's socio-political writings, it would be incorrect to talk about an outright political silence. In fact, in a lecture entitled 'Las tierras de Dios' (112–44) and delivered to a New York audience in autumn 1931, Gallegos launches an unreserved satire of Gómez, as well as his predecessor Cipriano Castro. The lecture presents the two *caudillos andinos* as primitive men, dropped by the 'torbellino creador' in the middle of the Venezuelan wilderness (120). Gallegos explains that even though this type of men have found their way to cities and disguised their nakedness with 'galones y charreteras doradas, y algunas medallas y cruces resplandecientes', they remain at bottom ignorant and savage thugs (117). However, underneath the light-hearted satire it is possible to perceive a resigned pessimism, which clashes with Gallegos's earlier vehemence and optimism. Most notably, Gallegos docilely admits in 'Las tierras de Dios' that for the time being it is impossible to foresee the end of the traditional *caudillo* system, because Venezuelans (and by extension most Latin Americans) seem incapable of dealing with political organizations. The Venezuelan nation's only hope therefore appears to be a benevolent and forward-thinking leader, who will replace the despots in whose grip Venezuela has been wrestling since her independence (140).[2] Significantly, both the image of the barbarous man born out of the furious elements and Gallegos's resigned acceptance of the never-ending procession of *caudillos* also found their way into *Canaima*, a novel on which Gallegos had started working in the early months of 1931, following a research trip to Venezuelan Guayana.[3] It would not be out of place to say that *Canaima*, which was initially published in Madrid, gives vent to much of the disillusionment experienced by Gallegos during his exile in the United States and Spain. Whereas in *Doña Bárbara* Gallegos is determined to find a solution to Venezuela's socio-political problems, and fittingly ends the novel with an optimistic image of one straight road towards the future, in *Canaima* he appears sceptical about the success of projects of reform in regions inhabited by savage *hombres machos*. By enumerating the multiple social ills of Venezuelan Guayana without, however, posing solutions to most of these ills, Gallegos evokes a pessimistic atmosphere completely foreign to the readers of his earlier novel. Moreover, the treatment that Gallegos gives to regional and national concerns in *Canaima* reveals a further development in his socio-political thought. While in *Doña Bárbara* Gallegos bridges the gap between the regional and the national by repeatedly using the *llanos* as an allegory of the Venezuelan nation, the narrator of *Canaima* draws only few analogies between the jungle environment of Venezuelan Guayana and Venezuela as a whole. *Canaima* accordingly marks the beginning of a movement towards more specific, regional concerns, a movement which will indeed bear its fruits in Gallegos's later novels. In the meantime, the ambiguity surrounding the exact borderline between regional and national issues, which still persists in *Canaima*, provides the necessary harness for attacking *gomecismo* in this novel, which generally focuses on a set of socio-economic problems characteristic of the Guayana region.

Although Gallegos originally decided to write a novel about Venezuelan Guayana because he wanted to complete what Gustavo Luis Carrera has aptly called 'una especie de mosaico novelístico de la geografía de su país', the setting of *Canaima* also proves fertile ground for Gallegos's recently developed pessimism with regard to socio-historical progress.[4] While Venezuelan Guayana, with its mysterious jungles, exuberant natural resources, and promises of golden cities, has for centuries cast a spell on explorers (with Gallegos being no exception in this sense), it has nevertheless for long remained a profoundly isolated region. Writing as late as the 1980s, the historian John V. Lombardi talks about 'the still undeveloped Guayana Highlands' and further points out that it was only in the second half of the twentieth century that the region became connected to the rest of the Venezuelan nation, thanks to the construction of a proper road network.[5] Meanwhile, Judith Ewell, whose history of Venezuela was also published in the 1980s, discusses more specifically how the enormous potential of Venezuelan Guayana continues to a large extent unexploited, even though the region has been repeatedly identified by Venezuelans as '[a] repository of the national hopes'.[6] In short, the fate of Venezuelan Guayana illustrates the fact that Venezuela has developed unevenly, this being something that Gallegos tries to accentuate when addressing the region's socio-economic problems in *Canaima*. Indeed, according to my reading, Gallegos's decision to explore the ills of the rubber exploitation industry in a novel whose events take place sometime between 1911 and the early 1930s — during a period when the major rubber boom had already run its course — should not be seen as a sign of historical inconsistency.[7] On the contrary, the focus on the rubber industry allows Gallegos to emphasize in yet another effective way the fact that Venezuelan Guayana has been hopelessly left behind in the race for socio-historical progress. Furthermore, in the context of Gallegos's continuing attack on *gomecismo*, the lack of genuine socio-historical progress that characterizes Venezuelan Guayana exemplifies how the benefits of the programmes of modernization introduced by the *caudillo andino* overlooked whole regions and barely reached ordinary people. As both Ewell and William Sullivan have explained, while those close to the dictator prospered, the misery of the masses continued, as almost no money was spent on public health and education, with the inhabitants of isolated rural regions witnessing few, if any, changes.[8] What is more, besides pinpointing the limits of the socio-economic changes introduced by the Gómez regime, Gallegos demonstrates in *Canaima* that the dictator's attempts to curtail the power of the tyrannical regional *caudillos* in no sense marked the end of corruption and violence. Using the decline of the fictional Ardavín family as an example, Gallegos laments the way in which the fall of the original regional *caudillos* merely implied the replacement of one group of thugs by another, which this time was handled by the *caudillo andino* himself.[9]

However, in *Canaima* Gallegos does not merely limit himself to criticizing the socio-economic changes associated with the Gómez regime, but unlike anywhere before, he puts his own, often overly optimistic models of socio-political progress under keen scrutiny. As the nostalgic reminiscences of the lost prosperity of the mines of Venezuelan Guayana and the lengthy pedagogical dialogues about the wasted hydroelectric potential of the region's waterfalls indicate, what Gallegos is essentially doing in *Canaima* is depicting a region that is at an unfruitful stage of transition. In fact, throughout the novel Gallegos openly expresses his doubts over whether one single model of development can be applied with equal success to all social and geographical spectra of the Venezuelan nation. For the time being, he nonetheless fails to formulate an innovative socio-political agenda that would provide a constructive outlet for his changing ideas about the nation's relationship with progress. Drawing on the image of the *caudillo* born out of a 'torbellino creador', Gallegos devises the character of Marcos Vargas, who at first appears to have the potential to become the benevolent and innovative *caudillo* that the author delineated in 'Las tierras de Dios'. However, not only do Marcos's endeavours of social reform come to nothing (the implication being that his failures will be redeemed by his son), but he further fails to reshuffle in any noteworthy way the repressive patriarchal order of the nation-family. Just like Santos Luzardo — Gallegos's other kind-hearted *caudillo* — Marcos Vargas is essentially a *criollo* patriarch, that is to say, a conventional guardian of the old hierarchical society. Indeed, Gallegos's unwillingness to subvert the age-old social order, which provided the necessary framework for traditional *caudillismo*, finds a pointed expression in the way in which he chooses to eliminate any factors that might pose a threat to Marcos's patriarchal authority. Most importantly, Gallegos deems Marcos's passionate love for the strong-willed Aracelis as hopeless and chooses instead to unite his hero in the end with the characterless Aymara. In point of fact, Marcos's marriage to the Indian Aymara allows Gallegos to smuggle in the theme of *mestizaje*, thus forcibly brushing aside the novel's concerns about Venezuela's complicated relationship with progress, through a schematic device employed in his earlier novels as a standard solution to the nation's socio-historical contradictions.[10]

Rather understandably, various critics have been led astray by the optimistic closing image of the *mestizo* Marcos Vargas (the younger) sailing towards a better future along the Orinoco. To be more precise, many of these critics have misinterpreted *Canaima* as an optimistic allegory that anticipates the successful fulfilment of national, or even supranational, aims. For instance, Pilar Almoina de Carrera sees 'el futuro [como una] virtualidad encarnada por el hijo de Marcos Vargas', while Françoise Pérus asserts that Gallegos in *Canaima* advocates '[el] reordenamiento de la cultura nacional en torno a este nuevo "mestizaje" étnico y cultural'.[11] Janine Potelet in turn goes so far as to place Marcos Vargas *hijo* in the wider context of the Latin American racial theory debate by referring to José Vasconcelos's notion of the *mestizos* as 'la raza cósmica', and to José Carlos Mariátegui's powerful declaration that 'el porvenir de la América latina depende [...] de la suerte del mestizaje'.[12] By interpreting the central message of *Canaima* simply in terms of its optimistic closing image, these critics have overlooked not only the structural and thematic complexity of the novel but also the pivotal fact that only limited narrative attention is paid to Marcos Vargas's relationship with the Indian Aymara, the mother of his mixed-race son. The intention of the current chapter is to focus on these previously ignored defining features of *Canaima*, which in fact make the novel stand apart from Gallegos's more conventional, earlier works of fiction. I will pay particular attention to how Gallegos's manipulation of the novel's temporal and structural factors supports his contention that the economy of the Guayana region went into decline during the early decades of the twentieth century, despite its natural riches, because of the lack of effective historical progress. I will argue that the struggle between linear, progressive time and various cyclical times, inherent in the structure of *Canaima*, manifests the persistency with which Venezuelan Guayana resists being incorporated into a new stage of history. In addition to studying the implications that narrative time and structure have in the novel, I will also explore in depth the representative function of the novel's heterosexual romances. I will illustrate how the extremely forced, allegorical alliance between Marcos and Aymara is throughout the novel overshadowed by the purely romantic love that connects Marcos to Aracelis — the wealthy daughter of an Italian merchant. My intention is to point out that the lack of vigour that characterizes Marcos's relationship with Aymara indicates that Gallegos is no longer convinced about the feasibility of interracial love as a standard solution to the complex, often region-specific, problems of the Venezuelan nation.

II

While the romance and subsequent marriage of Aymara and Marcos are merely glossed over in the novel's penultimate chapter, Marcos's passion for Aracelis starts to blossom as early as the section 'Marcos Vargas' (Chapter 1), and persists until the end of the novel. Substantial references are made to Aracelis and Marcos's relationship in as many as nine sections, with the relationship being the centre of narrative attention in sections as varied as 'Claro de luna', 'La Bordona', '"Musiú" Vellorini toma medidas', and 'Remansos y torrentes'. Unlike the subdued Aymara, Aracelis establishes herself as Marcos's match from the very start by sealing their mutual affection with a *bofetada* during their initial encounter. As the narrator points out, for a young man like Marcos who has up to that point lived in '[un] mundo [...] rudo y viril', there could have been no more appropriate way for love to announce its existence than through a violent smack.[13] However, at the outset, when Marcos is not yet completely devoted to the principles of fierce *hombría*, he makes no secret of the fact that he has become totally enchanted by Aracelis's beauty and haughty behaviour. For example, when Manuel Ladera jokingly insinuates, on their arrival to Yuruari, that Marcos might fall in love with one of the local girls, the latter observes that 'esa diligencia, como que [ya] está hecha' (17). Slightly later on, in the section 'Claro de luna', Marcos's enigmatic statement gains momentum as we find out that Aracelis is Ladera's niece. Marcos's decision to buy Ladera's fleet of carts and to establish himself in Upata is likely to have at least something to do with the fact that Aracelis lives with her family in this particular town. Moreover, in the section 'Claro de luna' Marcos declares his love for Aracelis tongue-in-cheek, in front of the whole Ladera family, when stating that it is unnecessary for the local girls to baptize him at the famous 'Piedra de Santa María' — in order to make sure that he marries 'una upatense'– because he is already 'confirmado' (31). Regardless of Aracelis's imploring 'señas negativas', Marcos further riles her by explaining to everyone how he still carries the marks of the confirmation on his cheek, marks that he believes are destined to persist 'mientras viva' (31). Aracelis in turn verifies in the midst of laughter and exclamations of disapproval the assumption that it was effectively she who 'confirmed' Marcos with the *bofetada*, after which she goes on to point out that the other girls should stay clear of Marcos because he belongs to her. Indeed, recognized by *señora* Ladera as '[una] muchachita loca [...] [quien] [h]ace y dice cuanto se le ocurre' (31) Aracelis is an unusual young woman, who readily challenges the social conventions of her time and place. In point of fact, she even defies the power structures of the traditional patriarchal family, as is illustrated in the later section 'Remansos y torrentes', where she explains to her cousin Maigualida that she will not allow her father to separate her from Marcos by sending her away to France: 'a mí no me [puede] arrea[r] por delante como a la pazguata de mamaíta, que no quiere ir y, sin embargo, no protesta. No sé qué voy a hacer, pero yo encontraré el modo de salirme con las mías' (167). Considering Aracelis's headstrong character, it is no surprise that the tempestuousness of her passion for Marcos is not limited to the initial *bofetada* and the scandal that it provokes; the relationship of these two young lovers is throughout the novel staged as a series of mock fights and power struggles. An analysis of the section 'La Bordona' provides an excellent insight into the exact laws of attraction that make Aracelis and Marcos gravitate towards each other.

The section 'La Bordona' opens with a description of how Aracelis and Marcos flirt through the bars of Aracelis's window on a romantic night of 'constelaciones del trópico y [...] estrellas fugaces' (75). In this section, which pulsates with sexual tension, Marcos repeatedly calls Aracelis 'Bordona' — using 'el sobrenombre familiar que [...] se les aplica a las hijas menores' — and provokes her by telling her to keep her fiery passion under control, through his cries of '¡Apaga, Bordona!' (75). Aracelis in the meantime alternates her declarations of love — '¡es que te quiero tanto, chico! ¡Tanto, tanto, tanto!' — with vehement reproaches as she calls Marcos '[o]dioso' and 'bicho antipático' (76). While Aracelis feels hurt by the fact that Marcos seems incapable of uttering actual words of affection, the narrator clarifies that this inability to express his feelings does not mean a lack of caring:

> A Marcos Vargas se le atragantaban las ternezas. Estaba enamorada de ella, le parecía la más linda de todas las criaturas, la única apetecible entre todas

> las mujeres y se deleitaba en contemplarla; pero también parecíale que no era de hombres demostrar ternura ni manifestarse enamorada de mujer alguna como no fuese por los modos violentos del apetito de posesión. El amor que inspiraba Aracelis era puro y delicado, pero el rudo ambiente viril en que se delineara su carácter impedíale ya exhibir la porción fina de sus sentimientos y sólo el buen humor podía dulcificar la aspereza a que debiera inducirlo su bronco concepto de la hombría. (77)

As this passage reveals, Marcos is devoted to Aracelis, but the 'rudo ambiente viril' in which he is becoming increasingly immersed forces him to keep in check the emotions that he only a few sections earlier expressed rather openly. What is more, we soon learn that, even though Aracelis complains about Marcos's apparent lack of feelings, she is essentially on the same emotional plane as he because she also is a product of the violent environment which she inhabits. In her adventurous eyes 'lo masculino mientras más rudo, más fascinante [...] resultaba' (77). Illustratively, one of the many ways in which she expresses her affection for Marcos in 'La Bordona' is by celebrating his daring and ruthless exploits, such as beating the thuggish José Francisco Ardavín in a game of dice, in which the two men use the clients of their respective cart-fleet companies as bets. In fact, both the vehemence of Aracelis's love for Marcos and her acceptance of the crude principles of *hombría* find a further, even more powerful, expression in the sections 'Remansos y torrentes' and 'Unas palabras de Ureña' (Chapter 11). By this stage Marcos has already been fully transformed by the violent jungle environment and by the act of killing Cholo Parima — two experiences that have caused him to abandon '[e]l amor [...] puro y delicado' in favour of 'los modos violentos del apetito de posesión' (77). Correspondingly, in the section 'Remansos y torrentes' Marcos asks Aracelis to go with him to explore the Guayanan wilderness 'como se van las mujeres con los hombres que les gustan' (168). Though deeply upset by the fact that Marcos does not wish to marry her but treats her instead like 'una mujercita del pueblo', we find out by the end of the subsequent section that Aracelis has nevertheless decided to accept Marcos's disrespectful proposal (168–71). Thus, it is only thanks to the momentary re-emergence of Marcos's humane side, which makes him leave his lover without a farewell so as not to cause her any additional harm, that Aracelis is saved from the fate of a concubine.

Marcos's drive to consummate his passion for Aracelis without marrying her springs originally from his desire to take revenge on Aracelis's Italian father, Francisco Vellorini, who from the very beginning opposes the thought of his daughter marrying Marcos. While Francisco Vellorini is known for his fondness for local proverbs and mannerisms and for being married to an *upatense*, the narrator reminds us repeatedly that marrying his sophisticated, half-Italian daughters to *criollos* does not form part of his plans. Accordingly, when Francisco discovers that Marcos is courting Aracelis he starts immediately plotting a trip to Europe, with the specific aim to 'quitarle de la cabeza a la Bordona unos amorcitos que parece tener con ese Marcos Vargas' (78). At this early stage, Marcos is not too taken aback by Francisco Vellorini's scheme. Indeed, he even tries to reason to himself that by sending Aracelis away, Francisco is doing him a favour: '[es] mejor [...] andar escotero' on the road of adventure that he has chosen (81). However, after his experiences in the ruthless jungle, Marcos becomes accustomed to dictating his own rules and no longer allows the whims of others to influence his actions. An excellent example of how Marcos's character is toughened by his jungle experiences is provided in the section 'De regreso', where Francisco Vellorini tries to close Marcos out of his family through a business proposal. Francisco explains to Marcos that the reason why he considers him the right man to take charge of the Vellorini family's 'negocio del purguo y de las minitas de oro' is because he does not belong to the family; as Francisco puts it, 'ya que he tenido la desgracia de perder a mi hermano no quiero hacer negocios de ningún género con nadie a quien me unan, *o puedan unirme en lo futuro*, nexos de familia' (158, emphasis added). Yet Francisco Vellorini's rejection of Marcos as the potential husband to his daughter, on the grounds that he is not racially the half-Italian Aracelis's equal, is by no means the only instance in the novel where racial politics play an integral role in determining the course and the outcome of heterosexual love. In fact, in *Canaima* Gallegos ultimately undermines the power of exclusively personal love, giving instead preference to heterosexual alliances, which can be held up as model solutions to Venezuela's persistent social and racial contradictions.

Significantly, Marcos's in many ways unsuccessful love affair with Aracelis unravels against the backdrop of Gabriel Ureña's perfect romance with Manuel Ladera's daughter Maigualida. The analogical nature of these two relationships is accentuated both by the fact that Gabriel Ureña can be regarded as Marcos's bookish alter ego (an important point to which I shall return later), and the way in which Marcos and Gabriel court girls who belong to the same family (Manuel Ladera is Aracelis's maternal uncle). Initially, Maigualida and Gabriel's love seems far more doomed than that of Marcos and Aracelis. Even though Maigualida and Gabriel have already been sweethearts as adolescents, by the time of their re-encounter some fifteen years later Maigualida has witnessed the death of one of her suitors at the hands of the violent José Francisco Ardavín, who has sworn that she will be his 'o de nadie' (34). Despite the strong attraction she feels for Gabriel, Maigualida is therefore compelled to ask him to stay away from her house as much as possible, in order to protect his life. Given his hatred of demonstrations of *hombría*, Gabriel resignedly accepts Maigualida's request and consequently saves his character from the stain of homicide, which, as we have seen, poisoned Marcos's love for Aracelis.

Indeed, Gabriel and Maigualida get a reward for their patience in the end, after José Francisco Ardavín loses touch with reality; in the section 'Remansos y torrentes' the young couple is finally able to enjoy 'el buen amar, sin éxtasis delicuescentes, con la dulce gravedad de la dicha bien gozada', in an idyllic country setting (166). As the reader soon learns, this love idyll is built on such secure foundations that it cannot be shaken by the actions or words of jealous intruders. Hence, Marcos's lascivious gazes at Maigualida fail to provoke Gabriel's anger, and his reproaches concerning the way in which Gabriel did not act on his feelings at an earlier point, but waited for outside forces to dictate the course of his affections, fall on deaf ears. However, even though Maigualida and Gabriel's love is highly romantic, it differs from the purely personal love that exists between Marcos and Aracelis, owing to its wider social implications. While Francisco Vellorini tried to shut Marcos out of his family by means of a business proposal, Maigualida's widowed mother on the other hand invites the still hesitant Gabriel into the Ladera family by stating: 'Tu entrada en la familia sería la salvación para nosotros [...] nuestra [fortuna] desaparecerá pronto [...] si un hombre de tus condiciones no le hace frente a su administración' (165). As *señora* Ladera's statement indicates, in addition to formalizing emotional ties, marriages provide a useful medium through which to establish alliances of convenience that ideally benefit both parties involved. In fact, although this is not necessarily explicit at first glance, Gabriel Ureña and Maigualida's romance successfully cuts across the racial (and regional) spectrum. The wider socio-historical implications of Gabriel Ureña and Maigualida's relationship are already laid out in the section 'Palabras mágicas', which narrates in retrospect the lovers' initial encounter at the age of fifteen. In this section, specific attention is paid to the fact that Gabriel Ureña's love for Maigualida triggered his social awakening — it was through his encounter with this exotic young woman from Venezuelan Guayana that he grew aware of the social injustices and wasted potential of the Guayanan wilderness. Moreover, it is undoubtedly no coincidence that Maigualida enters the narrative following an enumeration of the wonderful objects that Gabriel's uncle brings from the jungle, objects which include 'un precioso chinchorro tejido por los indios arecunas del alto Caroní' and a miniature 'ranchería de indios con su churuata y sus curiaras' (43). Apart from categorizing Maigualida with these Indian artefacts, the narrator explores Maigualida's close association with the Indians also in the later section 'Mitología griega y solución lógica', where attention is paid to how 'el interesante rasgo indio' deepens on Maigualida's face as she grows older (164). In short, the marriage between Gabriel, a *criollo* from Caracas, and Maigualida, an *upatense* with Indian blood, is an example of a stereotypical national romance; this marriage does not only unite the *criollo* with the Indian, but it also represents an alliance between the city and the untamed countryside. Yet by constantly keeping the personal dimension of Gabriel and Maigualida's romance in the foreground, Gallegos is able to make this thoroughly representative marriage appear far more convincing than the relationship between Marcos and the Indian Aymara, which functions as the novel's main allegorical relationship.

Marcos's marriage to Aymara is portrayed as a marriage of convenience from the very outset. Just as Gabriel Ureña was invited by *señora* Ladera to join the Ladera family in order to defend the family's assets, the Indian *cacique* Ponchopire offers his sister Aymara to Marcos in the hopes that Marcos will help to protect his tribe from other white intruders. While Aymara demonstrates an obvious interest in Marcos, questions of emotion play only a secondary role in this marriage, as is confirmed by the blunt way in which Ponchopire tells his sister: 'Tú serás la mujer del racional. Saca de ese hombre el mayor provecho para ti y para tu gente' (186). All in all, Marcos's relationship with Aymara has none of the witty dynamism that characterized Marcos and Aracelis's romance. Aymara never seems to question or challenge Marcos's patriarchal authority, but instead spends most of her time skulking silently around her husband. On one occasion the narrator even points out how Aymara has for some time been listening to Marcos's conversation with Ponchopire, 'sin que [Marcos] lo advertiese' (190). Nowhere in 'Aymara' or 'El racional' — the two sections that focus on Marcos and Aymara's relationship — does Marcos have a conversation with his Indian wife, who mainly communicates through 'risa[s]', 'gruñidos', 'gestos', 'señas', and 'gemidos' (186, 190, 192). The only time Aymara utters an actual sentence is when she expresses her love for Marcos by stating 'yo queriéndote tanto, tanto, tanto' (192), a statement that provides a crudely Indianized version of Aracelis's declaration of love in the section 'La Bordona'. Besides, in spite of Aymara's words of love, the attraction between Marcos and Aymara is generally depicted as far more sexual than romantic. Even Aymara's introduction into the narrative coincides suggestively with her sexual awakening, which in turn is triggered by the presence of Marcos at the *veladas*, where the Indian men congregate in order to share their daily experiences:

> Durante aquellas veladas, Aymara, sabrosa y arisca como apetecible y espinosa la carne del pez homónimo, ya sintiendo las urgencias de la mujer que despuntaba en ella se refugiaba a lo más oscuro de la churuata para contemplar a su gusto al racional, encendidos los ojos de lumbre de amor; pero si Marcos, buscándola entre el mujerío atento a la charla de los hombres alcanzaba a descubrirla y se quedaba mirándola, ella rebullía y se acurrucuba más en la sombra, mezclando la risa con los gruñidos, anticipos del instinto con que suele entregarse la india voluptuosa y huraña. (186)

As insinuated among other things by the references to 'las urgencias de la mujer' and the animal-like delight with which Aymara anticipates her physical surrender to Marcos, the 'lumbre de amor' that lights her eyes is mainly that of sexual desire. Moreover, the fact that Marcos perceives Aymara in equally erotic terms is betrayed by the way in which he tells Ponchopire that he likes his sister 'más que el piraricú del pescado de su nombre' (186) — an assertion that links Marcos's feelings for Aymara with the act of savouring the flesh of the fish with which she is believed to have a spiritual link.[14] On the whole, in the two sections that explore Marcos and Aymara's relationship, there seems to be an underlying implication that racial difference somehow augments erotic desire. The notion that this elevated sexual desire has less to do with Marcos and Aymara as individuals than with cross-racial attraction is further corroborated by the yearning glances that Marcos exchanges with the mysterious green-eyed Huarequena who appears in Ponchopire's village, much to Aymara's distress. We are told that while the rest of the villagers express their respect for Ponchopire — who is delivering a discourse about the recent events of the village — by staring at the ground, 'Marcos Vargas [...] no hizo sino contemplar a la huarequena, quien a su vez se atrevió a sostenerle la mirada varias veces' (191). Yet the relationship between Marcos and Aymara seems rather forced regardless of the powerful sexual magnetism which marks Marcos's interactions with Indian women, because it lacks completely the psychological depth of the novel's other heterosexual relationships. If we additionally take into account Aymara's resigned nature and her almost complete muteness, it becomes more and more evident that she is a thinly sketched character who fulfils a representative role in the novel. As a matter of fact, Aymara's lack of individuality and her purely sexual appeal make her not only an archetypal Indian woman, but also an unresisting, and therefore ideal, tool in the process of *mestizaje*, which Gallegos continues to promote in *Canaima*.

Essentially, Aymara enters the narrative in the penultimate chapter of the novel with the specific purpose of mothering Marcos's *mestizo* son who, as critics have noted, stands as a symbol for a better future. However, the doubts that Marcos himself has about his relationship with Aymara, and even about the child that they are expecting, call into question the efficacy of *mestizaje* as a solution to national and regional problems. In fact, Marcos still longs for Aracelis in the sections 'Aymara' and 'El racional', even though one of the main aims of these two sections is to depict his relationship with Aymara. For instance, at the beginning of 'Aymara', Marcos's earlier, tenderly mocking phrase, '¡Apaga, Bordona! ¡Apaga, que nos quemamos!', fuses together with the image of a burning jungle, in what we can assume to be Marcos's drug-induced hallucinations (183). And in 'El racional' the sight of an old newspaper from Ciudad Bolívar — the only token of 'el mundo civilizado' that Marcos has stumbled upon in the last three years — brings to his mind Aracelis's passionate words, '¡es que te quiero tanto, tanto, tanto!' (189–90). What is more, the newspaper in question is conveniently brought to Ponchopire's village by the *mestizo* sons of a mysteriously murdered *criollo cacique*. These primitive and superstitious *mestizos*, who believe that the village's witch doctor can determine the cause of their father's death through physical contact with the dead man's 'objetos [...] de [...] uso personal' and his 'mechones de cabellos y [...] uñas', present the results of *mestizaje* in a truly negative light (189). Marcos does not fail to notice this fact, as can be seen from the way in which he moves his gaze mechanically from 'la profunda estupidez que expresaban los rostros de los mestizos' to 'el vientre de Aymara', where his child is already developing (190). Indeed, after establishing the unpleasant connection between his unborn child and the slow-witted *mestizos*, Marcos starts avoiding Aymara's company intentionally, and even contemplates leaving the Indian village altogether. Although the section 'El racional' ends with the reconciliation of Aymara and Marcos, this reconciliation should not be read as a sign of hope, but rather as proof of how Marcos has simply accepted the circumstance that he will be facing 'el porvenir sin esperanzas' by the side of Aymara and her fellow Indians (192). Overall, Marcos's lack of affection for Aymara and the feeling of revulsion he experiences on seeing the dead *cacique's* mixed-race sons do not help in any way to prepare the ground for the novel's closing image of the *mestizo* Marcos Vargas as the personification of a better future. One could obviously make a case based on the fact that unlike the ignorant *mestizo* sons of the dead *cacique*, Marcos Vargas (the younger) is about to receive a decent education. As the narrator points out, Marcos sends his son to Gabriel Ureña because he wants his *caraqueño* friend to educate him 'como está educando a sus hijos' (194). Yet even this interpretation fails to be thoroughly convincing if we take into account how Marcos's own, expensive education in a British boarding school in Trinidad did him little good. Considering the way in which education failed to keep Marcos away from the violent adventures of the Guayanan jungles, it appears unlikely that it will have the desired effect on his partly Indian son, who after all has spent his early days in a primitive Indian village, located in the middle of this very wilderness.

III

The pessimism that compromises Gallegos's representation of interracial love and *mestizaje* as effective socio-historical solutions further permeates the temporal and structural organization of *Canaima*. Surprisingly, no sustained analysis of the narrative structure of *Canaima*, or the way in which time functions within this structure, can be found in the otherwise substantial criticism on the novel. Both Maya Schärer Nussberger and Françoise Pérus have accurately acknowledged the existence of two contradictory and competing temporal forces in *Canaima*, one of which is cyclical and repetitive, and the other linear and progressive, but neither critic addresses the issue of how these two forces are played out on the structural level in any significant detail.[15] Besides, both Pérus and Schärer Nussberger oversimplify matters by arguing that the cyclical time in *Canaima* represents the time of myth, a reading that fails to acknowledge the inherently destructive nature of cyclical time in *Canaima*. According to my interpretation, cyclical time in *Canaima* cannot be defined as mythical time because, although the time of myth is cyclical and unprogressive, like the cyclical time in this particular novel, it is not regressive and destructive. A more careful analysis reveals that the cyclical pattern in *Canaima* is furnished by the omnipresence of the mysterious evil spirit, Canaima, 'el dios frenético, principio del mal y causa de todos los males [...] [l]o demoníaco, sin forma determinada y capaz de adoptar cualquier apariencia' (121). Indeed, throughout the novel, the evil spirit slows down the pace of the central narrative of Marcos by increasingly making him a victim of its cyclical and violent logic. And it is ultimately the counterforce of Canaima that prevents Marcos from turning into a social reformer, capable of working towards a convincing and practical set of solutions to the various socio-historical problems of Venezuelan Guayana.

The central narrative of *Canaima* is organized along the apparently linear trajectory of Marcos, his wanderings in the vast lands of Venezuelan Guayana, and the character development that results from his experiences. Before readers become attuned to the reigning, cyclical logic of Gallegos's Guayana, which is a world governed by Canaima, they are likely to approach *Canaima* as a *Bildungsroman*. There are numerous references to the fact that Marcos has the necessary characteristics of a social reformer, though it is implied that these characteristics need some further development. Already as a child, Marcos displays skills of leadership and secures the respect of others as '[el] cacique querido por su carácter expansivo y franco, al par que respetado por la fuerza de sus puños' (10). Moreover, we are told that it is against Marcos's very nature to conform to established social conventions and rules. As he himself confesses, 'a unos pueden imponerle con reglamentos la disciplina que han inventado otros para el público grueso [...] mientras que otros [...] tienen que escoger la suya por sí mismo' (15). Yet Marcos's extraordinary potential is most pointedly recognized by his friend Gabriel Ureña who, as late as in the section 'Unas palabras de Ureña' (Chapter 16), sees Marcos as a man capable of fighting the social injustice which afflicts Venezuelan Guayana:

> En esta tierra hay para ti un camino trillado y una gran obra por emprender. Más de una vez te he oído decir que aspiras a construirte tu vida a tu medida propia. ¿No la conoces ya? ¿No la sientes tal cual es? Por unas cuantas palabras que de regreso del Guarampín me dijiste en Upata comprendía que habías encontrado la plena medida de ti mismo y vislumbrado la obra a que debías dedicarte. Presenciaste la iniquidad y hasta la has sufrido en ti mismo [y] tienes el impulso generoso que se necesita para consagrarse a

combatirla [...] Cuando la vida da facultades, y tú las posees, repito, da junto con ellas responsabilidades. Este pueblo todo lo espera de un hombre, del Hombre Macho que se dice ahora, y tú, ¿por qué no?, puedes ser ese mesías. (170–71)

In this passage Gabriel Ureña is trying to push the disorientated Marcos onto what he considers to be the right path for him. The absolute trust that Gabriel Ureña has in Marcos's potential as a social reformer appears all the more striking when considered in the light of the fact that he expresses this trust at a time when Marcos has been profoundly transformed by his jungle experiences, and his name already carries the stain of homicide. Indeed, Gabriel Ureña seems to believe that the violent social injustice that Marcos witnessed in the jungles of Guarampín has provided him with the necessary grounding for acting against cruelty and corruption. By drawing Marcos's attention to his extraordinary 'facultades' and by envisioning how he could become 'el mesías' of the exploited people of Venezuelan Guayana, Gabriel further tries to convince Marcos that his life has a greater purpose. Essentially, Gabriel's suggestion that '[un] Hombre Macho' can turn into a 'mesías' if he uses his talents constructively, goes so far as to nullify the violent deeds that Marcos has by this point committed, deeds which Marcos himself believes stand in the way of any generous, future actions.

On the whole, Marcos's character development is not an uncomplicated process, but full of twists and turns. Most notably, the ease with which Marcos becomes seduced by the cult of *hombría* can be seen as an example of moral decline rather than evolution. As early as the section 'Ases y suertes' (Chapter 4), Marcos's actions start being dictated by the principles of *hombría*; as the narrator points out, Marcos's imprudently courageous behaviour during his dice game with José Francisco Ardavín has its roots in the fact that 'en él se había desatado ya la fuerza que [...] impulsaba a todos a la afirmación violenta de la hombría' (38). Meanwhile, the way in which Marcos increasingly reacts against social injustices gives the impression that he is a man who learns through confronting difficulties. While in 'Unas manchas de sangre' Marcos still jovially pushes aside Manuel Ladera's pessimistic vision of the socio-historical ills of Venezuelan Guayana, at the end of the section 'Camino de los carreros' he begins his fight against these ills by making sure that Manuel's murderers are brought to justice, despite their connections with the local *cacique*, Miguel Ardavín. Moreover, after observing closely the brutal living and working conditions of the *purgüeros*, whose work he supervises in the jungle, Marcos further comes to understand that 'el trato afable y la superficial camaradería' are simply not enough, but more radical measures are necessary for alleviating the misery of the enslaved workers (134). In short, a reader who is familiar with other works by Gallegos, such *Doña Bárbara*, is likely to presume that Marcos, the budding social reformer, will eventually turn out to be another Santos Luzardo, capable of tracing a road, 'uno solo y derecho hacia el porvenir'.[16] Indeed, this expectation is nurtured by Gabriel Ureña's certainty that there exists for Marcos in Venezuelan Guayana 'un camino trillado y una gran obra para emprender' (170). However, in reality Gallegos merely mockingly plays in *Canaima* with the reader's expectation that the novel will in the end offer some straightforward solution to the socio-historical problems of Venezuelan Guayana. The reader becomes increasingly aware of the fact that expectations in *Canaima* usually turn out to be misplaced, and progress, be it individual or socio-historical, fails due to the cyclicality that determines all actions in the world of Canaima. Hence, the prospect that the novel will sooner or later offer some kind of coherent, practical solution to the region's ills appears increasingly improbable. Nevertheless, the interplay between expectation and the consequent disappointment is maintained until the end of the novel, even when circumstances no longer foster hope. A striking example of this technique can be found at the very end, in the penultimate chapter of the novel (Chapter 18, section 'El racional'), that is, at a point when Marcos has already renounced his travels and become a subdued settler in the Indian village. After listening to the Indian prophecies of how the time of changes is at hand, Marcos begins to contemplate the possibility of doing something substantial for the benefit of the Indians, who have since the time of the conquest been abused by the white man:

> ¿Sería posible — se preguntaba — sacar algo fuerte de aquellos indios melancólicos? ¿Quedarían rescoldos avivables de la antigua rebeldía rabiosa bajo aquellas cenizas de sumisión fatalista? [...] ¿no sería él capaz de reunir bajo su mando todas aquellas comunidades dispersas en un vasto territorio y a la cabeza de ellas emprender aquella obra grande que una vez le aconsejara Gabriel Ureña? Decirle al blanco explotador: '¡Fuera de aquí! ...' Y crear un gran pueblo indio... (191)

Although Marcos seems to have strong doubts about the feasibility of mobilizing the Indians for a project of social reform, as is implied by the way in which most of his ideas concerning reform are formulated as questions, he nonetheless is here entertaining highly ambitious plans. Disappointingly, the hope inherent in Marcos's speculations is immediately undermined by the further questions that he poses to himself: in addition to querying the limits of his own intellectual preparation, he also wonders if '¿no sería ya la raza indígena [...] algo total y definitivamente perdido para la vida del país?' (192). As the pessimistic tone of the remainder of the section reveals, Marcos's momentary optimism only makes him realize more fully the fact that neither he nor the Indians have what it takes to push forward social reform. The section draws to a close with the narrator lamenting the gloomy future that awaits Marcos and the Indians, and closes fittingly with a defeatist image of Marcos and Aymara gazing at the wasted potential of the Ventuari river whose waters are referred to as '[a]guas perdidas sobre la vasta tierra inculta' (192). Considering the way in which the section in the end relapses into defeatism, the function of the earlier reawakening of false expectations appears to be to make the tone of the conclusion of this specific section, as well as that of the novel itself, all the more pessimistic.

The expectation that Marcos's trajectory will in the end turn out be progressive and the impression that it is actually linear are further fostered by the way in which the trajectory records chronological time. The trajectory presents systematically the most important turns in Marcos's life in the order in which they occur. Pivotal temporal markers that help to create the impression of linearity can be found in the early and late parts of *Canaima*, making it possible to establish the almost exact temporal framework of Marcos's life and consequently that of the historical period in which his story unfolds.[17] The first crucial temporal marker can be found in the section entitled 'Marcos Vargas', which is the section that introduces the eponymous character. The narrator draws attention to the way in which for the Indians, who continue to call Ciudad Bolívar by its colonial name, Angostura, 'no ha pasado el siglo y pico de la república' (9). Taking into account the fact that the first Venezuelan republic was founded by Simón Bolívar in 1811 during the Venezuelan war of independence from Spain, this statement places the beginning of Marcos's trajectory in the years immediately following 1911. Moreover, in the same section Marcos enters a British boarding school in Trinidad 'con dieciséis años cumplidos', and subsequently returns to his native Ciudad Bolívar after 'cuatro [años] de internado y disciplina inglesa' (11). At the beginning of the next section, 'Por el camino y ante la vida', Marcos leaves Ciudad Bolívar again, having '[a]caba[do] de cumplir los veintiún años, que lo hacían dueño de sus actos' (14). After this, the narrative moves forward slowly for most of the novel, recording Marcos's life on what is often a daily, and sometimes even an hourly, basis. However, towards the end of the novel there are significant lacunae in chronology. At the beginning of Chapter 17 it is hinted that 'unos tres años' (or more) have passed since the events of Chapter 16 (171). Significantly, a more specific temporal marker appears in the section 'Oro' of Chapter 17. In this section, Marcos's close friend Arteaguita, who has not seen Marcos since his complete retreat to the wilderness, is surprised by the fact that he looks 'como de cuarenta pasados cuando apenas transponía los veinticinco' (178). In Chapter 18, which describes Marcos's life in the Indian village, attention is, on the other hand, drawn to the pregnancy of Marcos's Indian wife, Aymara. Effectively, in '¡Esto fue!', the concluding chapter of the novel, we are told that Marcos has a son — 'un joven como de doce a catorce años' (194).[18] Considering that Marcos, in 'Oro', was about twenty-five, he must be at least in his late thirties by the end of the novel because he has an adolescent son. Hence, the central, organizing narrative covers a period of approximately twenty years. As Marcos's trajectory begins in the years immediately following 1911, the final section is most probably set in the early 1930s, thus bringing the narrative events right up to the historical moment when Gallegos was writing his novel.

IV

Even though a wealth of evidence, on first reading, seems to suggest that Marcos's trajectory is constructed on an intrinsically linear axis, a sustained analysis of the narrative structure of *Canaima* reveals that the progressive linearity of the trajectory is in fact merely illusory. Despite the often exact temporal markers, time in *Canaima* (both the novel and the represented world) is predominantly cyclical. My intention is to demonstrate in the next two sections that Marcos's failed struggle with the world governed by Canaima is cleverly mimicked by the way in which his trajectory becomes entangled with, and is retarded by, the various cyclical temporal-spatial matrices of the novel.

The key to understanding the temporal-spatial organization of *Canaima*, as well as that of its represented world, can be found in the episodes discussing Juan Solito. This mysterious character, who has been described by critics such as Juan Liscano and Armando Rojas Guardía as a *criollo* version of Merlin, provides an insight into the organizational logic of the world of Canaima.[19] Indeed, already when introducing Juan Solito to Marcos, Manuel Ladera warns that underneath his scruffy appearance, Juan Solito 'lleva oculto un filósofo' (21). Significantly, in this same episode Juan Solito goes on to explain, referring to himself in third person as always, that he has derived his knowledge from the trees: 'Los palos del monte [...] le han enseñao su sabiduría' (23). As this enigmatic statement implies, Juan Solito is able to 'communicate' with his environment, and he is therefore much in accord with his surroundings. What is more, we are told that when Marcos encounters Juan Solito the second time, 'en lo más intrincado del monte', he comes across as 'ni cazador de tigres [...] ni tampoco espectador del paisaje, sino más bien como *sumido* en él' (82, emphasis added). In other words, Juan Solito is not only in harmony with the landscape that surrounds him but he is an integral part of it. However, this perfect integration with his environment does not imply that he has anything to do with the destructiveness that characterizes the savage territory, which is presided over by the evil spirit of Canaima. On the contrary, unlike Marcos, whose actions are dictated by the violent principles of his environment, Juan Solito is able to use his perfect comprehension of the logic of the world of Canaima in beneficial ways. His small-scale acts, such as mysteriously 'tying' an animal's or a person's steps in 'la forma del bejuco donde se atocan el principio y el fin' (84), so as to prevent the animal or person from leaving a particular place, show us how the inherently cyclical logic of the Guayanan environment can be manipulated to meet one's own ends. Juan Solito thus has what the novel seems to suggest is the right attitude for triumphing over the cyclicality and violence associated with Canaima.

Juan Solito tries to explain to Marcos the logic of the world of Canaima, but the way in which the latter constantly misinterprets his words only emphasizes the profound contradiction between the mindset of Marcos and the *telos* of his environment. On top of this, Marcos's habit of jumping to conclusions leads Juan Solito to state that '[l]as palabras son como los caminos, que cuando no se conocen piden baquianos. No basta decí: "Por aquí voy a reventá a tal parte"; es menester que tal parte esté en la punta del camino' (83). In addition to criticizing Marcos's hastiness, Juan Solito's words are also worthy of attention because they imply the need to know where one is going. By denouncing directionless wandering, these words implicitly criticize the fact that Marcos has no agenda, destination, or a clear aim towards which he is working. Even more importantly, the emphasis put by Juan Solito on '[los] pasos [amarraos que] están siguiendo la forma del bejuco donde se atocan el principio y el fin' (84) clearly evokes the way in which in the world of Canaima every road is inevitably circular in essence; as Schärer Nussberger has put it, 'los caminos de *Canaima* revelan [...] la renuncia [...] [del] camino "civilizador" soñado por Santos Luzardo'.[20] Yet Marcos, with his faulty interpretation of his environment, fails again to understand the crucial lesson inherent in Juan Solito's references to 'pasos amarraos', and he literally tries to look for the 'bejuco mágico' (84), leading Juan Solito to a further realization of the incompetence of his student. Besides, it is undoubtedly of uppermost importance that both occasions on which Juan Solito makes reference to 'pasos amarraos' take place when Marcos is on the road. The first occasion is recorded very early on in the novel, at the end of Chapter 2, this chapter having suggestively opened with a section entitled 'Por el camino y ante la vida'. The second, more elaborate encounter that Marcos has with Juan Solito takes place in the final section of Chapter 8, following Marcos's confident declaration, at the end of the previous section, that it is not bad to be left 'solo por su camino y ante la vida' (81).[21] The repetition of the expression 'por el [o su] camino y ante la vida' and the reappearance of Juan Solito in Chapter 8 forms a kind of cycle itself, drawing the reader's attention to the lack of genuine progress between Chapters 2 and 8. What is more, the juxtaposition of the venture of setting out on the road with the notion of 'pasos amarraos', and the cycle formed by the repeated material, imply that Marcos's own steps are tied, and his apparently linear trajectory is in reality circular.

The interpretation that Marcos's trajectory is inherently circular finds further support in the fact that the ending of *Canaima* evidently mirrors its beginning. In '¡Esto fue!', the concluding chapter of *Canaima*, material from the opening section, 'Pórtico', is repeated with few or no alterations (I will explore the significance of these alterations more carefully when discussing the novel's ending). The material in question is mainly related to the description of the hydrographic system formed by the Orinoco and its various tributaries. In the opening section as well as in the concluding chapter, various references are made to tributaries such as Ventuari, Maipure, and Atures, with particular emphasis being placed on the fact that the waters of these tributaries are essential 'para que sea grande el Orinoco' (3–6, 192–94). Furthermore, both make significant allusions to boats travelling along the Orinoco, and include in their introductory paragraphs the energetic exclamation '¡–Nueve pies! ¡Fondo duro!' (3, 192), which refers to the depth of water and the condition of the riverbed when navigating. On top of this, in the concluding chapter, in which the younger Marcos Vargas travels to a school in Caracas along the Orinoco, we are told that '[a]poyado sobre la barandilla del puente de proa va *otra vez* Marcos Vargas' (194, emphasis added).[22] The 'otra vez' suggests that the elder Marcos Vargas must have also made a journey of some consequence along the Orinoco earlier on, most probably when travelling to and from his British boarding school in Trinidad. As a matter of fact, the mysterious *vapor*, whose journey upriver is followed in almost minute detail in the opening section of the novel, invites further speculations along these same lines. The anonymity of the *vapor* gives rise to the impression that it could in theory be carrying either Marcos Vargas or his son back from their respective schools in Trinidad and Caracas. While there is not enough evidence to determine that this is actually the case, already the indisputable repetitiveness of the novel's concluding chapter is enough to prove that Marcos's apparently linear trajectory is grounded in a dominant temporal-spatial matrix that is cyclical, and his trajectory accordingly bends back on itself. Throughout the novel he is merely walking around in a circle, which he in the end completes in the form of his son, Marcos Vargas, who then begins the trajectory all over again.

V

In addition to the all-encompassing cyclical temporal-spatial matrix of *Canaima*, it is essential to acknowledge the existence of various smaller, cyclical organizational units in the novel. In fact, in *Canaima* these smaller cyclical matrices can help the reader to distinguish the novel's dominant cyclicality long before reaching the end. Hence, I will now move on to explore how the cyclicality is played out throughout the novel, for instance, in the episodes discussing life in provincial towns. Aside from focusing on the particular way in which time functions within these towns, I will also make reference to how the composition of specific textual units, such as sections and paragraphs, often mirrors the cyclical organizational principle of the world of Canaima, a principle according to which the beginning and the end must always touch.

The subnarrative of provincial towns intermingles repeatedly with the central narrative recording Marcos's trajectory. Out of the fifty sections in *Canaima*, thirty-eight are set partly, or fully, in one of the provincial towns, in their immediate outskirts, or on the road between them. Additionally, the provincial towns play a particularly significant role in the first half of the novel, wherein Marcos's trajectory proceeds almost exclusively between them. Marcos first travels from his native Ciudad Bolívar to Upata to take over Manuel Ladera's fleet of carts, then from Upata to San Félix in the company of Manuel Ladera whom he is helping to transport some livestock, and then from San Félix back to Upata again. After an extended stay in Upata, Marcos goes to El Callao in order to attract some more clients for his transportation company, after which he finally sets out for the jungle at the beginning of the second half of the novel, following a brief spell in Tumeremo. Marcos's trajectory in the first half of *Canaima* accordingly consists of various unprogressive routes that can be most accurately described as 'numerosas vueltas del protagonista sobre sus propios pasos', an expression used by Pérus to describe the stagnant nature of the central trajectory of *Canaima* in general.[23]

The lack of progress that characterizes Marcos's trajectory in the first half of *Canaima* is also accentuated by the cyclical structure of a number of sections (e.g. 'Por el camino y ante la vida', 'Claro de luna', and 'También Marcos Vargas').[24] In these cyclical sections the section title is either repeated in the final paragraph of the section or material from the first paragraph of the section is recycled in the final one. As illustrated in the section 'Por el camino y ante la vida', which marks the beginning of Marcos's adventures as he departs from his native Ciudad Bolívar, this technique can be used to subvert the progressive drive of the content, by displaying the underlying cyclicality of Marcos's trajectory. Yet the main function of the cyclical sections is to emphasize the cyclical nature of time and experience in the provincial towns of Venezuelan Guayana. As part of his comprehensive study of the temporal-spatial organization of provincial town novels, Mikhail Bakhtin has identified the key features of the kind of cyclical time that generally determines the rhythm of life in provincial towns. Much of what Bakhtin says about time in provincial towns can help us to understand better the function that this particular type of time has in *Canaima*. According to Bakhtin, in traditional provincial towns:

> There are no events, only 'doings' that constantly repeat themselves. Time [there] has no advancing historical movement; it moves rather in narrow circles: the circle of the day, of the week, of the month, of a person's entire life. A day is just a day, a year is just a year — a life is just a life. Day in, and day out the same round of activities are repeated, the same topics of

conversation, the same words and so forth. In this type of time people eat, drink, sleep, have wives, mistresses [...], involve themselves in petty intrigues, sit in their shops or offices, play cards, [and] gossip.[25]

Bakhtin's evocation of this cyclical time, which is characterized by repetitiveness and monotony, captures impeccably the atmosphere of stasis that dominates in provincial towns, including the ones portrayed in *Canaima*. Moreover, as Bakhtin explains elsewhere in his essay, the cyclicality of time in provincial towns not only implies the lack of 'advancing historical movement', but it actually opposes 'the progressive forces of history', making life 'a senseless running-in-place at one historical point, at one level of historical development'.[26] Indeed, as I will now illustrate, the inhabitants of the provincial towns of Venezuelan Guayana, with whom Marcos associates closely and frequently, are portrayed as a people who live in the past and the present and display no desire to break the stagnant cycles of their small-town lives.

The fact that the residents of the provincial towns of Venezuelan Guayana seem contentedly resigned to the lack of change is already suggested by the way in which the same jokes are successfully repeated over and over again. A striking example is the joke that concerns the tradesmen brothers, Francisco and José Vellorini, whom the clients refer to as 'Vellorini el bueno y Vellorini el malo' respectively (26). Behind the humorous epithet lies Francisco Vellorini's trick of sending any clients making unprofitable proposals to José, whom he advises in advance to reject the proposals, therefore turning his far more benevolent brother into a scapegoat. Though this strategy has been repeated so many times that 'ya no había quien se lo creyera' (27), referring to the Vellorini brothers by their nicknames has become an amusing tradition both in Upata and Tumeremo. Another source of amusement relates to the chubby Childerico's habit of boasting that 'yo tengo mi corcel y algún día lo jintearé' (74), whenever he suspects that he is being ridiculed by his acquaintances. By taking Childerico's words literally, the *upatenses* enjoy speculating maliciously about what kind of 'horse' Childerico might be alluding to when he talks about his 'corcel'. Surprisingly, even Aracelis's way of behaving is to some extent determined by the uneventful life of Upata, despite all the references made to her adventurous nature. In fact, thanks to his intimate relationship with Aracelis, Marcos is in constant danger of being absorbed permanently into the cyclical life of Upata. Suggestively, in the section 'La Bordona' — which as we have already seen records a conversation that Marcos and Aracelis have through a window grille — Aracelis tells Marcos that she has asked a shooting star 'que nos conserve toda la vida junticos, así como estamos en este momento' (75). Although her request could be read as that of any young lover who does not wish the moment to pass, the statement is likely to have further implications, considering the fact that Aracelis presents an alternative destiny of settling down. After all, by wishing that she and Marcos could become 'conserv[ados] toda la vida junticos, así como est[án] en este momento' she is requesting that they could be stationary in time and space, and this obviously means that she would always have Marcos with her in Upata. Moreover, Aracelis's conversation with Marcos reveals also that her mindset is essentially no different from that of the other inhabitants of the provincial towns. In her conversation with Marcos she recreates a number of past incidents in which he has been involved, including his unusual dice game with José Francisco Ardavín and his practical jokes during the local treasure hunt — incidents which she then fleshes out with her own, seemingly irrelevant commentaries. Dwelling on the audacity with which Marcos has reinterpreted local jokes, power hierarchies, and legends provides a major source of entertainment for Aracelis.

Overall, the past is regarded by the inhabitants of the provincial towns of Venezuelan Guayana as a dominant presence that continues into the present, rather than as a historical phase that has been left behind. Illustratively, when the *Españolito* produces a document that appears to 'corroborar una vieja leyenda' concerning '[unos] lingotes de oro' (58), which were buried by the Spanish monks on the eve of independence, the whole of Upata becomes mobilized in a passionate treasure hunt. The legend about the treasure takes such a powerful hold on the collective imagination of the *upatenses* that it helps to distract completely the people's attention from the recent murder of Manuel Ladera, who after all was well-liked and respected by his fellow townsmen.[27] Even more strikingly, the mining town of El Callao is defined chiefly in terms of its literal golden past. Filled with nostalgia, the *jefe civil* of El Callao, Apolonio Alcaraván, paints a vivid picture of a multicultural, prosperous, and lively mining town where '[n]o se cerraban las puertas de los botiquines para los turnos de negros que tres veces al día [...] salían de la mina, ni en ellos se bebía sino champaña y *brandy* fino' (91). Meanwhile, the already ageing 'negra Damiana', whose parents both used to work at the old gold mine, physically clings on to the residues of El Callao's golden past by washing the sands of the Yuruari river where 'pepitas de oro' can still be found (92). In the end, the general lack of historical development in the provincial towns is underlined by the allusions made in the concluding chapter, '¡Esto fue!', to how 'todavía la negra Damiana continúa lavando las arenas' while 'Childerico continúa diciendo que él tiene su corcel y algún día lo jineteará' (193). Almost twenty years after the original references, life in provincial towns still keeps on rotating on the same stagnant axis.

Yet the atmosphere of stasis that characterizes the provincial town episodes already finds a pronounced expression earlier on, in the constant present of the American Míster Davenport and his companions, which is described in the section 'El varadero', located at the dead centre of *Canaima*. While Míster

Davenport, who enjoys retelling amusing stories about the various 'travesuras de muchachos' (93) committed by his group of friends, might not appear to have a different mentality from the other inhabitants of provincial towns, he is, however, unlike them in that he is aware of the inactivity that surrounds him, though he is for the most part unwilling to admit his own idleness. In fact, as is implied throughout 'El varadero', stasis is not an exclusive characteristic of the provincial towns of Venezuelan Guayana, but a far more general characteristic of the Guayana region as a whole. Even though Míster Davenport criticizes the people of Venezuelan Guayana for asking 'permiso a una pierna para mover la otra', and claims that the innate 'flojera' of the Guayanese is the very cause of 'el paludismo', he as a foreigner has not been immune to all inactivity-related diseases (96). Effectively, Davenport explains that foreigners like himself, who have been left 'varados' in Venezuelan Guayana, are victims of '[una] enfermedad incurable [...] [que] [s]e llama chinchorro, [y] que es la enfermedad más traidora de esta tierra' (98). Davenport then goes on to describe humorously the nature of this disease in more detail:

> ¡el chinchorrito, el chinchorrito! Cuando yo digo esta cosa, quiero decir todo lo que significa el trópico para los hombres que no hemos nacido en él. Tú decides marcharte, porque ves que por adentro de tí ya no anda bien la cosa, y el trópico te dice, suavecito en la oreja: 'Deja eso para después, *musiú*. Hay tiempo para todo.' (99)

As Davenport's words suggest, the Guayanan tropics seduce foreigners into abandoning their journeys with the promise of a more relaxed life where time is not immediately pressing. Additionally, the 'chinchorro', or hammock, as a symbol for the tropics alludes to ways in which Venezuelan Guayana fosters lethargic inactivity in foreigners; accepting a life devoid of any significant, productive action is a requirement for fully adapting to the tropical environment. The powerful hold that the 'chinchorro' disease has on Davenport is conveyed by the confidence with which he boasts about how he keeps 'busy' riding around on his mule and drinking imported whisky while employing 'términos y giros criollos', which have made him popular among the locals (94-95). Besides, it is worth noting that although at first glance Davenport's anecdotes about foreigners who have caught the 'chinchorro' disease and been left 'varados' in Venezuelan Guayana might not seem to have an immediate relevance to the *criollo* Marcos, who appears as a mere listener in the episode, a more careful analysis reveals that this is not the case. As a matter of fact, these anecdotes prefigure the way in which Marcos will renounce his journey and become immersed in the cyclical rhythm of life of the Indian village, where he settles down.

Marcos's integration into the life of the Indian community in Chapter 18 is described in similar terms, sometimes using the very same symbols, as the acclimatization of foreigners to Venezuelan Guayana. Marcos spends his first days in the Indian village, lying 'en [un] chinchorro de urdimbre sutilísima tejida con plumas de raros pájaros de la selva', and experiencing 'la suave voluptuosidad de una paz profunda' while contemplating 'sencillas escenas de comienzos de mundos' (184). Surely, one can recognize in this sensual portrayal of Marcos lying in his exotically decorated 'chinchorro', savouring the feeling of immersion in the voluptuousness of a peace stimulated by his new environment, an echo of the earlier description of how the seductive voice of the tropics softly whispers in the ear of the foreigner lying in his 'chinchorro', and lures him to renounce his journey. Furthermore, while Davenport's almost perfect integration into his new environment finds expression in his thorough adaptation to the relaxed lifestyle of the inhabitants of Venezuelan Guayana, the extent to which Marcos adopts the lifestyle of the Indians is conveyed by his assimilation of the cyclical rhythm of the Indian village. Marcos participates in daily activities such as fishing, at night-fall joins the other men in the circle around the fire, and takes part in rites and festivities, which are dictated by the movements of the moon. However, it is essential to point out that despite its apparently harmonious nature, the cyclical time of the Indian village is not an inherently idyllic time. Adapting to the life of the Indians, who pick lice with '[un] éxtasis animal' (184) and eat from 'una sola fuente, donde todos metían [...] [sus manos] nada limpias' (185–86), implies regressing on the evolutionary scale. In point of fact, whereas the stagnation of the provincial towns presented an obstacle for historical development, the lands of the Indians, which are evocatively described as 'tierras melancólicas que se quedaron atrás en la marcha del mundo' (185), exist outside history altogether. Marcos reaches the full understanding of this circumstance when he finds a newspaper from Ciudad Bolívar among the belongings of the mysteriously murdered *criollo cacique*. By being described as 'de un día indeterminable [...] por haber desaparecido el trozo que contenía la fecha' (189), the newspaper gives visual expression to the way in which calendar-time, and by extension historical time, becomes inconsequential even for a *criollo* when living in these lands outside history. Overall, Marcos's realization that he too has lost the notion of time helps him to recognize that his life is not heading in a desirable direction.[28] In other words, like the foreigners who have been left 'varados' in Venezuelan Guayana, Marcos senses in his heart that 'ya no anda bien la cosa' (99). Yet just like these foreigners, who are unable to leave Venezuelan Guayana — which Davenport wittily refers to as 'esta tierra pegajosa' (98) — Marcos cannot escape from the Indian village, because Aymara 'le [ha] aprisionado las huellas' (190). Indeed, by being located in the penultimate chapter of *Canaima*, at the very threshold of the novel's end, this direct reference to 'tied steps' works as a powerful reminder of the overall cyclicality and futility of Marcos's trajectory.

VI

Though Marcos's trajectory is from the very beginning of the novel hamstrung by the inherently cyclical logic of the Guayanan environment, it nevertheless retains its misleading linear impression well up to the point when Marcos enters the jungle in Chapter 12, in a section suggestively entitled 'Canaima'. In this section descriptive material is dominant, with Marcos's name just 'popping up' here and there, as if Marcos were present only in the background, like the landscape or vegetation would normally be in a novel, while the jungle — the core of the world of Canaima — plays the central role.[29] Aside from the episodes featuring Juan Solito, this particular section provides the best insight into the workings of the cyclical and repetitive logic which determines all aspects of life in the tropical, Guayanan environment. The section opens with the repetition of the word 'árboles', the same word being additionally repeated in groups of two and three at intervals throughout the whole episode, conveying a feeling of nausea and entrapping monotony. Further descriptive characteristics are added to the subject 'árboles', as well as the basic feature of repetition, through tautology:

> ¡Árboles! ¡Árboles! ¡Árboles! ... La exasperante monotonía de la variedad infinita, lo abrumador de lo múltiple y uno hasta el embrutecimiento. [...] La grandeza estaba en la infinitud, en la repetición obsesionante de un motivo único al parecer. ¡Árboles, árboles, árboles! Una sola bóveda verde sobre miríadas de columnas afelpadas de musgos, tiñosas de líquenes, cubiertas de parásitas y trepadoras, trenzadas y estranguladas por bejucos tan gruesos como troncos de árboles. ¡Barreras de árboles, murallas de árboles, macizos de árboles! (119)

In other words, repetition in the jungle consists of different variations of what in principle is the same; while the motif itself is constant it incessantly changes in form. Yet this sustained conservation of the tree motif certainly does not mirror the logic of generative *eterno retorno* of the renewal of plants. On the contrary, as is suggested throughout the jungle episodes, the jungle is the cradle of a malevolent cyclicality that hinders the socio-historical development of Venezuelan Guayana, and entraps individuals in a never-ending cycle of violence and cruelty. As already shown in the section 'Canaima', the jungle environment has a profoundly dehumanizing effect on those who dare to penetrate its boundaries. The narrator introduces us to the underlying dynamics of this process of dehumanization by describing the feeling of desperation that the jungle environment engenders in the hearts of people who get lost in its green monotony:

> El infierno verde por donde los extraviados describen los círculos de la desesperación siguiendo sus propias huellas una y otra vez, escoltados por

> las larvas del terror ancestral, sin atreverse a mirarse unos a otros, hasta que de pronto resuena en el espantoso silencio, sin que ninguno lo haya pronunciado, la palabra tremenda que desencadena la locura: — ¡Perdidos! Y se rompe el círculo, cada cual buscando su rumbo, ya totalmente desligado del otro, bestia señera y delirante, hasta que vuelven a encontrarse en el mismo sitio donde se dispersaron, pero ya no se reconocen porque unos momentos han bastado para que el instinto desande camino de siglos. (120)

As this passage illustrates, '[e]l infierno verde' turns human beings into captives, whose actions are dictated by the jungle's intoxicatingly cyclical and repetitive logic. Thus, the people who get lost in the jungle end up 'siguiendo sus propias huellas una y otra vez'; it is as if, on entering the jungle, their steps had been tied in order to ensure that their progressive trajectories are thwarted. The references to 'las larvas del terror ancestral' and to the way in which a few moments are enough 'para que el instinto desande camino de siglos' further indicate that with each circle the men complete, they become increasingly like their primitive ancestors. Essentially, this transformation means that the men lose their collective spirit and become fixated on their survival as individuals. At first the men do not dare to 'mirarse unos a otros', soon after which their group breaks up with each man embarking on his own course, 'ya totalmente desligado del otro'. As the narrator notes, when the men finally meet again, after having completed their respective circles, 'ya no se reconocen'. In addition to delineating the early stages of the dehumanization process that men undergo in the jungle, the fate of these lost people also highlights more generally the degenerative nature of repetitive cycles: instead of marking progress, each new turn in a cycle simply implies further decay and destruction. While I will explore later in this chapter the important, wider implications that these degenerative cycles have for all aspects of life in Venezuelan Guayana, I would for now like to focus on the particular changes that the jungle environment instigates in Marcos's character.

Marcos initially enters the jungle as the foreman of the Vellorini brothers' *empresa purgüera*, following his assassination of Cholo Parima, an act that marks his definite break with the so-called civilized world. From the moment Marcos shoots Cholo Parima in the section 'Las horas menguadas' (Chapter 11), narrative tension begins to build. Not only does Canaima gain an increasingly powerful hold on Marcos after his arrival in the jungle, but it is in this particular environment that Marcos comes face to face with the social injustices of Venezuelan Guayana. Thanks to his friendship with Encarnación Damesano, one of his loyal *peones*, Marcos acquires a deeper understanding of '[el] alma de su pueblo' and learns to perceive 'la íntima rebeldía bajo la total sumisión aparente' (129). Effectively, Marcos loses all remaining vestiges of optimism, after witnessing how Encarnación Damesano dies from a snake bite acquired in the depths of the jungle, where Encarnación ventured with the specific purpose of finding some rubber to harvest. To be more precise, the death of this witty *peón* makes Marcos even more acutely aware of 'la tremenda injusticia que divid[e] a los hombres en Vellorinis y Damesanos', that is to say, into exploiters and the exploited (135). Driven by a completely new type of sombre mood, Marcos penetrates the depths of '[el] bosque antihumano' (136) at the end of the section 'El mal de la selva', only to stumble across further instances of social injustice. Originally, Marcos's plan is to find 'Sute' Cúpira — a fearless *bandolero* who roams the Guayanan wilderness with his 'doce [...] apóstoles' (137) — in order to express his gratitude for the way in which Cúpira's men tried to save Encarnación Damesano by bringing him back to Marcos's camp. However, Marcos does not maintain his high opinion of Cúpira and his followers for long, as he soon realizes that they are just another group of men who ruthlessly exploit the weak. Illustratively, in the section entitled 'Tarangué', Marcos gets infuriated by the fact that Cúpira and his gang make fun of 'los indios humillados y vencidos' by encouraging them to inhale large quantities of intoxicating 'yopo' during a ritual dance (145). At the end of this particular section Marcos sides with the Indians and openly provokes Cúpira and his men by calling them an 'Hatajo de bandidos que [...] explotan [a los indios] inicuamente' (146). In short, already at this point, Marcos seems prepared to give vent to the anger — which has been fermenting in his soul since his original homicidal act — by committing yet another violent deed.

The pressure that accumulates in Marcos's soul over the jungle episodes is further mirrored by the tension that builds up throughout the jungle in anticipation of the coming storm. As a matter of fact, both reach their electrifying breaking points at the beginning of the chapter entitled 'Tormenta',[30] which records Marcos's return to the Vellorini *purguo* station, after his rendezvous with Cúpira's men in the depths of the jungle:

> Regresó a la estación del Guarampín [...] agudizado por la fatiga del viaje el maléfico influjo de la selva. Pero no sólo él sufría sus extraños efectos, ni todo eran aberraciones de espíritu. El fenómeno obedecía también a causas naturales y todos los seres vivientes que poblaban la selva lo experimentaban de algún modo.
>
> Aproximábase el término de la estación lluviosa y hacía varios días que reinaba esa tregua que se toman las lluvias antes de desatarse en los tremendos chubascos finales del invierno tropical. Calmas enervantes y prolongadas durante las cuales el silencio de la fronda inmóvil sentíase cargado de presagios angustiosas [...] y sobre el inmenso condensador de la selva se iba acumulando la electricidad para el cataclismo de las descargas que pronto la estremecerían hasta la raíz más soterrada. (146)

The opening of the chapter 'Tormenta' thus lays out explicitly the intrinsic connection between Marcos's tormented soul and the dense atmosphere of the jungle, a connection which will be developed throughout the chapter. The quoted passage also establishes the fact that the accumulating tension has its origin in 'el maléfico influjo de la selva', which is gaining an increasingly powerful hold on all the inhabitants of the jungle as the storm draws closer. Indeed, in the first half of the chapter, significant attention is paid to the 'frenesí de crueldad' that overtakes human beings, during the prolonged hours of expectation (147). Most notably, the *peones* become possessed by an urge to torture and mutilate 'insectos o bestezuelas inofensivas' (147), in whose suffering they then take sadistic pleasure. In extreme cases this brutality escalates to the level of self-harm, as Marcos discovers when he comes upon a rubber worker, who is trying to cut off his own index finger. Yet Marcos himself is certainly not free from 'el maléfico influjo de la selva', as can be seen from the way in which he stops the act of mutilation from taking place by striking the rubber worker cold-bloodedly with the handle of the *machete*, until he writhes in pain on the ground. In so doing, Marcos falls into a trap: by opting to crush violence with further violence, he is actually drawn closer to the evil spirit that he is trying to fight. As I will show through a close reading of the *tormenta* episode, although Marcos thinks that he gains a deeper understanding of himself during the violent storm, which eventually breaks out, it is in fact during this pivotal episode that he succumbs entirely to the malignant influence of Canaima.

Before providing a detailed analysis of the storm and its effect on Marcos's character, however, it is worth pointing out that critics have unanimously acknowledged that the *tormenta* functions as the central crisis of *Canaima*. For instance, both Juan Gregorio Rodríguez Sánchez and Potelet call the 'Tormenta' chapter 'el clímax', while Liscano refers to it as 'el punto cenital de [la] novela', and Schärer Nussberger strongly agrees.[31] Furthermore, as Pérus observes, the importance of the episode is accentuated on the structural level, as it is '[el] primer capítulo de la novela que no se subdivide, como los anteriores, en varios apartados, para marcar con ello y en el plano estrictamente formal, el momento de mayor confluencia y precipitación de los caudales narrativos'.[32] Yet the secondary literature on this particular chapter still leaves scope for further exploration, as critics have overlooked especially the way in which the *tormenta* episode addresses the issue of the true nature of Marcos's trajectory. In point of fact, I would suggest that the episode summarizes on a symbolical level the various changes of direction to which Marcos's trajectory is subjected throughout the novel.

In the 'Tormenta' chapter much emphasis is put on the 'vereda ancha, larga y recta' which Marcos follows in the jungle, the expression being repeated with small alterations five times altogether (148–50). According to my interpretation, the 'vereda' is intended as an implicit symbol of Marcos's trajectory and as a rather obvious reminder of Santos Luzardo's road, 'uno solo y derecho hacia el porvenir'.³³ As Marcos walks along the 'vereda', usual notions of time and space are subverted, and as a consequence the 'vereda' loses its apparent linear direction. Thus, Marcos finds it impossible to determine if he has walked '[u]na hora, quizá dos' or 'sólo algunos minutos' (148). Significantly, the fusion of all time into one and the same moment brings to mind the constant present of the provincial towns where time's passing seems to make little difference, as well as the time of the jungle itself, where there is no 'otra vez' but only 'todavía' (123).³⁴ Moreover, the reader's attention is further drawn to the fact that the 'vereda ancha, larga y recta [...] se hundía por los dos extremos en los verdes abismos' (148). The 'vereda', with its beginning and end sinking into hallucinatory perspectives, gives rise to the impression that the 'vereda' is a curved line, this image capturing the way in which Marcos's trajectory on a larger scale bends back on itself. What is more, throughout the *tormenta* episode Marcos alternately abandons and picks up the 'vereda', just as he resumes his apparently linear trajectory after long stays in provincial towns. The last time he returns to the 'vereda', when the storm has already begun, the 'vereda' suddenly ends 'contra el bosque intrincado' (152). The sudden end of the 'vereda' both mimics Marcos's absorption by the jungle environment and the way in which his trajectory will lose its course completely after the *tormenta* episode. While Marcos had no clear idea before the storm of where his path was taking him, he now literally loses any remaining vestiges of the path itself. Following the initial puzzlement caused by his experiences during the storm — which is described in Chapters 15 and 16 — Marcos starts dashing hither and thither in order to prove his *hombría*. Correspondingly, the narrative tempo accelerates from Chapter 16 onwards by omitting long periods of time; approximately three years have passed between Chapters 16 and 17 and another twelve to fourteen years pass between Chapters 18 and 19. Hence, the events of Marcos's life after the storm are in general briefly glossed over, his most adventurous years being mainly referred to in retrospect by the *caucheros* in Chapter 17. These time gaps and the altered narrative tempo help to emphasize the fragmentary nature of Marcos's experience during the years following the *tormenta*, years which he in fact spends roaming aimlessly around the Guayanan wilderness, before ultimately settling down in the Indian village.

In order to understand the reason why Marcos's trajectory loses its course from the *tormenta* episode onwards, thereby disappointing expectations of him as a social reformer, it is, however, necessary to consider the metamorphosis that Marcos undergoes during the storm. Rodríguez Sánchez has captured the very essence of this metamorphosis, as well as that of the 'Tormenta' chapter in general, when he states that:

> El capítulo 'Tormenta' [...] supone el bautismo de Marcos Vargas, su consustanciación con la selva. Es la ruptura con su mundo anterior, el

elemento símbolico que detiene el proceso redentor y que envuelve al protagonista que, a partir de ese momento, desiste de su empresa y se convierte en un integrante más del mundo inconcluso.[35]

Marcos's transformation into just another element of the jungle is already foreshadowed early on in the *tormenta* episode by the corresponding humanization of the vegetal world, which with its 'mil pupilas asombradas' contemplates Marcos 'desde cada una de las hojas de todas las ramas del bosque' (149). Effectively, Marcos himself also anticipates his decisive battle with Canaima and the natural world that the spirit stands for. As the narrator notes, the motivation behind his theatrical undressing at the outbreak of the storm is to measure himself in his nakedness against the full forces of Nature. Moreover, as the following passage illustrates, the borderline between Marcos's physical, especially inner, self, and the outer world of the jungle, becomes increasingly blurred during the storm:

> Las raíces más profundas de su ser se hundían en suelo tempestuoso, era todavía una tormenta el choque de sus sangres en sus venas, la más íntima esencia de su espíritu participaba de la naturaleza de los elementos irascibles y en el espectáculo imponente que ahora le ofrecía la tierra satánica se hallaba a sí mismo, hombre cósmico, desnudo de historia, reintegrado al paso inicial al borde del abismo creador. (151)

With the storm palpitating in his veins, Marcos fuses with the furious elements in this powerful passage, which borders on the fantastic. Yet the key image of the passage is undoubtedly that of Marcos putting down roots in the ground on which he stands — an image which prefigures his occasional transformations into a tree. As a matter of fact, slightly later, in the section entitled 'Contaban los caucheros', a direct link is drawn between Marcos's transformations into a tree and the state of being possessed by Canaima. Following a night filled with terrifying cries, which make one of Marcos's Indian helpers conclude that '[s]iendo Canaima gritando en la cabeza del siburene', Marcos confesses that on waking up 'sentía el cuerpo [...] como si alguna vez hubiera sido de madera' (174–75).[36] In the light of all this evidence, the image of Marcos putting down roots in the 'suelo tempestuoso' during the storm should not be seen as a harmonious coming together with nature. Indeed, the notion that Marcos emerges from his baptism by the elements as '[un] hombre cósmico, desnudo de historia, reintegrado al paso inicial del abismo creador' carries with it further negative implications. Although, at first glance, not being burdened by the sins and mistakes of one's ancestors might appear to be a positive thing, having no history also has its drawbacks. In fact, the most significant outcome of the storm is that Marcos loses touch with progressive, historical time for good, as he becomes immersed in the constant present of the Guayanan wilderness. Generally speaking, Marcos's break with historical time and the image of his putting down roots both suggest that he comes to a figurative standstill, a standstill that marks the end of his active struggle with the force of Canaima, and hence also that of his plans of social reform. On the whole, Marcos does not emerge from the storm with a better understanding of how to tackle Venezuelan Guayana's socio-historical problems; instead he incorrectly comes to assume that, just like the storm he too should be full of '[i]ra' and 'cólera' when faced with 'la iniquidad que no permit[e] el optimismo en [su] corazón generoso' (151). As his first frenzied and then submissive behaviour demonstrates, unlike Juan Solito, who is at one with his surroundings, Marcos never learns to master the jungle environment but instead becomes an unresisting puppet of the ferocious forces that he is trying to conquer. Hence, Marcos does not in the end turn out much better than the *caudillos andinos*, whom Gallegos in his essay 'Las tierras de Dios' (112–44) describes as having been born out of a similar 'torbellino creador' (120).

VII

The profound pessimism that pervades Gallegos's treatment of the theme of social reform in *Canaima* finds a further expression in the fact that Marcos is not the novel's only failed social reformer. As I mentioned earlier, when discussing the novel's representative heterosexual relationships, the *caraqueño* Gabriel Ureña should be regarded as Marcos's bookish alter ego. Initially, Gabriel seems to ooze potential: in the section 'Las palabras mágicas', which focuses on his childhood, the *voces clamantes* of Venezuelan Guayana's injustices already call out to him as he studies maps of the region's vast deserts and jungles (44). He thus becomes conscious of the need to fight these injustices at a far earlier stage than Marcos, who becomes fully aware of the iniquity that surrounds him only after witnessing it himself. The contrasting emotions that the closeness of the untamed lands of Venezuelan Guayana evoke in Marcos and Gabriel — as they contemplate the waterfalls of Caroní for the first time — provide an excellent insight into the highly different psyches of these two characters:

> Hundiendo la mirada en las nieblas mañaneras [Gabriel Ureña] quedóse en silencio largo rato reviviendo los sueños de la adolescencia, cuando inclinado sobre el mapa le parecía oír las palabras cabalísticas clamando en el desierto. Detrás de aquellas lejanías estaban las tierras de la violencia impune, el vasto país desolado del indio irredento, las misteriosas tierras hondas, calladas, trágicas ...
> También Marcos Vargas callaba [...] Si los saltos del Caroní eran enormes fuerzas perdidas, también lo eran todavía sus vehementes inclinaciones hacia la aventura de gran escenario: la selva sin fin, el vasto mundo del itinerario gigantesco vislumbrado a través de los cuentos de los caucheros, sembrado de hermosos peligros. (45)

Gabriel is here clearly being haunted by the need to do something about the social injustices and wasted potential of the wilderness of Venezuelan Guayana. Although he is intensely drawn to the mysteries of these sparsely inhabited lands, Gabriel's way of regarding these lands as the home of 'la violencia impune' and '[el] indio irredento', suggests that he nevertheless resents the fact that these lands remain untamed and uncivilized. Marcos in the meantime seems barely interested in the wasted potential of Venezuelan Guayana's vast territories, but is instead annoyed by how his conventional occupation as the owner of a cart-fleet company holds him back from exploring these lands.[37] Effectively, Marcos views these barbaric lands, which are strewn with dangers, as the ideal setting for tantalizing adventures. Yet even though Marcos and Gabriel have very different understandings of the possibilities offered by Venezuelan Guayana, they nevertheless take pleasure in each other's company. As the narrator points out in the section 'Camino de los carreros', the secret of this 'mutua simpatía' lies in the fact that the two men actually complement each other (51). While Gabriel is a theoretician of social reform, who is well-read in the region's myths and history, Marcos rejects bookish learning from his childhood and generally assumes an active approach to life. In other words, together the two men have the necessary traits of a successful social reformer but individually they either lack the theoretical grounding of Venezuelan Guayana's socio-historical issues, or the talent to turn speculative ideas into productive actions. Whereas Marcos squanders his potential and energies in aimless demonstrations of *hombría*, Gabriel's drive for social reform crumbles as a result of his phlegmatism. Regardless of the ambitious dreams that Gabriel entertains as a child, he becomes a 'telegrafista por apatía, por aceptación de un *modus vivendi* en un sentido de menor resistencia, ya que su padre lo había sido y desde niño le enseñó el oficio' (64). He further allows outside forces to dictate his actions and life-decisions when promising Maigualida to stay away from her house, in order to avoid the wrath of José Francisco Ardavín, a promise which he keeps until his rival goes completely insane. And finally, by marrying Maigualida, Gabriel renounces any remaining possibilities of turning into a social reformer; as Gabriel puts it, when he is trying to push the responsibility of social reform onto Marcos, his marriage requires him to dedicate his life fully to 'lo personal y prudente' (170). All in all, Gallegos's decision not to present us with an ideal social reformer in whom a sharp intellect blends with a drive for action — as he nevertheless did in *Doña Bárbara* with regard to the character of Santos Luzardo — highlights in yet another way the substantial revisions to which the author is subjecting his theories of socio-historical progress in *Canaima*.

However, the sense of failure that accompanies every mention of social reform in *Canaima* cannot be exclusively attributed to the deficiencies of the novel's potential social reformers. As a matter of fact, at various points the novel conveys the impression that the socio-historical ills are so robustly grounded in the milieu of Venezuelan Guayana that they appear unconquerable. A closer look at the depiction of cycles of exploitation and violence — both of which are closely related to the cycles of generations — reveals that while each cycle in *Canaima* might have its own specific end, it is merely a variation of a perpetual principle of violence or exploitation.[38] In other words, the end of one cycle is devoid of significance because it merely marks the beginning of yet another similar one. Indeed, as Apolonio Alcaraván perceptively points out to Marcos, though in a far more light-hearted context, the story of the inhabitants of Venezuelan Guayana can be best described as '[un] cuento de nunca acabar' (93).[39]

Throughout *Canaima* significant emphasis is placed on the essentially cyclical nature of the social exploitation which forms part of the everyday life of Venezuelan Guayana. Manuel Ladera explains, as early as Chapter 2, that Guayana's natural riches such as 'purguo y oro' are essentially the region's 'maldición', because they increasingly corrupt people, tempting them away from traditional occupations, such as cultivating the land (17). By helping to exploit the natural resources for the greedy *empresarios*, the workers themselves become exploited 'por medio del sistema del avance' (17). As the narrator further points out in Chapter 15, at the end of each season of exploitation many of the workers 'no tra[en] sino deudas', and even those who have been 'más laboriosos y prudentes o más afortunados' squander their earnings 'en horas de parranda' (156). Both kinds of men return the next year, either in order to pay their debts to the *empresario*, or with the intention of making a fair sum of money which this time will not be misspent. Furthermore, the cycle of enslavement is passed on to the next generation, as is indicated by expressions such as '[l]a esclavitud que a veces [...] heredan los hijos con la deuda' (18) and '[la] hipoteca del hombre sin rescate que a veces pasaba de padres a hijos' (104). Similarly, the prerogative of violent leadership also passes from one generation to another, as is suggested by the way in which the Ardavines have held the 'cacicazgo' of the Yuruari district '[d]esde lejanos tiempos' (32). Though the Ardavines of the past are described as 'hombres valerosos' (32), the contemporary Ardavines, on the other hand, merely display signs of degeneration: José Gregorio Ardavín retires from civilization and later dies de 'la repugnante enfermedad del carare' (32), Miguel Ardavín is thrown into a prison, and the generally cowardly José Francisco Ardavín goes completely insane and starts wandering around aimlessly, 'desgarrada la ropa' and 'babeante la boca' (163). Yet the decline of the Ardavín family does not mark the end de 'la sangrienta historia de las revueltas armadas' of the Yuruari district of Venezuelan Guayana (32).[40] On the contrary, as Marcos learns when he encounters the new *jefe civil* of Tumeremo, 'la política antiardavinista [...] no consist[ía] [...] sino en la suplantación de la violencia de unos por la de otros' (115).[41] Moreover, Marcos himself is not able to break the cycle of violence and adventure initiated by his two older brothers, both of whom are now dead. Marcos acknowledges that by buying Manuel Ladera's fleet of cart he was trying to please his mother, who was afraid to lose yet another son to the dangers of the *aventura cauchera*. However, by moving to the Yuruari district, where the cart-fleet transportation company operates, Marcos's path crosses that of Cholo Parima, the murderer of one of his brothers. As a result of this circumstance, Marcos eventually becomes involved in the kind of violent actions that he was trying to avoid in the first place. Marcos's role as perpetuator of the cycle of violence is accentuated by the very structure of the paragraph in which he describes the irony of his situation to Manuel Ladera, the cyclical effect being achieved in this particular instance by the way in which the paragraph opens and closes with the exclamation '¡Lo que son las cosas!' (20).

VIII

The fact that the cycles of generations are closely linked with those of exploitation and violence, both in Venezuelan Guayana and more specifically in the life of Marcos, underscores the pessimistic connotation that all cycles have in *Canaima*. It is certainly no coincidence that the overarching cyclical temporal-spatial matrix of *Canaima* produces a cycle of generations, with the younger Marcos Vargas in the end picking up the trajectory his father had renounced, hence announcing the commencement of yet another cycle. While the misleadingly encouraging image of the *mestizo* Marcos Vargas as a new, more educated, social reformer has prompted critics to interpret the ending of *Canaima* as a promise of a better future, a systematic analysis of the concluding chapter '¡Esto fue!' reveals that the novel ends on a decidedly pessimistic note. In point of fact, there exists a profound contradiction between the optimistic image of the younger Marcos Vargas, and the structural implications and overall mood of the concluding chapter.

The ending of *Canaima*, which consists almost exclusively of repeated material, marks the triumph of the ruinous cycles. Illustratively, the concluding chapter '¡Esto fue!' opens with a virtually exact repetition of the description of the Orinoco that originally appeared in the introductory section, 'Pórtico':

> Bocas del Orinoco. Puertas, no bien despejadas todavía, de una región por donde pasó la aventura que aridece el esfuerzo y donde clavó la violencia sus hitos funestos. Aguas de tantos y tantos ríos por donde una inmensa tierra inútilmente se ha exprimido para que sea grande el Orinoco. ('¡Esto fue!', 192)

> Bocas del Orinoco. Puertas, apenas entornadas todavía, de una región donde imperan tiempos de violencia y de aventura [...] ¡Agua de mil y tantos

ríos y caños por donde una inmensa tierra se exprime para que sea grande el Orinoco! ('Pórtico', 3–5)

The central message of the passage as it appears in '¡Esto fue!' is that only a few minor changes, and absolutely no productive developments, have taken place in the years that have passed between the beginning and the end of the narrative. Thus, the 'puertas' that in the opening section were 'apenas entornadas' continue 'no bien despejadas todavía' in the repeated description, suggesting the way in which the world of Canaima still remains to a large extent undiscovered and full of enigmas. Moreover, the general function of the minute but significant alterations in the diction and format that appear in the later passage is to accentuate the negative development that has occurred between the two points. For instance, the substitution of the expression 'agua de mil y tantos ríos' for 'aguas de tantos y tantos ríos' means exchanging a description of the exuberance of the Orinoco for an insinuation of monotonous enumeration. In the later version, the glorifying tone of the earlier version is further subverted by the exclusion of the exclamation marks and by the introduction of the adverb 'inútilmente' into the description of how the 'inmensa tierra' drains 'para que sea grande el Orinoco'. The past tense of the repeated passage additionally emphasizes the impression that any opportunities that might have existed are now gone for good. Overall, the optimistic expectation of coming adventures that is apparent in the earlier version is replaced in the later version by an atmosphere of renunciation and disillusionment resulting from the victory of violence.

Significantly, this repetitive opening of the concluding chapter sets the tone for the rest of the chapter, where the central concern seems to be to exhibit the negative nature of change in its various aspects. Not only are the positive outcomes of technological progress directly called into question by the allusion to how 'el progreso *aparente* del camión' has replaced 'los carros de los antiguos convoyes' (192, emphasis added), but various references are made to the fact that the economy of Venezuelan Guayana is now in decline. While life in the provincial towns continues rotating in the same monotonous cycles as before, with 'la negra Damiana' still washing the sands of the Yuruari and Childerico declaring that he has his 'corcel', the sands 'ya no arrastran oro' and in Childerico's shop '[ya] no hay mucho que vender' (193). Furthermore, even the apparently positive comments concerning Gabriel Ureña's farm, *Tupuquén*, where '[l]a tierra produce, los ganados se multiplican, los hijos crecen y van saliendo buenos' (193) fails to convey a picture of genuine socio-historical progress. As Schärer Nussberger has pointed out, the prosperity of Gabriel Ureña's farm and family 'queda incluída en el ámbito estrecho de un "idilio pastoril," de una vida que no se abre verdaderamente al futuro'.[42] Generally speaking, the concluding chapter of *Canaima* emphasizes the fact that the situation of Venezuelan Guayana has only worsened over time, and the past, which with its numerous social problems was nowhere close to idyllic, appears as more attractive than the present.[43] The overwhelming nostalgia for the past is expressed by the exclamation '¡Esto fue!' of the chapter title, this exclamation being repeated six times at short intervals throughout the chapter, conveying a sense of cyclicality. Each statement about the current state of affairs ends with the exclamation '¡Esto fue!' — the reference to the past reminds the reader that the present situation is merely a new, more degenerate variation of the older cycle we have come to know in the novel. The message of the victory of the ruinous cycles is even accentuated by the cyclical structure of the concluding chapter: only the beginning (the first two paragraphs) and the end (the last paragraph) make references to the hydrographic system of the Orinoco, almost directly quoting material from the opening section of *Canaima*. As a matter of fact, the cyclical structure of the concluding chapter mimics the more general temporal-spatial organization of the novel, which consists of a number of smaller, cyclical organizational units embedded in a larger, overarching cyclical matrix.

The likelihood that the new cycle begun by the younger Marcos Vargas at the end of *Canaima* will merely repeat his father's lack of productivity is clearly anticipated by the overtly negative understanding of change that prevails in the concluding chapter. Perhaps at first glance, the final image of the younger Marcos Vargas travelling 'hacia el porvenir', his journey aided by the current of the Orinoco, might indeed appear to contradict this interpretation and encourage the optimistic reading favoured by various critics. After all, according to literary tradition, travelling with the current towards the mouth of the river symbolizes travelling forwards in time, while travelling towards the origin of the river implies travelling backwards in time. However, a closer inspection of the representation of rivers in 'Pórtico', the novel's opening section, reveals that in the world of Canaima even traditional ideas attached to rivers as symbolical analogues of temporal succession are subverted. In 'Pórtico' the different phases of the Orinoco, as it flows towards the sea, are first described in terms of human chronology, the final stage suggestively consisting of how the river 'ya viejo y majestuoso [...] despide [a] sus hijos hacia la gran aventura del mar' (4). The progressive temporal scale offered by this description is, however, almost immediately undermined by the account of the journey of the anonymous *vapor*. Ascending evolutionary stages are attained as the *vapor*, whose 'marcha es tiempo', travels upriver; 'la soledad de las plantas' gradually gives way to emblems of animal life, including 'salvajes rajeos' and 'huellas de bestias', as well as to tokens of human habitation such as 'trochas del indio', 'tarimbas de palma', and 'gritos de un lenguaje naciente' (4). Hence, rather confusingly travelling both downriver and upriver involves advancing towards a more developed stage of existence.⁴⁴ As the two contradictory temporal gauges offered by the Orinoco illustrate, in the world of Canaima the beginning and end are also identical in temporal terms: both mark the accumulation of all time and the point zero from which the regaining of time can begin all over again. In fact, as we have already seen, in this profoundly cyclical world, where the subject's steps are always tied, it does not make any difference in which direction one chooses to travel because one will still always reach the point which is simultaneously the beginning and the end. And ultimately, in such a world there cannot exist a true opening 'hacia el porvenir' (194).

In the final analysis, *Canaima* does not offer anything close to a coherent model for solving the socio-historical problems of Venezuelan Guayana, but instead devises an apparently comforting ending that once again aims to reawaken the reader's (false) expectations. Essentially, the introduction of the younger Marcos Vargas as another potential social reformer merely pushes any possible solutions outside the boundaries of the novel, thus assuring the further continuation of '[el] cuento de nunca acabar' (93). Yet one should not allow the novel's instrinsic pessimism to overshadow the fact that *Canaima* marks a pivotal turning point in Gallegos's ideas about nationhood and socio-historical progress. His growing disillusionment with regard to interracial love as a standard solution to Venezuela's complex problems, as well as his discontent with the concept of an ideal social reformer, clear the ground for substantial thematic and structural revisions. As I will illustrate in the next two chapters, after rejecting his previously oversimplified model of social reform, Gallegos begins in novels such as *Pobre negro* and *Sobre la misma tierra* to explore new paths to socio-historical progress, paths that are not solely built around interracial love and *mestizaje*. Even though the traditional narrative framework of interracial romance still persists to different degrees in these later novels, Gallegos proceeds to expose the framework's crevices and to experiment with what critics have classified as fragmentary narrative structures. Also, Gallegos's representation of the figure of the potential social reformer undergoes further, major changes in *Pobre negro* and *Sobre la misma tierra*: the main characters of these novels are no longer exclusively *criollo* patriarchs but also women and/or mixed-race individuals. Indeed, the rather forced image of the younger, *mestizo* Marcos Vargas as a potential social reformer recovers some credibility when considered in the wider context of Gallegos's novelistic production, as this image can be seen to anticipate the more active parts played by mixed-race individuals in Gallegos's later Venezuelan novels. Instead of being depicted as mere end products of interracial love, the *mestizos* of these later novels are diligent participants in national and regional affairs, that is to say, individuals who are capable of either succeeding or failing in their endeavours, depending on their distinct characters and skills. By presenting as potential social reformers individuals who belong to marginal social groups because of their race or gender, Gallegos comes to undermine successfully the traditional *criollo* and patriarchal order of the nation-family. Moreover, Gallegos's understanding of nationhood develops from *Canaima* onwards, as he begins drawing more reasonable connections between regional and national concerns. By the time he writes *Sobre la misma tierra* he has realized that while the fate of one particular region can rarely exemplify that of the Venezuelan nation, regional projects can nevertheless contribute to national well-being. All in all, by resorting to innovative yet realistic socio-political agendas, Gallegos finds in *Pobre negro* and *Sobre la misma tierra* a way out of the cycles of desperation that characterize *Canaima*.

Notes to Chapter 1

1. Rómulo Gallegos, 'Una renuncia', in *Una posición en la vida*, ed. by Lowell Dunham (Los Teques: Ediciones del Gobierno del Estado Miranda, 1985), pp. 110–11 (p. 110). Subsequent page references to Gallegos's socio-political writings appear in parentheses in the text.
2. Whilst Gallegos acknowledges already in his 1919 essay 'Las causas' (15–22) that change might have to be initiated by an individual, at this early stage he sees the rule of the *caudillo civilizador* as a purely transitional stage on the path to democracy.
3. See Efraín Subero, 'Génesis de *Canaima*', in *Canaima*, ed. by Charles Minguet, Colección Archivos (Madrid: CSIC, 1991), pp. 309–16, for a discussion of the various different phases of the writing of *Canaima*.
4. Gustavo Luis Carrera, '*Canaima* y sus contextos', in *Canaima*, pp. 317–24 (p. 323).
5. John V. Lombardi, *Venezuela: The Search for Order, the Dream of Progress* (Oxford: Oxford University Press, 1982), pp. 10, 27.
6. Judith Ewell, *Venezuela: A Century of Change* (Stanford: Stanford University Press, 1984), p. 17. As Ewell further points out, in a letter to Cipriano Castro in 1900 the Venezuelan politician and scholar César Zumeta stated that 'Guayana is our reserve and future. Exploit it, General, and neither fortune or history will ever forget your name' (17, author's translation). It should, however, be borne in mind that with the discovery of major oil fields in Zulia in the 1920s, Venezuelan Guayana, just like many other previously economically attractive regions, lost some of its allure.
7. See Zephyr Frank, 'The International Natural Rubber Market 1870–1930' <www.eh.net/encyclopedia/article/frank.international.rubber.market> [accessed 5 September 2010]. Frank notes that by 1914 Malaysia had already overtaken South America's biggest rubber exporter, Brazil. After this point the rubber exploitation industry moved to South East Asia for good.
8. Ewell, p. 37; and William M. Sullivan, 'Situación económica y política durante el periodo de Juan Vicente Gómez, 1908–1935', in *Política y economía en Venezuela 1810–1976*, ed. by Alfredo Boulton (Caracas: Fundación John Boulton, 1976), pp. 247–71 (pp. 263–64).
9. In the late nineteenth century, when Antonio Guzmán Blanco was the President of Venezuela, regional *caudillos* enjoyed a high degree of autonomy; as Lombardi puts it, '[i]n the federal system managed by Antonio Guzmán Blanco, local caudillos governed their localities in any way they saw fit so long as public order was not greatly disturbed and the local government supported the national government' (192–93). Yet as Edwin Lieuwen, *Venezuela*, 2nd edn (London: Oxford University Press, 1965), observes '[w]ith

the coming to power of the *andinos* at the turn of the century, the pattern of political control of the nation by regional *caudillos* had come full circle' (43). Whilst Castro had already successfully weakened the power of the *caudillo* system, Gómez made further efforts to centralize Venezuelan politics. In Ewell's words, 'By 1922 [...] Gómez had built a new national administration which was stronger and more unified than anything that Venezuela had experienced since the colonial period' (59).

10. *Mestizaje* is presented as the appropriate solution to Venezuela's socio-historical contradictions in both *La trepadora* (1925) and *Doña Bárbara* (1929).
11. Pilar Almoina de Carrera, 'Canaima: arquetipos ideológicos y culturales', in *Canaima*, pp. 325-39 (p. 339); and Françoise Pérus, 'Universalidad del regionalismo: *Canaima* de Rómulo Gallegos', ibid., pp. 417-72 (p. 434).
12. Janine Potelet, 'Canaima, novela del indio caribe', in *Canaima*, pp. 377-416 (p. 412). Potelet is here referring to José Vasconcelos's *La raza cósmica* (1925) and quoting from José Carlos Mariátegui's *Siete ensayos de la realidad peruana* (1928).
13. Rómulo Gallegos, *Canaima*, ed. by Charles Minguet, Colección Archivos (Madrid: CSIC, 1991), p. 14. Subsequent page references appear in parentheses in the text.
14. The narrator explains in the section 'Ángulos cruzados' that the *nahual* is the name given by the Indians to what they believe to be the '*alter ego* o segunda encarnación del yo' (123, emphasis in original).
15. Maya Schärer Nussberger, 'Canaima: la vuelta al mito', in *Rómulo Gallegos: el mundo inconcluso* (Caracas: Monte Ávila, 1979), pp. 187-243; and Pérus, pp. 421-31.
16. Rómulo Gallegos, *Doña Bárbara*, ed. by Domingo Miliana, Letras Hispánicas, 5th edn (Madrid: Cátedra, 2004), p. 468.
17. Whilst critics have generally neglected the temporal framework of *Canaima*, a significant exception is Michael Doudoroff in his introduction to the English version of the acclaimed critical edition of the novel. Doudoroff speculates that '[t]he telegraph had come to Upata, so most of the adventures occur after about 1890; a motion picture is shown, but there are no automobiles, so the later events probably take place before 1920' (Rómulo Gallegos, *Canaima*, ed. by Michael J. Doudoroff, trans. by Will Kirkland (Pittsburgh: University of Pittsburgh Press, 1996), pp. xi-xviii (p. xvii)). However, by reading historical time from technological advancements such as the 'telegraph', the 'motion picture', and 'automobiles' instead of looking for precise numerical temporal markers in the novel, Doudoroff ultimately erects a faulty temporal framework. Moreover, he also makes a significant mistake in suggesting that there are no automobiles in *Canaima*. In '¡Esto fue!', the final chapter of the novel, specific attention is drawn to the way in which 'el progreso aparente del camión' has overtaken 'los carros de los antiguos convoyes' (192).
18. '¡Esto fue!' is a self-contained chapter, which is not divided into sub-sections.
19. Juan Liscano, 'Las tres novelas mayores: *Doña Bárbara, Cantaclaro y Canaima*', in *Rómulo Gallegos multivisión*, ed. by Isaac J. Pardo and Oscar Sambrano Urdaneta (Caracas: Ediciones de la Presidencia de la República, 1986), pp. 195-225 (pp. 222-24); and Armando Rojas Guardía, 'Canaima o la nostalgia de un héroe', in *Canaima ante la crítica*, ed. by Lyll Barceló Sifontes-Abreu (Caracas: Monte Ávila, 1995), pp. 149-68 (p. 158-59).
20. Schärer Nussberger, p. 197. Here it should be recalled that Schärer Nussberger fails to acknowledge the eminent relevance that her claim has in terms of the socio-historical reality of Venezuelan Guayana, because she does not believe that *Canaima* is tied to a specific country or region.
21. The substitution of 'el camino' for 'su camino' seems to imply that Marcos is in the later section more in charge of his destiny and the road that he is taking. Yet the

'control' suggested by the word 'su' is almost immediately overturned by Juan Solito's denunciation of directionless wandering in the episode that follows.
22. Critical controversy surrounds the source of the deliberately vague expression 'la capital', which is identified as the younger Marcos Vargas's destination. Both Liscano, p. 220, and Waldo Ross, 'Meditación sobre el mundo de Juan Solito', in *Canaima ante la crítica*, ed. by Lyll Barceló Sifontes-Abreu (Caracas: Monte Ávila, 1995), pp. 45–59 (p. 47), insist that the younger Marcos Vargas travels to Ciudad Bolívar. María del Carmen Porras, 'Entre los peligros de la desmesura y las limitaciones de la normalidad: *Canaima* de Rómulo Gallegos', *ALPHA: Revista de artes, letras y filosofía*, 18 (2002), 43–62 (p. 61), on the other hand, claims that he is sailing to Caracas. Overall, Caracas does appear as the more plausible alternative. The attention drawn to the way in which 'es el Orinoco quien lo va sacando hacia el porvenir' (194) implies that his journey is actually aided by the Orinoco, and he must therefore be travelling downriver towards the sea. Besides, *nota explicativa* 132 of the Charles Minguet edition specifically points out that at the time when Marcos Vargas's story is set, passengers from the Guayana region had to 'mecerse y marearse en un oleaje costero del Este, por 15 días de cabotaje angustioso, en barcos que eran una amenaza y una tortura' (212) in order to reach Caracas. Although the original purpose of this explanation is to illustrate why the journey in question was not popular, making it common for parents to send their children to boarding schools in Trinidad instead, it nevertheless also reveals that steamships from the ports of the Orinoco basin did sail to Caracas via the ocean. On balance, it appears more likely that Gabriel Ureña, himself a *caraqueño*, would have sent his sons, as he is now sending the younger Marcos, to a school in Caracas rather than to one in Ciudad Bolívar.
23. Pérus, p. 434. Whilst Pérus's expression 'numerosas vueltas del protagonista sobre sus propios pasos' describes well Marcos's trajectory in the first half of the novel, it is far less applicable to the second half, where the emphasis is on jungle episodes and Marcos's later, spontaneous adventures. As I will explain later in this chapter, the cyclical logic of the world of Canaima is explored in new ways in the second half of the novel. Moreover, in the light of the evidence relating to the linear impression of Marcos's trajectory, which has been addressed above, I find it impossible to agree with Pérus's generalizing statement that '[la] principal característica [de la trayectoria de Marcos] consiste en que no se *presenta jamás* como lineal y progresiva' (434, emphasis added).
24. With the exception of the concluding chapter, '¡Esto fue!', there are few sections with an evidently cyclical structure to be found in the second half of *Canaima*. This change in narrative style helps to make the rhythm of the narrative of the second half less predictable, accordingly stressing the increasingly fragmentary nature of Marcos's experience. Whilst there are also various cyclical sections to be found, for instance, in *Doña Bárbara*, these are more evenly distributed over the whole novel than in *Canaima*. Although cyclical sections, such as 'Uno solo y mil caminos distintos' (Chapter 4, 'Primera Parte'), 'Los rebullones' (Chapter 8, 'Segunda Parte'), and 'La hora del Hombre' (Chapter 5, 'Tercera Parte'), at times slow down the progressive drive of *Doña Bárbara*, in contrast to *Canaima*, the cyclical counterforce furnished by these sections does not hinder the novel from ultimately putting forward an agenda of sociohistorical development.
25. Mikhail Bakhtin, 'Forms of Time and of the Chronotope in the Novel', in *The Dialogic Imagination: Four Essays by Mikhail Bakhtin*, ed. by Michael Holquist, trans. by Caryl Emerson and Michael Holquist (Austin: University of Texas Press, 1981), pp. 84–258 (pp. 247–48).
26. Ibid., pp. 229–30. Bakhtin makes this statement whilst pointing out that, though the cyclical time of provincial towns resembles the cyclical time of the idyll in a number of

27. As the narrator points out in the section 'El tesoro de los frailes' (57–60), Miguel Ardavín encourages the fraudulent enterprises of *Españolito* with the specific purpose of distracting public attention away from the murder of Manuel Ladera, which was committed by Cholo Parima at the orders of José Francisco Ardavín.
28. Other factors that make Marcos fully aware of the fact that his life is not heading in a desirable direction include 'la profunda estupidez' (190) imprinted on the faces of the dead *cacique's mestizo* sons and Aymara's pregnancy.
29. Just like *Doña Bárbara*, which dwells on life on the *llanos*, *Canaima* too can be categorized as a *novela de la tierra*. The Spanish American *novelas de la tierra* have been criticized for focusing on the natural world to such an extent that they often pay limited attention to questions of characterization and plot. My analysis of *Canaima* illustrates that lengthy descriptions of nature do not necessarily have to compromise the literary quality of a novel. For a discussion of the role that nature plays in *Canaima*, see Carlos Fuentes, 'Rómulo Gallegos: la naturaleza impersonal', in *Valiente mundo nuevo: épica, utopía y mito en la novela hispanoamericana* (Mexico City: Fondo de Cultura Económica, 1990), pp. 97–121.
30. As I will explain in more detail below, apart from the concluding chapter '¡Esto fue!', 'Tormenta' is the only chapter in the novel, which is not divided into subsections.
31. Juan Gregorio Rodríguez Sánchez, 'El "Pórtico" de *Canaima* como totalidad', in *XIX congreso internacional de literatura iberoamericana* (Caracas: Ediciones del Centro de Estudios Latinoamericanos Rómulo Gallegos, 1980), pp. 249–57 (p. 255); Potelet, p. 395; Liscano, p. 143; and Schärer Nussberger, p. 220.
32. Pérus, p. 447.
33. Gallegos, *Doña Bárbara*, p. 468.
34. When discussing the different stages in the development of butterflies that Marcos witnesses in the jungle, the narrator explains how

> [u]n día, recién llegado, estando allí fue la lluvia de falenas. Millares, millares de gusanos que de pronto comenzaron a caer de las ramas de todos los árboles. Y *treinta días después, estando allí, no otra vez sino todavía, pues era como el tiempo no hubiese corrido*, fue la eclosión de las crisálidas, el repentino florecimiento del aire. (123, emphasis added)

35. Rodríguez Sánchez, p. 255.
36. As Potelet, p. 383, explains in footnote 32, 'siburene' means 'jefe indígena en los dialectos Caribes'. However, in 'Contaban los caucheros' the Indian helper evidently uses the term to refer to his *criollo* boss, Marcos Vargas.
37. Directly after lamenting the fact that he has not yet been able to explore the Guayanan wilderness, Marcos goes on to contemplate the various downsides of being an owner of a cart-fleet company. In his adventurous mind his new occupation appears monotonous, as it basically consists of 'ganarse la vida, simplemente, recorriendo una y cien veces los mismos caminos detrás de [los] carros' (46).
38. When discussing cycles of generations, I do not use the word 'generation' merely to refer to stages of descent such as grandfather, father, and son, but I also employ it when distinguishing between the more specific stages of peer succession (e.g. between brothers and cousins of a fairly similar age).

39. After telling Marcos '[una] buena porción del anecdotario propio y ajeno de la vida picaresca de El Callao', Apolonio Alcaraván concludes that it is impossible to narrate everything because 'sería cuento de nunca acabar, porque El Callao, como todo Guayana, es una universidad donde los hombres se lo pasan estudiando travesuras de muchachos y celebrándoselas unos a otros' (93).
40. When discussing the violent past of the Yuruari district, Gallegos points out that political violence is by no means an exclusive characteristic of the district in question, but an integral part of Venezuelan history in general. This is one of the few instances in the novel where Gallegos draws a direct analogy between the socio-political situation of Venezuelan Guayana and that of the Venezuelan nation.
41. As Sullivan, pp. 250–51, explains, Gómez initially gained the support of the Venezuelans, who had grown tired of the constant threat of civil war, with his slogan 'Paz, Unión y Trabajo'. This slogan promised

> paz que libraría el país de la pesadilla de la guerra civil que había amenazado a Venezuela desde 1892; trabajo que permitiría a los venezolanos obtener los beneficios de éste sin amenaza alguna de interferencia y unión que acabaría con el faccionalismo, las luchas intestinas y las rivalidades entre los partidos que habían dividido al país a todo lo largo de la historia. (251)

However, in reality the elimination of the often region-specific *faccionalismo* simply brought in a new type of violence. By installing his friends and family members in important political and administrative positions, Gómez assured the continuous persecution and purging of his opponents. In Ewell's words, there were basically three options left for critics of the Gómez regime: 'martyrdom, prison, or exile' (37).
42. Schärer Nussberger, p. 234, endnote 10.
43. The nostalgia for the past which is expressed in '¡Esto fue!' can be regarded as an elaborate version of the earlier glorification of the past that is apparent in the provincial town episodes.
44. When studying the way in which the Orinoco is described in the opening section of *Canaima*, Pérus correctly observes that 'el remontar el curso de los ríos [...] [no] coincide con un retorno hacia los sucesivos "pasos perdidos"' (423). Pérus, however, fails to acknowledge the two contradictory temporal analogues offered by the descriptions of the Orinoco in this section, and instead plays down the importance of succession by arguing that '[t]odos los tiempos históricos y míticos coinciden aquí y se yuxtaponen en un mismo paisaje' (423). Pérus's use of the expression 'pasos perdidos' alludes to the Cuban Alejo Carpentier's novel *Los pasos perdidos* (1953), where the protagonist-narrator's journey towards the origins of the Orinoco involves travelling backwards in Venezuelan history.

CHAPTER 2

Alternative Paths to Progress in *Pobre negro*

I

Pobre negro (1937) stands out for being the first novel that Gallegos published after his return to Venezuela in 1936, following the death of dictator Juan Vicente Gómez. Although *Pobre negro* provides a fictional interpretation of the socio-political events that led to the Venezuelan Federal Revolution of 1858–63, critics including Mónica Marinone and Pedro Díaz Seijas have insinuated that the new, highly unstable socio-political atmosphere that Gallegos encountered in 1936 might have exerted influence on the novel.[1] In fact, Antonio Scocozza and Doug Yarrington have gone as far as to claim that the principal focus of *Pobre negro* is the political situation generated by the end of Gómez's regime, and that Gallegos merely displaced his story in time by situating it in nineteenth-century Venezuela.[2] While dictator Gómez's death in late 1935 undeniably marked the beginning of a new political era, it was initially followed by scenes of complete chaos: there were protests and widespread looting and vandalism as the people realized that the old order had definitively collapsed.[3] On the whole, the argument that in *Pobre negro* Gallegos draws on these immediate socio-political consequences of Gómez's death appears all the more convincing if we consider the fact that he also addresses these consequences directly in his speech 'Soy un hombre que desea el orden', which he delivered to the Venezuelan congress in April 1937, only a couple of months after the publication of his novel.[4] As Gallegos explains in his speech, the end of *gomecismo* instigated a period of transition, that is to say, a gradual yet forceful movement from autocracy to genuine democracy. Throughout the speech, Gallegos insists that the socio-political disorder that accompanied the collapse of the Gómez regime ought not to be viewed in a purely negative light; on the contrary, the disorder holds within it the seeds of a new, less hierarchical social order (150). In fact, Gallegos explores this same, productive, relationship between disorder and order in *Pobre negro*, which, as I will show in the present chapter, is a novel that also records in more than one way a transitional period in Gallegos's socio-political thought.

Overall, the interpretation that *Pobre negro* has two different historical points of reference remains justifiable, even if we choose to assume, as Juan Liscano amongst others has done, that Gallegos had already almost finished *Pobre negro* before returning from exile.[5] During the last three years of his life Gómez's declining health had been the source of widespread and constant speculation, which had been keenly exploited by the political opposition.[6] Gallegos, who had left Venezuela in 1931 precisely because he wished to avoid being absorbed into the corrupt politics of the Gómez government, doubtless followed the news concerning Gómez's death carefully, waiting for the moment when he could finally return to his native country. For Gallegos, as for millions of Venezuelans at home, the awareness that Gómez's almost thirty-year-long dictatorship was finally coming to an end presaged a significant turning point in Venezuelan history. The time of change was at hand. Indeed, I consider it highly probable that it was the approaching end of Gómez's era which encouraged Gallegos to draw lessons from an important, earlier moment of socio-political change. My analysis will accordingly assume that *Pobre negro* addresses various events and debates which took place in the 1930s, but unlike Scocozza, I will not disregard the meaningfulness of the novel's nineteenth-century setting. As a matter of fact, by focusing on the build-up to the Federal Revolution, and on the revolution itself, Gallegos explores a historical period that effectively laid out the fragmentary and unstable foundations of the Venezuelan nation.[7] Gallegos himself points out in 'Soy un hombre que desea el orden' that it is incorrect to portray Gómez as the one and only source of Venezuela's socio-political ills. In Gallegos's words, the dictator should rather be regarded as the natural end-product of '[un] largo período de involución hacia la barbarie que venía siguiendo el país casi desde los mismos comienzos de la República' (150). In the light of this evidence, I would like to suggest that in *Pobre negro* Gallegos's aims are in fact twofold: on one hand he seeks to understand why Venezuela remains a socially and politically divided nation in the 1930s, and on the other, he tries to project towards the future the type of structural change that the Federal Revolution promised, but ultimately failed, to introduce into Venezuelan society. What is more, throughout the novel, Gallegos uses the conflicted atmosphere of hesitation and change, which is furnished by both the Federal Revolution and Gómez's death, to question, and cautiously to revise, some of his own key ideas and models relating to progress in Venezuela.

As illustrated in Chapter 1, Gallegos already abandons his overly optimistic and linear view of socio-political progress in *Canaima*, where he turns the novel's main protagonist and potential social reformer, Marcos Vargas, into a victim of the inherent cyclicality that governs all the temporal and spatial elements of the Guayanan environment. In *Pobre negro*, Gallegos's originally straightforward understanding of progress breaks down even further, as he moves closer to admitting that no 'standard' progressive agenda can be successfully applied to the different social, ethnic, and political sectors of the Venezuelan nation. Correspondingly, in terms of structure, Gallegos departs in *Pobre negro* significantly from the orderly *Bildungsroman* format, where the story line is usually constructed along the trajectory of one specific hero. Instead Gallegos achieves a disorderly effect by experimenting in *Pobre negro* with a relatively complex narrative plot, consisting of multiple narrative trajectories which correspond to the novel's various main characters (Pedro Miguel, Luisana, Cecilio the elder, and Cecilio the younger) — each trajectory epitomizing a possible, alternative path to progress. By identifying a *mestizo* (Pedro Miguel) and a woman (Luisana) as potential social reformers, Gallegos illustrates his increasing disenchantment with the type of the *criollo* intellectual, whom in his earlier novels and essays he had regarded as having the exclusive ability to lead the uneducated masses towards progress. In line with this change of view, both of the Cecilios, who answer the description of the stereotypical *criollo* intellectual, fail to act effectively during those moments of socio-political change when they should in theory have put their pre-eminent education into practice. In fact, in *Pobre negro* Gallegos additionally rejects the idealistic concept of an almost messianic, intellectual man of action — this rejection process having originally begun in *Canaima* — by accentuating the circumstance that no individual man (or woman) possesses all the necessary qualities required for carrying out a project on a national scale. Moreover, while in *Canaima* we could perceive a sharp movement from a national to a regional focus, the even more specific issues of race and gender become central in *Pobre negro*. Essentially, Gallegos's increased concern with matters relating to race and gender — which will indeed be resumed and developed in *Sobre la misma tierra* — reflects his growing disillusionment with his previously relatively unproblematic vision of the Venezuelan nation. However, it is worth noting that this concern was originally prompted at least to some extent by actual socio-political events that took place in Venezuela in the 1930s, and these events further determine the type of expression that issues of race and gender find in *Pobre negro*.

Though *mestizaje* is fundamental to Gallegos's socio-political thought in general, *Pobre negro* is, with the exception of *La trepadora* (1925), the only Gallegos novel that concentrates predominantly on ethnic difference, and explores in depth the incorporation of black people into the Venezuelan nation-family — *mestizaje* being usually associated in Gallegos's oeuvre with indigenous peoples. Focusing on the highly conspicuous ethnic difference of the black people seems clearly to help Gallegos to accentuate the persistence of the contrasting and competing racial-cultural elements, which, as he explains in socio-political essays such as 'Las causas' (15–22), can be still regarded as the source of the social divisions of twentieth-century Venezuela. Yet as Henry Cohen has pointed out, Gallegos's rather sudden and short-lived shift in interest to the fate of black people was likely to have been prompted even more specifically by the immigration debate that gained momentum in the 1930s.[8] Throughout the Gómez era, the Venezuelan economy had depended to a large extent on black Antillean labour. As Winthrop R. Wright notes, '[t]he majority of stevedores, miners, and coastal agricultural workers came from the Antilles'.[9] However, officially there had been since the late nineteenth century a strict ban on non-white immigration: whereas the immigration of white Europeans and North Americans into Venezuela was encouraged, the entry of non-white (especially black) individuals was opposed by members of the Venezuelan elite on grounds that these coloured individuals would further degenerate the nation's genetic stock. In his detailed account of the 1930s immigration debate, Wright pays specific attention to the way in which the Venezuelan elite continued clinging to their age-old racist attitudes, regardless of the wave of socio-political change that swept across Venezuela in the years immediately following Gómez's death.[10] Indeed, between 1936 and 1937 the immigration debate merely intensified, as registered in several articles which set forth the 'outright dangers' posed by black immigrants. For instance, Wright notes that the 27 August 1936 issue of the newspaper *Panorama* openly expressed alarm at the rate at which black West Indian workers were entering Venezuela, while further depicting these West Indians as a threat not only to the Venezuelan workers, whose jobs they were taking, but to the integrity of the entire Venezuelan society.[11] Furthermore, this persistent racist attitude was officially codified in the immigration and colonization legislations of 1936 and 1937, which renewed '[the] exclusive policy of admitting whites only'.[12] Considering these socio-historical circumstances, the emphasis that Gallegos places on the necessity and benefits of the incorporation of black people into the Venezuelan nation-family in *Pobre negro* can be justifiably read as a response to a contemporary debate. Moreover, Gallegos's concern regarding the role of black people in Venezuelan national life further anticipates the policies instigated by his political party, Acción Democrática, which during the 1940s would repeatedly criticize Venezuela's restrictive immigration laws as part of its more general campaign against racial discrimination.[13]

In parallel with his sudden interest in the fate of the black people, Gallegos's explosive concern for women's emancipation is also likely to have been triggered by a set of contemporary events, which raged at the time he was composing his novel. Although the Federal Revolution, as well as the period of social upheaval that preceded it, gave women the opportunity to take on unusually active roles, it is certainly no coincidence that the mid-1930s, when Gallegos was writing *Pobre negro*, bore witness to an unprecedented women's liberation movement in Venezuela.[14] As the historian Elisabeth J. Friedman has explained in her seminal book on the topic, 'women's organizing formed a distinct part of the explosion of civic activity following the death of dictator General Vicente Gómez in December 1935'.[15] Yet women had started organizing themselves already before this date; the Asociación Cultural Feminina (ACF) — the first significant Venezuelan women's rights movement — was officially founded in October 1935. From the start the members of ACF, the so-called *acefistas*, fought to improve the social role and cultural level of Venezuelan women. Amongst other things, they organized night schools for working-class women, campaigned for women's suffrage, and demanded the reform of the misogynistic Civil Code, which automatically awarded custody of children to the husband. The notably more moderate Asociación Venezolana de Mujeres (AVM) was, on the other hand, established in February 1936, that is, almost immediately after Gómez's death. Unlike the *acefistas*, the AVM members did not aim to challenge established gender norms. Rather, they sought to improve women's living standards by appealing to the important role that they played in the education and nurturing of the future generations of Venezuelan citizens. Along with these two major coalitions, numerous smaller women's organizations sprung up all over Venezuela particularly between 1936 and 1937: some of these groups described themselves as feminist while others held to traditional Catholic values. Despite their varying degrees of radicalness, collectively these organizations brought women to the foreground of Venezuelan national life, something that could not be ignored by the new political parties that formed after Gómez's death. In fact, most of these parties supported the call for women's suffrage. Gallegos no doubt followed the actions of these women's groups closely because of his deep-rooted interest in socio-political change in general. However, his non-fictional writings additionally reveal a direct interest in issues concerning the socio-political position of women. For instance, in his 1941 campaign speech, 'Había aquí una lección por dar' (182–99), Gallegos specifically insists that women should have the right to vote because 'no es cosa probada que haya más virtud ciudadana [...] en el hombre que en la mujer' (197). Indeed, when women's suffrage was finally obtained in 1947, it was introduced by President Rómulo Betancourt, who was a member of Acción Democrática, the party that Gallegos had helped to found in 1941.

By focusing on minority groups such as women and black Venezuelans, while further acknowledging the variety of paths to progress, *Pobre negro* strives to be ideologically more subversive and innovative than *Doña Bárbara* and *Canaima*. Still, it is worth noting that just as he had done in these earlier novels, Gallegos continues representing *mestizaje* in *Pobre negro* as the primary basis of a new, less hierarchical society, and as a standard precondition for wider socio-historical change in Venezuela. Yet as I will illustrate in the current chapter, *mestizaje* is always a double-edged process, because though it aims to reconcile different ethnic groups and to incorporate the oppressed sectors of the society into the nation-family, its ultimate outcome is homogenization. In fact, a careful analysis reveals that even the various trajectories of the main characters of *Pobre negro* are embedded within an all-encompassing narrative framework of heterosexual, conciliatory love, through which Gallegos had already in his earlier novels conveyed the desirability of *mestizaje* as a solution to Venezuela's social contradictions. Essentially, Gallegos's way of imposing order on the novel's experimental plots by enclosing them within a highly traditional narrative framework mimics the manner in which, on the thematic level, he constantly backs away from the radical positions that he momentarily embraces. As a result, *Pobre negro* comes across as a profoundly indecisive novel which persistently fails to harmonize its multiple driving impulses. The rather limited critical literature on *Pobre negro* fails to account for, and to analyse, the meaning and wider implications of this indecisiveness, and instead simply dismisses the novel for not attaining the literary and aesthetic quality of Gallegos's three major novels, *Doña Bárbara, Cantaclaro,* and *Canaima*. By insisting on measuring *Pobre negro* against the standard expectations of a Gallegos novel, critics including Ulrich Leo and Orlando Araujo have ignored the possibility that Gallegos may have been deliberately trying to push traditional, formal boundaries in the novel.[16] The intention of the current chapter is to fill the gap in the existing criticism by exploring in depth the connection between the conflicting pulls of innovation and hesitation that can be sensed at work on both the thematic and structural levels of *Pobre negro*. I will suggest that the various narrative trajectories of *Pobre negro*, which occasionally almost hide the framework of romance, reveal Gallegos's increasingly questioning attitude towards the viability of conciliatory, interracial love, and the consequent *mestizaje*, as effective solutions to Venezuela's various social problems and inequalities. At the same time, I will also examine how Gallegos's more subversive ideas and narrative techniques constantly fail to achieve their full potential — this circumstance having undoubtedly much to do with the fact that these ideas and techniques are constrained by an inherently traditional narrative framework. Though I wish to demonstrate that there exists a close correspondence between the novel's formal hesitation and its socio-political message, I will at times also draw attention to interesting instances where the correspondence breaks down, and consider why this happens. Overall, the underlying intention of the current chapter is to determine to what extent Gallegos succeeds in *Pobre negro* in establishing a feasible model for a less hierarchical Venezuelan nation-family, in spite of social and textual contradictions.

II

Pobre negro explores the fundamental socio-political contradictions of the Venezuelan nation through the framework of two generations of heterosexual relationships between black (or partly black) men, and white, upper-class women, living in the newly independent Venezuelan Republic. The earliest important historical marker is without a doubt the birth of the tormented Ana Julia Alcorta, the female protagonist of the novel's first interracial relationship. We are told that Ana Julia, who is often also referred to as 'la Blanca', 'vino al mundo junto con la guerra que conmovió el sosiego de la familia Alcorta, acomodada a la tranquila existencia de la Colonia, y sus primeros años discurrieron en un ambiente de sobresalto'.[17] As this statement implies, Ana Julia's birth coincides with the earliest Venezuelan wars of independence from Spain, which took place in the years 1810 and 1811. The fulfilment of the romance between second-generation Luisana Alcorta and Ana Julia's mixed-race son, Pedro Miguel, on the other hand, not only closes the storyline of the novel, but coincides meaningfully with the end of the Federal Revolution, which at least aimed to lay out the foundations of a new, less hierarchical society. Considering the fact that the Federal Revolution ended in 1863, and that the first significant battles for independence were fought in 1810, it can be deduced that *Pobre negro* records approximately the first fifty-three years of the history of the Venezuelan Republic. And these were indisputably critical years in the development of the Venezuelan nation. As Antonio Isea has accurately pointed out, independence itself had merely meant 'la precaria ruptura del cordón umbilical que [...] unía [Venezuela] a [...] España'.[18] Consequently, the novel's two heterosexual relationships, and in a broader sense the lives of the characters involved in these relationships, as well as the lives of the novel's other central characters, unfold over a period of profound historical change, and thus clearly encompass and intertwine with wider historical narratives.

An illustrative indication of the way in which the personal often stands for the socio-historical in *Pobre negro* can already be found in the section 'El extraño mal', which introduces the character of Ana Julia and describes at length the symptoms of her mysterious illness. Overall, the 'extraño mal' which marks almost the entire life of Ana Julia should not be merely understood as the sexual frustration of an individual woman, or as a symbol for the entrapment of Venezuelan women in the novel's nineteenth-century, or possibly even twentieth-century, context.[19] A careful analysis reveals that Ana Julia's repressed sexuality, which is painfully struggling to find an expression, also functions as an implicit symbol for the collective fate of the various oppressed sections of Venezuela's population, which are increasingly striving to become recognized participants in national life. In *Pobre negro* the black people are without a doubt presented as the most prominent group within these oppressed masses. In fact, as the narrator explains, Ana Julia is not only haunted by '[una] extraña dolencia', but also by '[u]na impresión ya casi visual de cierta sombra proyectada sobre ella, de algo espantosamente negro, que fuera a echársele encima por momentos' (11). On one level, this 'sombra [...] de algo espantosamente negro' certainly points to the way in which Ana Julia will eventually give in to her desire for a black man during her random sexual encounter with the slave, Negro Malo.[20] However, the description of Ana Julia's formative childhood years reveals that the same unsettling events that lay the grounds for the development of her psychosexual condition also exacerbated Venezuela's already tense political and racial atmosphere. The events discussed include, for instance, '[l]a emigración del catorce', which is triggered by the arrival of the royalist leader José Tomás Boves, and the rape of a white girl by an anonymous 'negro de estatura descomunal', who is then stoned by the furious white mob as a punishment (12).[21] In the light of this evident connection between individual and socio-historical affairs, the 'sombra', which is merely waiting for the right moment to materialize fully, can additionally be interpreted as foreshadowing the Federal Revolution, in which the clashes between the nation's different social, racial, and political groups will reach their climax. Moreover, if we consider the fact that the Federal Revolution is depicted throughout *Pobre negro* as a significant moment when the *black* people force their way to the surface of Venezuela's national life and history, the 'sombra [...] de algo espantosamente *negro*' (11, emphasis added) appears to be an extremely fitting metaphor for the Federal Revolution. Furthermore, the link between Ana Julia's yearning for sexual satisfaction and the urge of the black people to become acknowledged citizens of the Venezuelan nation is further underlined by the circumstance that Ana Julia's sexual encounter with Negro Malo does not merely mark the fulfilment of a forbidden erotic fantasy. After all, it is during this illicit act that Ana Julia conceives Pedro Miguel and thereby sets in motion the process of *mestizaje*, which is presented in *Pobre negro* as the ideal means through which to incorporate the black people into Venezuelan national life.

As I already noted in passing, Ana Julia's sexual frustration also points very distinctly to the entrapment of the Venezuelan woman, and hence the desire for erotic satisfaction can additionally be read as suggestive of the wish for a wider-scale emancipation of women. I will address this important issue of the emancipation of women more fully later when I discuss Luisana's trajectory. For now, I would point out that the historical narratives of the liberation of the black people and the emancipation of women are indeed closely interwoven throughout *Pobre negro*. A basic comparison of the social roles of the protagonists of the novel's two interracial relationships reveals that these two pivotal, historical narratives unfold, on the whole, according to a similar rhythm. The novel's first couple — Ana Julia and Negro Malo — are still essentially impotent prisoners of the stereotypes imposed on them by the patriarchal *criollo* society. Negro Malo is a slave and his actions are therefore dictated by the *capataz* under whose supervision he toils, while Ana Julia only seems to have the choice between marriage and becoming a nun. Though the novel's second couple, Luisana and Pedro Miguel, still live in a society where women and coloured men are generally considered as inferior, significant change has, nevertheless, taken place. The patriarchal society is in the process of losing its traditional equilibrium. Most noticeably, Pedro Miguel is no longer a slave but a free man (though as I will explain below he owes this freedom mainly to his condition as a *mestizo*). Luisana, on the other hand, challenges the traditional role of the woman repeatedly, and does not find it necessary to act as the passive member in the love affair. She even teases out a declaration of love from the obstinate Pedro Miguel in the section 'Una declaración de amor'. Furthermore, as I will now move on to explore, social change, especially the emancipation of women and of black people, also affects the ways in which heterosexual desire finds its fulfilment.

Ana Julia and Negro Malo's spontaneous sexual encounter, in the section suggestively titled 'Noche de embrujamientos', is not preceded by any kind of amorous prologue. Threatened by the night's mysterious shadows and intoxicated by the persistent beat of *el tambor*, which mimics the palpitations caused by sexual arousal, Ana Julia and Negro Malo are drawn to each other as if under a spell. Through their socially scandalous encounter, both momentarily subvert the roles imposed on them by society. Ana Julia disappoints the expectations placed on her as the daughter of a respectable, land-owning family by engaging in premarital sexual intercourse with a black man, while Negro Malo rebelliously rises from his submissive position by possessing the white daughter of the man who owns him. Yet the narrator chooses to condemn the putative immorality of these actions, accordingly indicating that the existing social norms ought not to be overthrown in such a way. Indeed the illicit encounter has profoundly negative consequences in the long term for both participants. Negro Malo becomes a constant fugitive, and Ana Julia's spirit not only subsides 'en los negros remansos de la melancolía' (28), but she actually dies after giving birth to Pedro Miguel. The novel's main couple, Pedro Miguel and Luisana, on the other hand, fall in love in the critical atmosphere prompted by the social unrest of mid-nineteenth-century Venezuela. And, despite its prevailing constraints, this is a society where the anticipation of coming change already makes it possible to translate interracial desire into respectable romance. Unlike Ana Julia and Negro Malo, Pedro Miguel and Luisana do not rush into consummating their desire. The romance between Pedro Miguel and Luisana develops extremely slowly, with both characters trying to suppress their feelings for as long as possible. Although they meet for the first time as adolescents in 'Día de acontecimientos' (Chapter 2, 'Primera Jornada'), neither of the two explores consciously his or her feelings for the other before the 'Tercera Jornada', which ends with a declaration of love ('Una declaración de amor'). Moreover, it will take the entire 'Cuarta Jornada' before Luisana and Pedro Miguel finally find themselves in the position to envision the fulfilment of their romance in the novel's final section, 'La capitana'. Significant emphasis, moreover, is placed on the fact that both Pedro Miguel and Luisana successfully manage to resist their sexual impulses. Despite her erotic reveries in 'Las aleluyas de la enfermera', Luisana does not become '[una] hembra expuesta al azar de los apetitos' (146). Similarly, Pedro Miguel, in 'El desertor', desists from his violent plan to rape Luisana, and instead docilely surrenders his wounded body into the care of Luisana's nursing hands. In other words, *Pobre negro* narrates a progressive movement from a destructive and random sexual encounter to a healing romance, hence cementing the new type of social order on a peaceful and loving unification, instead of a radical, momentary subversion.

The novel's two heterosexual relationships should in fact be seen as two different stages in the wider national project of *mestizaje*. Consequently, the protagonists of these two relationships ought to be regarded as tools of this particular project. Ana Julia notably acknowledges her involvement in an enterprise on a wider scale when she exclaims, ' — ¡Dios mío! ¿Por qué me has escogido para esto?' (11), while twisting under her convulsive desire for sex. Furthermore, as already indicated above, neither Ana Julia nor Negro Malo seem to be in charge of their own actions in the section 'Noche de embrujamientos'. For instance, when Negro Malo glimpses the Casa Grande at the end of the track that he has been following, he asks himself in some confusion, '¿qué vengo buscando yo por aquí?', and slightly later on, he approaches the unconscious Ana Julia 'contra su voluntad' (23). Ana Julia, in the meantime, is 'ya insensata' when 'encamin[ando] al callejón de los caobos gigantes' (24), where her path crosses with that of the also delirious Negro Malo. Overall, Ana Julia and Negro Malo's one-off encounter, which is only addressed at any significant length in the sections 'Noche de embrujamientos' and 'El salto más allá del límite', functions as a preliminary event. The fact that the encounter is less important in itself than in propelling the process of *mestizaje* is further emphasized by the way in which after these two sections, the narrative rather disruptively leaps ahead to discuss Ana Julia and Negro Malo's *mestizo* son, Pedro Miguel, in the section 'El cachorro'. Understandably, the rather rough union between Ana Julia and Negro Malo could not be held up as the model for the socio-racial solution which is promoted in *Pobre negro*. In the words of Ulrich Leo, the very nature of the encounter dictates the need for yet another 'unión entre negro y blanca no solamente sexual, sino de verdadero amor', which will accordingly appear as 'conciliador, positivo, solucionante y armonizante'.[22] The absolute continuity between the novel's two interracial relationships is further accentuated by Pedro Miguel's awareness that by falling in love with Luisana, he becomes an unresisting tool of the very same project in which his parents had been involved:

> Sintió que el destino insistía en escoger otra víctima para llevar adelante una obra ya iniciada, que su vida dejaba de pertenecerle desde aquel momento para formar parte del plan ineludible, y se asustó que esto ocurriese junto con un desbordamiento de dulzuras interiores nunca imaginadas. (189)

But while Pedro Miguel feels scared about the role that destiny has imposed on him, Luisana is excessively excited about being part of this wider-scale project begun by her aunt, Ana Julia. In fact, in the sections 'Las aleluyas de la enfermera' and 'La nueva Luisana', which record Luisana's immediate impressions and actions after acknowledging her feelings for Pedro Miguel, the object of her affections occupies a surprisingly minimal place in her thoughts. Instead, Luisana is entirely absorbed in thinking of herself as 'La Blanca reaparecida' (144, 146) and contemplating how she will turn Ana Julia's shameful lapse into conciliatory and productive love.

However, while the heterosexual relationships of *Pobre negro* convey lucidly the message of *mestizaje* as a desirable solution to Venezuela's racial problems, the rigid schematism of these allegorical relationships also has its limitations, as it undermines the very naturalness of the driving forces of love and erotic desire. Ulrich Leo and Juan Liscano have discussed the weaknesses of the main love-plot of *Pobre negro* — that is, the romance between Luisana and Pedro Miguel — and both have agreed that it does not seem psychologically plausible. Liscano accurately notes that Luisana and Pedro Miguel appear as an unconvincing match. In his words, 'ninguna de [las] actuaciones [de Pedro Miguel] [...] lo presentan y definen como naturaleza [...] [capaz de] atraer una personalidad tan rica y hermosa como Luisana'.[23] Leo, for his part, points out that Luisana and Pedro Miguel's love affair lacks completely the kind of emotional vigour that would make it convincing. He explains that Luisana and Pedro Miguel do not fall in love because they are inclined to do so, but in order to 'conducir a su "fin" una "acción" inventada de antemano, y a la cual deb[en] someterse los carácteres, en lugar de que ellos fueran los que la dominaran y hasta la produjeran'.[24] Furthermore, it is worth adding that the forced nature of the central love-plot of *Pobre negro* is also emphasized by the fact that far less narrative attention is dedicated to this love-plot than one would expect in a novel proposing heterosexual romance as a conciliatory solution. To begin with, the romance does not become the centre of primary attention until the 'Tercera Jornada', after which it is again set aside for almost the entire 'Cuarta Jornada'. Besides, out of the forty-eight sections of *Pobre negro*, only seven focus directly (and at significant length) on either of the novel's two romantic relationships.[25] And yet I think it is crucial that these relationships play such an integral part specifically at the beginning and the end of the novel. Indeed, the way in which the action of *Pobre negro* is propelled into motion by a description of sexual fulfilment, and brought to a conclusion with an allusion to romantic fulfilment, underlines the fact that the heterosexual relationships of *Pobre negro* function above all (though not exclusively) as framing-devices.

Overall, the separate trajectories of Pedro Miguel and Luisana and the personal development undergone by these two characters are explored in far more depth than the romantic relationship itself.[26] Although the interracial romance is absolutely crucial to the novel's central thesis of *mestizaje*, it nonetheless often seems to function as a mere backdrop to these personal trajectories that provide more particularized interpretations of historical change. Moreover, in addition to Luisana's and Pedro Miguel's trajectories, the tightly intertwined trajectories of the Cecilios, the novel's two socio-political theoreticians, receive a significant amount of narrative attention in *Pobre negro*. I will now move on to explore how these trajectories of the novel's four main characters illustrate the contention that the concepts of progress and emancipation can mean different things to, and may be experienced differently by, divergent types of people, living in the same country, during the same historical epoch. I will also consider the circumstance that though the trajectories are markedly progressive in intention, none of them can be regarded as a model for a successful progressive agenda. While presenting Pedro Miguel, Luisana, and the two Cecilios as potential social reformers, Gallegos, however, harshly delimits the agency of each of the characters by making them somehow incapable of productive action in a wider arena.

III

Although I do not agree with critics such as Hilda Marban and Mónica Marinone, who have rather reductively argued that the plot of *Pobre negro* revolves solely around the character Pedro Miguel, I will, nevertheless, continue the analysis of what I consider to be the novel's equivalent trajectories by looking at the trajectory of this particular character.[27] After all, Pedro Miguel's trajectory provides an especially significant case-study because he is the personification of *mestizaje*, which as I have already argued is the socio-racial solution that Gallegos proposes throughout *Pobre negro*.

Pedro Miguel's path from being 'el repudiado de [la] familia' (51) to becoming a fully-fledged member of the Alcorta family through his romantic unification with Luisana is almost certainly intended to represent a model path along which the marginalized black people should proceed in order to become accepted members of the Venezuelan nation-family. Yet a closer look at this parallel scenario reveals its underlying complexities. No doubt Pedro Miguel is extremely concerned with the destiny of the black people. Already at a young age he reads radical publications, such as 'El Sin Camisa' and 'El Trabuco', to the illiterate black slaves of the neighbouring *haciendas* ('Candiles en la oscuridad') and, later on, he unjustifiably warns them to mistrust the well-intentioned liberal reforms of Cecilio the younger ('La revelación'). What is more, Pedro Miguel finally puts his defiant ideas into practice by becoming the highly esteemed leader of a troop of black *guerrilleros* in the Federal Revolution ('Cuarta Jornada'). But although Pedro Miguel sides with the black people up to the section 'El desertor', one of the final sections of the novel, he is not the 'pobre negro' of the novel's title. On the contrary, he is what Richard Jackson has identified as a recurrent character in Latin American literature, the 'superior' mulatto, who is presented as the suitable leader for the ignorant black masses.[28] And in the case of Pedro Miguel, his partially white blood does not only make him a legitimate leader but also qualifies him as the white Luisana's suitor — a role unavailable to his fully black father, who could only possess Ana Julia momentarily and secretly in the dreamlike 'noche de embrujamientos' (20). What is more, Gallegos's opting for a *mestizo* hero rather than a black hero, who would merely become involved in the process of *mestizaje* through an interracial relationship, suggests that for him the ultimate aim of interbreeding is not so much the mixing of races, but rather literal and intellectual 'whitening'.[29] Indeed there is plenty of evidence in *Pobre negro* that, within the novel's scheme, the black people must lose their racial and ethnic difference and embrace the homogenizing cultural identity of the white Venezuelans in order to become true citizens of the nation. Highly suggestive in this sense is the way in which all of Pedro Miguel's tutors are white *criollos*. As Antonio Isea observes, it is '[e]l padre Mediavilla [...] [quien] canaliza en Pedro Miguel un deseo de cambio socio-racial' while '[l]os dos Cecilios [...] son los encargados de [su] educación formal'.[30] Illustratively, Cecilio the younger imposes on Pedro Miguel a liberal, though specifically *criollo*, understanding of Venezuela's socio-historical situation by reading him those sections of the book he is writing, which according to Pedro Miguel's own self-conscious words, 'más a mi alcance estarán, seguramente' (154). Furthermore, Gallegos strategically establishes the connection between the black man's socio-political advancement and the notion of 'whitening' as early as the section 'El salto más allá del límite', where Negro Malo's impressions following his sexual encounter with Ana Julia receive significant attention. As a result of his contact with Ana Julia's white body, Negro Malo undergoes a process of purification and eventual symbolic rebirth, which is described with the help of various elaborate and highly suggestive similes. We are told, for example, that his newly acquired state of mind evokes 'el agua turbia de las avenidas del monte, que [...] poco a poco va volviéndose clara', and '[el] alba cándida, de un día ya perenne, que hubiese invadido una caverna' (24). Later in the same episode, Negro Malo is figured as 'un rey sonriente [que] contemplaba su reino, que era toda la tierra', after which the narrator further clarifies that Negro Malo owes his new (imaginary) social status to the sensation that 'ya no era negro' (25). However, while Negro Malo envisions the effects of 'whitening' as revitalization and cause for jubilation, a study of the contradictions and complexities of Pedro Miguel's character reveals more cogently the difficulties inherent in this socio-racial process, as opposed to its possible benefits.

Though the *mestizo* Pedro Miguel represents the necessary socio-racial goal of Venezuela, his very condition as a *mestizo* makes him simultaneously a microcosmic 'campo de lucha entre dos razas irreconciliables' (97). In theory he could obviously become a peaceful mediator between these two hostile races, as Cecilio the younger insinuates when he optimistically views Pedro Miguel as the potential incarnation of '[la] armonía constructiva de una nación' (98). In practice, however, Pedro Miguel not only shows no interest in being a mediator between the two racial camps, but he also fails as a promoter of the rights of the blacks because of the constant struggle between conflicting and competing impulses that takes place within him. It is as if Pedro Miguel's white blood, and to some extent his *criollo* education, prevent him from siding fully with the black people, whose cause is, nonetheless, very close to his heart. As Pedro Miguel himself puts it, Cecilio the younger's disclosure concerning his multiracial parentage in 'La revelación' merely replaces his 'rencor contra el mantuano [...] [por] dos rencores' — one of which is now also directed against the black people (116). This said, it is nevertheless Pedro Miguel's wavering attitude towards the white people, or the *mantuanos* as he calls them, that conveys most effectively his confused sense of identity. One moment he hates the members of the Alcorta family for having cast him out of the family as a newborn, and the next he becomes a humble cultivator of their land and desperately yearns for their acceptance. Pedro Miguel's susceptibility to feelings of both attraction and repulsion towards the members of the Alcorta family is captured well in the section 'Décimas y fulías', which describes how the black people celebrate the *fiesta de mayo*. During the celebrations Pedro Miguel tries contemptuously to ignore Cecilio the younger and Luisana, who are sitting at '[una] discreta distancia de amos' (96), but he nonetheless casts 'rápidas miradas furtivas' (100) in their direction, and when they leave their seats, he 'emp[i]ez[a] a no encontrarle interés al velorio' (103). An even more illuminating example can be found in the section 'El desertor', which explores in detail Pedro Miguel's strikingly sudden changes of mind with regard to the Alcortas, and more specifically his conflicting feelings towards Luisana. The section begins with Pedro Miguel angrily musing how '[n]o se había lanzado a la guerra [...] por la causa del pueblo, sino por ahogar en sangre el amor a Luisana Alcorta' (243). He thus blames her for the homicides that he has committed and marches towards 'La Fundación', the Alcorta family's ranch, determined to punish her for being the cause of '[el] traicionero amor' (243). Pedro Miguel's troops have already set 'los cacaotales de La Fundación' (243) on fire, and he himself is planning to bring to a climax 'todo el posible horror de una vida' by raping Luisana as revenge (244). Although Pedro Miguel climbs up the stairs of the Casa Grande with his sabre in his hand, the fairy-tale atmosphere, which is evoked by the description of 'los escalones, invadidos por los matorrales que ya rodeaban el vetusto caserón' (245), already undermines Pedro Miguel's sinister intentions and thus prepares the ground for the coming shift in mood. Met by Cecilio the elder, Pedro Miguel loses his wrathful feelings, respectfully takes off his hat, and finally allows Cecilio to lead him 'por el brazo ya inerme [...] hacia el interior de la casa' (246). Entering the Casa Grande, once again completely seduced by the wish to belong to the Alcorta family, Pedro Miguel turns his back on the black people, this time for good. Over the course of an episode that scarcely fills four pages, Pedro Miguel's feelings towards the white people have accordingly shifted from bitterness and vengefulness to subservience and regained fondness.

As demonstrated by this shifting attitude towards white people, Pedro Miguel's trajectory is marked by constant hesitation, and a lack of definite direction. In fact, Pedro Miguel also finds it difficult to make decisions in a more general sense, and when he does make an apparent decision, he normally does not adhere to it. At various points in the narrative the reader is led to believe that Pedro Miguel is about to take the decisive step that will make him a social reformer who will work towards redressing the existing socio-racial imbalance, but time and again his plans to make a difference turn out to be futile daydreams. A detailed analysis of the highly ambiguous section '¿Qué te pasa, Pedro Miguel?' illustrates particularly well this interplay between expectation and subsequent disappointment. The section records the first night that Pedro Miguel spends in his old room, following his six-year absence from the house of his adoptive parents — this temporary exile having been the consequence of his earlier intention to 'provocar un levantamiento de esclavos' (75). After observing how his room, which formerly struck him as 'grande y alto' seems now a pokey 'ratonera', Pedro Miguel goes on to muse how proportions are not fixed, but can change over time (105). He continues musing about the question of proportions throughout the night, the obsessive cycles of his constantly more obtuse thoughts being conveyed by the way in which the expression '¡Las proporciones!' is repeated four times, and at increased intervals, in the passage describing his sleepless night (105–06). In the meantime he is also mesmerized by 'la representación imaginaria y casi alucinatoria de una gota de agua que insensiblemente y a largos intervalos manaba del encañado de[l] techo' (105-06). A shrewd connection is in fact established between 'las proporciones' and the 'gotera' through a shared rhythm. Just like the 'gotera', the exclamatory interjection surfaces in Pedro Miguel's thoughts at 'largos intervalos'; we are told that 'más de veinte minutos' pass between the first and the second time that Pedro Miguel thinks about 'las proporciones', and by the third time this happens, the candle that was 'entera' when he entered his room is 'ya casi consumida' (105). The by now obvious connection between 'la gotera' and 'las proporciones' is further underlined by the narrative statement that the falling of the imaginary drops 'coincidía precisamente con la vuelta de la exclamación a los labios [de Pedro Miguel]' (106). On top of this, we are informed that the 'gotera' represents 'el recuerdo de alguna gotera real cuando Pedro Miguel habitaba aquel cuarto', and hence functions as a vehicle through which 'alguna parte de su anterior experiencia trataba de filtrarse' (106). The interplay between Pedro Miguel's present situation and his past — a past marked by an inclination for rebellion — gives rise to the impression that the modifiable proportions that he is contemplating here are not merely those of his room. The suggestion that Pedro Miguel's musings have underlying socio-racial implications is backed by the fact that the Federal Revolution, in which he finally translates his beliefs into action, is referred to in *Pobre negro* as a war that aims to 'igual[ar] las desproporciones' (171). At first glance, Pedro Miguel seems to reach some kind of significant conclusion during his restless night, as is suggested by the reference to 'la idea fija' which he has in mind when contemplating the dawn (106). Furthermore, the act of suddenly abandoning his reveries in order to direct his steps hastily towards the house of Padre Mediavilla — who, after all, is the man who originally implanted in him the desire for socio-racial change — seems to suggest that Pedro Miguel is about to translate his newly conceived idea into a decisive action. However, by the time Pedro Miguel reaches the house, he has lost all the enthusiasm for his grand idea. Consequently, when Padre Mediavilla inquires about the purpose of Pedro Miguel's visit, the latter merely mutters stubbornly that '[e]n este momento parece que se me hubiera olvidado lo que me hizo venir hasta acá' (107). During this rather unproductive interview, Pedro Miguel becomes, nonetheless, 'nuevamente prisionero de la idea fija', which he also in this instance associates with the expression '¡Las proporciones!' (109). Though Pedro Miguel fails again to explicate his line of thought, the manner in which his conversation with Padre Mediavilla moves almost directly on to addressing issues of social unrest gives rise to the expectation that some further light will be cast on the actual meaning of the expression 'proporciones'. Yet the section finishes on an anticlimactic note, as Pedro Miguel replies to Padre Mediavilla's question '¿Qué te pasa, Pedro Miguel?', by stating, '— Eso es lo que yo quisiera saber' (110). Moreover, the repetition of the section title, '¿Qué te pasa, Pedro Miguel?', at the very threshold of the section's end, creates a cyclical effect, which accentuates the impression that Pedro Miguel's ideas about 'proporciones' have failed to progress. In other words, in this exemplary section marked by expectation, indecisiveness, and uncertainty Pedro Miguel's ideas have come full circle. In the wider allegorical context of *Pobre negro*, these uncertainties can additionally be read as a reflection of those of the whole socio-racial class to which Pedro Miguel belongs. Conscious of the imminence of historical change, the oppressed sectors of society, who in this particular case are the coloured (or partly coloured) people, begin increasingly to flirt with the idea of action, but their endeavours are still constantly restrained by a general lack of confidence and unpreparedness.

The theme of Pedro Miguel as a potential, though ultimately unsuccessful, social reformer is developed in the section 'La revelación', which follows on from '¿Qué te pasa, Pedro Miguel?'. In 'La revelación' specific attention is given to some of the practical reasons why Pedro Miguel fails to bring about any productive change, even though he wishes to free the black people from their subordinate status. While Cecilio the younger prepares the black slaves for the coming liberation by giving them primary education and their own little plots of land to cultivate, Pedro Miguel, on the other hand, merely tries to radicalize the blacks by claiming that the intention behind Cecilio the younger's reforms is not sincerely kind-hearted. Consequently, Cecilio the younger confronts Pedro Miguel, pointing out the fact that Pedro Miguel's radical ideas are likely to have only destructive results, owing to the absence of a specific agenda for improving the social position of the black people. As Cecilio the younger puts it:

> Esa gente tiene puesta en ti toda su confianza, y tú abusas de ella al fomentarle rencores, sin ofrecerles [sic] soluciones de sus problemas. [...] ¿Cuáles son tus planes? ¿Qué les ofreces a esa gente, en cambio de lo que me impides darles? Bien sé que no les doy todo lo que ellos necesitan y tienen derecho de reclamar; pero más no está a mi alcance por el momento, y de todos modos, algo es ya. En cambio, tú: ¿La rebeldía? ¿Simplemente la rebeldía? (114)

Defending himself against these accusations, Pedro Miguel in turn asks Cecilio the younger, '¿[q]ué culpa tengo de no saber lo que usted sabe?', thereby identifying the lack of education as the principal reason behind his incapability to conceive coherent, long-term plans (114). In fact, this verbal interchange between Pedro Miguel and Cecilio the younger captures well Gallegos's belief that any successful change must be brought about through a persistent and systematic process and not with 'un solo tajo de espada o un solo rasgo de pluma' ('El verdadero triunfo', 49).[31] Besides, Cecilio the younger's reproaches turn out to be all the more valid if we consider how Pedro Miguel's understanding of 'las reivindicaciones sociales' remains nebulous even during the Federal Revolution, in which he blindly leads his troops in vengeful and relentless attacks against *mantuanos* because of a 'falta de ideas claras' (215). Furthermore, Pedro Miguel's role as a leader is strikingly short-lived. By deserting his troops at the end of *Pobre negro*, Pedro Miguel simultaneously gives up all his ambitions and becomes a puppet, whose future destiny depends on the Alcortas. Indeed, when boarding the 'falucho' that will take him to 'la isla de Margarita', the wounded and self-disappointed Pedro Miguel comments on the Alcortas' decision to send him away from the Venezuelan mainland, by resignedly acknowledging that, '[g]anas de quedarme aquí son las que yo puedo tener; pero vida que otra salva a otro pertenece' (251). Finally, it is worth noting that Pedro Miguel makes this statement in the novel's concluding section, where Luisana is referred to as 'la capitana'. Undoubtedly, Luisana's appellative does not merely refer to the way in which she delivers orders relating to navigation, such as '[m]ande izar la vela' and '¡[v]enga viento!', when heading away from the mainland in the company of Pedro Miguel (252). The expression 'la capitana' also functions as an implicit reminder of the fact that at the beginning of the Federal Revolution it was Luisana who persuaded the vacillating Pedro Miguel to join the fighting by offering him the military title of 'capitán', which he vehemently rejected, this being part of Luisana's shrewd plan ('Hágote capitán'). The apparently playful, but intrinsically mocking, association of the rank of 'capitán/a' with Luisana rather than with Pedro Miguel, to whom it originally applied, reiterates the subordinate status against which Pedro Miguel tries to fight throughout *Pobre negro*, and thus underlines the coloured man's perpetually inferior role within the Venezuelan social hierarchy. What is more, this reversal of ranks emphasizes the impression that Pedro Miguel's failure as a social reformer derives ultimately not from his lack of education, but rather from the discriminatory assumption that a coloured man cannot by his very nature possess the level-headedness and determination required of a successful leader-figure.

IV

Luisana's behaviour differs from that of Pedro Miguel precisely because of her characteristically firm decisiveness and confident drive towards productive action. Unlike Pedro Miguel, Luisana does not allow her traditionally subordinate position to prevent her from turning most of her plans into well-designed actions. Consequently, Luisana's trajectory records her struggles to break the boundaries of domestic space and illustrates how she manages increasingly to engage in the life outside these boundaries. This said, Luisana and her sisters are, however, at first presented to the reader as 'las virtudes domésticas' in the section 'La herencia de Don Nadie' (36). Yet it does not take long for Luisana to distinguish herself from her conventionally feminine and dependent siblings. In the very same section in which she is referred to as '[una] virtud doméstica', her potential for action and leadership is already marked out by the way in which 'las hermanitas menores' regard her as a surrogate for 'la madre que han perdido' (36). Moreover, her extraordinary ability for finding the right solutions to others' problems develops even further when she grows into a young woman, as is suggested in 'Las vacaciones del humanista', in which her practical and active nature is described in the following manner:

> Fuese la hermana, la prima, la amiga o simplemente la vecina, ella tomaba a pecho la dificultad, el contratiempo o la angustia, y ya no los abandonaba hasta que les hubiese encontrado solución o remedio, desde la refección del vestido con que otra debía ir a la fiesta o al baile [...] hasta la tribulación mortal que fuese necesario compartir a la cabecera de un enfermo, días y noches consecutivos sin pegar los ojos. (73)

Highly illustrative in this sense are Luisana's reactions in 'El sacrificio' on finding out that her beloved brother Cecilio the younger is suffering from leprosy. While Luisana's and Cecilio the younger's father — Fermín Alcorta — is paralysed by grief and self-pity, Luisana takes the reins and proceeds immediately to 'salvar de la irreparable catástrofe lo que aún fuese viable' (90). But as Luisana herself acknowledges, her decision to renounce what has over time turned into a purely formal engagement with her pompous cousin Antonio de Céspedes, and to devote her life instead to nursing her brother, is not such an enormous sacrifice after all. On the contrary, it saves her from the oppressive destiny of women which she scornfully defines, in 'Disputas y vacilaciones', as '[c]uatro paredes, cuatro hijos...La infinita vulgaridad de una mujer entre mujeres, lavando mantillas, [y] acunando lloriqueos' (82). By moving with Cecilio the younger to the family ranch, 'La Fundación', Luisana grasps the opportunity to live outside the constraints of the conventional family unit, and it is thanks to this circumstance that she is able gradually to gain a good measure of independence.

In his 1949 lecture 'La pura mujer sobre la tierra' (396–425), Gallegos openly acknowledged his attraction to strong and seductive female characters and further suggested that Luisana is closely related to the notorious but enchanting Doña Bárbara. However, as I have already explained, Luisana is able to use her strength of character in order to carry out productive actions, while Doña Bárbara's determination and courage only find expression in violence and cruelty. Yet Luisana's occasionally masculine and provocative behaviour does in some respects evoke that of her novelistic predecessor. For instance, when realizing that she will eventually be left without the protection of male family members, Luisana begins to explore 'los caminos del varón', trying to find out everything she can about '[el] manejo de la hacienda' (146). And she does not feel intimidated when riding through the town unaccompanied, though she is completely aware of the 'malicias que levant[a] a su paso' (185). Even when it comes to love, she is not ready to be either passive or patient. She decides to 'tomar el amor que ya era suyo sin esperar a que se le declarase' (184) and finally wrings a proper declaration of love out of the hesitant Pedro Miguel.

The pivotal moment that prompts this kind of increasingly emancipated behaviour is that of Luisana's symbolic rebirth in the section 'Las aleluyas de la enfermera'. After breaking with her sisters, who have incorrectly been blaming her for an illicit affair with Pedro Miguel, Luisana experiences an unprecedented feeling of liberation. The usually sensible and purely practical young woman becomes momentarily childlike and carefree as she begins to 'saltar, correr, treparse a los árboles y encaramarse sobre los peñascos, reír, cantar, lanzar el grito a las resonancias del agreste silencio y soltar la lengua al disparate del pensamiento' (140). The impression that Luisana suddenly undergoes a metamorphosis is further underlined by the way in which the section 'Las aleluyas de la enfermera' is followed by a section suggestively titled 'La nueva Luisana', which additionally opens with a commentary on how 'Luisana había adquirido costumbres nuevas' (144). Nevertheless, it is in 'Las aleluyas de la enfermera' where we can find evidence pointing to the fact that at the heart of Luisana's rebirth lies her sexual awakening. Indeed in 'Las aleluyas de la enfermera' the main emphasis is placed on Cecilio the elder's alluring sketch of Luisana lying with her 'cabellos despeinados' on 'una gran piedra revestida de musgos y líquenes', looking like a virgin who is about to be sacrificed by the ancient barbarians (141). As becomes clear from the following extract, the conversation that Cecilio the elder and Luisana have about the picture during the drawing process captures well the episode's underlying ambiguity and unresolved eroticism:

> El acento llano del dibujante bromista [...] continuó:
> — ¡La había despeinado el frenesí fanático del sacrificador, y sus cabellos sueltos cubrían la piedra propiciatoria! [...] Su pecho subía hasta el cielo y bajaba hasta la profunda tierra.
> — ¡Uy! ¿A qué nombrar la pelona, cuando de tantos cabellos se trata?
> — Eso de la pelona es una desgraciada invención de un mal dibujante. Hermosa caballera tiene y de cada hebra una vida pendiente. ¡Ajá!...Esta línea...¡Sí, sí!...Habíamos quedado en que el pecho subía y bajaba...
> — Pero así no podrá verse en el papel.
> — Tú, calla y respira. Ya verás como sí aparece...¡Bueno! Ya salimos del pecho. Ahora puedes hablar todo lo que quieras, porque estamos en el rostro, y la palabra lo anima. (142)

With the strokes of his pencil, as well as by verbally describing Luisana's abundant 'cabellos', her 'pecho' which moves according to the rhythm of her deep breaths, and her vivacious 'rostro', Cecilio the elder not only awakens Luisana's dormant sexuality bit by bit, but he also revises the unimpeachable picture that the reader has built of her. Moreover, as Luisana's surprisingly naïve and coquettish replies imply, she responds to each stroke and insinuation, thus cooperating in the reconstruction process. Yet almost immediately after bringing to the surface Luisana's lively and erotic side, Cecilio the elder rejects the picture that he has just drawn and tears it 'en pedazos' which he then 'esparc[e] al aire' (143). Although on one level this can be merely regarded as an act with which Cecilio the elder destroys all the evidence of the morally dubious exchange that has taken place between him and Luisana, I think that the incident also has wider implications. In fact, Cecilio the elder's act of tearing up his controversial picture of Luisana resonates with the way in which Gallegos throughout *Pobre negro* depicts Luisana as a radical woman, with exceptional freedoms, but then diminishes these freedoms in order to ensure that, unlike her unredeemable predecessor Doña Bárbara, she will continue conforming to the conventional description of a respectable woman.[32]

As Marinone has observed, the narrator of *Pobre negro* 'fija autoritariamente un sistema de reglas estableciendo lo legítimo y lo ilegítimo en relación con las mujeres'.[33] And according to these 'reglas' many aspects of Luisana's behaviour during and since her rebirth in 'Las aleluyas de la enfermera' are classified as inappropriate. Some elucidation of what aspects of Luisana's behaviour are considered as unsuitable for a woman can be found in the section 'La capitana'. Though Luisana is at first boldly named 'la capitana', the narrator soon ridicules in a rather inconsistent manner her previously manly behaviour, and contentedly points out that she is not anymore 'la mujerona desviada hacia los caminos del hombre' (253). As the narrator also explains, by this stage she has further withdrawn from her active, and sometimes even aggressive, position in her relationship with Pedro Miguel and is no longer trying to 'tomar de éste el amor que aún no se atrevía a ofrecerle' (253). What is more, we are told that Luisana, whom acquaintances had in the past 'juzga[do] incapaz de verdadera ternura' (73), has become '[una] mujer auténtica' by falling tenderly in love with Pedro Miguel and trusting herself to his 'varonil protección' (253). Gallegos's insinuation in the final section of *Pobre negro* that Luisana does after all fit the picture of a traditional woman, while simultaneously presenting her as a harbinger of women's emancipation, is evidently contradictory and inconsistent. However, it is worth noting that Gallegos has also controlled Luisana's agency earlier in *Pobre negro*, particularly by delimiting her sphere of action. Although she is able to make a difference in the lives of her family members and acquaintances, often taking on duties that are not usually associated with women, she is not able to fulfil her dream of being 'libre para vestir[se] de hombre y echar[se] a andar por todos los caminos del mundo' (76).

Consequently, she cannot get directly involved in most of the events that are in the process of moulding the socio-political destiny of the Venezuelan nation: she can only enter the sphere of the nation's socio-political life through the various men in her life. For instance, she helps Cecilio the younger to finish his book about 'la estructura social y económica del país' (124) by transcribing his ideas when he can no longer 'manejar la pluma' (138). As another example, in 'Una declaración de amor' she bullies Pedro Miguel into getting involved in the Federal Revolution when he does not seem capable of making the decisive move. Indeed, one of the main reasons why Luisana chooses Pedro Miguel as her romantic partner, instead of Antonio de Céspedes, is precisely because she acknowledges that alongside and by means of Pedro Miguel she will more effectively be able to subvert traditional feminine boundaries, and to influence the course of socio-political events. As Luisana herself reflects, Antonio 'era un hombre ya hecho' and by his side she can merely be '[l]a esposa para la procreación y el cuidado del hogar y para completarle fuera de éste el adorno de su marcial persona'; in Pedro Miguel, on the other hand, 'había todo un mundo por crear' (183–84). The fact that Luisana is able to gain significant agency only in the company of Pedro Miguel who, according to traditional hierarchies, is her inferior both racially and socially, once again undercuts the degree of freedom with which she is endowed. Yet despite all these limitations on her freedom and sphere of action, Luisana remains the character who in *Pobre negro* most successfully translates her plans into productive deeds. In the context of the women's suffrage movements that were emerging at the time that Gallegos was writing *Pobre negro*, it seems probable that one of the functions of the energetic Luisana is in fact to make a statement about the possible benefits to be derived from the more active participation of women in the field of Venezuelan politics.

V

Overall, both Luisana and Pedro Miguel fail as social reformers, despite their fine intentions and apparent radicalism, because they are still to a significant extent restrained by the traditional stereotypes imposed on them by society — stereotypes that are often reinforced by Gallegos's narrator. The two Cecilios, in the meantime, suffer from no such constraints. As white *criollo* males they occupy a social position that needs no justification.[34] Interestingly, the trajectories of the two Cecilios are more closely intertwined than any of the other trajectories in *Pobre negro*; this fact occasionally gives rise to the impression that they actually share one single, bifurcating trajectory. To begin with, both Cecilios represent the same type of individual within Gallegos's microcosmic vision of the Venezuelan nation. They are *criollo* intellectuals who, despite belonging to a privileged social class, acknowledge (at least in principle) the need for social change even if it comes at the cost of sacrificing their class privileges. Apart from their shared name, the unity of the two Cecilios is established from the very beginning by the way in which they are introduced almost simultaneously in the section 'La herencia de don Nadie'. In this particular section further attention is drawn to the two Cecilios' shared passion for books and knowledge, thus giving rise to the partly misleading expectation that Cecilio the younger is destined to continue in the steps of the elder. Even more significantly, the two Cecilios act over and over again as Gallegos's spokesmen: their different points of view reflect Gallegos's own predominantly indecisive attitude towards radical change, as well as his persistent nostalgia for the old-fashioned patriarchal society which he is, nonetheless, trying to overthrow throughout *Pobre negro*.

In fact, Gallegos uses the two 'Cecilios' to put forward his own often conflicting ideas concerning the concepts of 'orden' and 'desorden', which in *Pobre negro* are intrinsically tied to the issue of progress, and especially to that of remedying existing social and racial inequalities.[35] Suggestively, Cecilio the younger's adherence to 'orden' and Cecilio the elder's faith in the creative force of 'desorden' — and not just the 'desorden' which characterizes periods of change but also that which is generated by Venezuela's diverse peoples, traditions, and regions — are already spelled out in 'La herencia de don Nadie'. During Cecilio the elder's ten-year absence, Cecilio the younger has imposed 'la tiranía del orden' on the elder's personal library, where works on disciplines as divergent as 'medicina', '[a]stronomía', 'botánica', and 'filosofía' usually coexist in '[una] babélica confusión' (35). Cecilio the elder's desire to transcend conventional boundaries, as opposed to Cecilio the younger's drive to impose them, is further accentuated in this section through references to the different types of occupations that Cecilio the elder has held during his wanderings. Over the years, the highly educated Cecilio the elder has maintained himself with the help of various 'oficios de artesanos', working as a 'sastre', 'ebanista', and 'albañil' at different 'extremos del país' (39). The socio-political significance of the concepts 'orden' and 'desorden' is, however, not fully spelled out until the section entitled 'Nostalgias y pedagogías'. Throughout this section the term 'desorden' is associated with revolutionary and progressive ways of thought, while 'orden' is linked with restrictive and old-fashioned socio-political models. For instance, Cecilio the elder tries to 'crearle [a Cecilio el joven] un espíritu revolucionario' through an unconventional teaching technique, which has as its aim to 'introducir en él desde temprano cierto desorden' (43). Even more instructive is the 'última lección' (46) which Cecilio the elder delivers to the adolescent Cecilio the younger before once again disappearing mysteriously from the lives of the Alcortas. Cecilio the elder's lengthy discourse to his nephew captures well the elder's political outlook, while drawing specific attention to the negative qualities of 'orden' and to the productive forces embodied in 'desorden':

> Se avecinan tiempos difíciles para nuestra patria y particularmente para las familias que, como la de los Alcortas y los Céspedes, empezaron a perder su preponderancia social y política con la guerra de la independencia; pero es necesario que tengas siempre presente que no hay que echar de menos lo que destruyó esa guerra, pues no era realmente nuestro. La colonia, con su espíritu de orden, y, por consiguiente jerárquico, no la produjo este suelo, sino que la toleró trasplantada, solamente. Era un jardín de plantas exóticas, muy bien trazado, muy apacible, muy señorial – ¡todo lo que se quiera! –; pero postizo y, por tanto, precario. [...] En cambio, lo que esa guerra puso en pie es lo genuinamente nuestro: la democracia del campamento, el mantuano junto con el descamisado comiendo del mismo tasajo [...], el empuje, la garra, el desorden. ¡Nuestro Señor el Desorden! ¡Bendito sea! Porque demuestra que este pueblo está vivo. (46–47)

'Orden', according to Cecilio the elder's interpretation, is thus closely associated with the colonial past, oppressive hierarchies and boundaries, as well as with artificiality. The liberating and vital 'desorden', on the other hand, surfaced momentarily during the wars of independence, which witnessed the temporary transgression of traditional socio-racial frontiers. And the future potential of the Venezuelan nation, as Cecilio the elder envisions it, lies necessarily in 'desorden', which he views as the nation's natural condition. The clever 'jardín' metaphor, moreover, plays not only with the widely exploited notion of the failure of the European colonizers to tame Spanish American nature, but also with the names of the central characters of *Pobre negro*.[36] The surnames 'Alcorta' and 'Césped', which belong to families that prospered under colonial rule, echo the Spanish colonizers' earnest intentions to turn the Venezuelan wilderness into a well-groomed 'jardín postizo'. This 'jardín' metaphor continues even into the 'Cuarta Jornada', as is made clear by the way in which Pedro Miguel comes to be known as Pedro Miguel *Candelas*, because of his habit of relentlessly burning the estates of the *mantuanos* that lie in the path of his troops. In so doing, Pedro Miguel literally destroys the artificial and restrictive boundaries imposed on land by the estate owners. Furthermore, the 'candelas' evoke an age-old tradition of the Venezuelan *llaneros*, which consists in burning the pastures in order to ensure that the land will regain its exuberance after the rainy season.[37] In the light of Cecilio the elder's 'jardín' metaphor, the 'desorden' that ensues from Pedro Miguel's 'candelas', can therefore be understood as a necessary step in preparing the land for the work of the 'Gran Sembrador', the name given by Cecilio the elder to the trend that will sow permanent change throughout Venezuela.

Rather disappointingly, Cecilio the elder's radical, and in principle persuasive, arguments and theories, such as the ones relating to the productive qualities of 'desorden', remain by and large mere innovative speculations. Though he emphasizes the need for socio-political change that will take into account Venezuela's natural inclination towards 'desorden' — that is, Venezuela's heterogeneity of peoples, cultures, and regions, as well as the country's hyperbolic nature — he fails to illustrate how this 'desorden' could be channelled productively in the right direction in order to produce a less hierarchical society. In fact, already Cecilio the elder's own lifestyle is marked by a lack of a clear direction or a concrete aim. To begin with, he never seems to have a proper destination in view when he sets out on the road. And although he is familiar with the divergent regions of Venezuela, and their respective peoples and traditions, he does not really put his knowledge to any effective use, but instead generally avoids giving coherent accounts of his journeys. For instance, when the adolescent Cecilio the younger tries to find out what 'las distintas regiones del país' are like, the elder simply replies with disdain that ' — Yo sé cómo son, pero a nadie se lo he preguntado' (46). In addition, Cecilio the elder actually seems to lose his faith over time in the productive nature of 'desorden'. Still in the section 'La convencioncita', Cecilio the elder seems elated at the fall of General José Tadeo Monagas's government, an incident that ushered in the Federal Revolution.[38] Full of enthusiasm, he writes on the wall the year of the event using 'un pedazo de carbón' while announcing prophetically that 1858 is '[el] [a]ño del Gran Sembrador', as well as the moment that marks the beginning of 'la gran cosecha de nuestro señor el desorden' (147–48). However, soon afterwards, in the section 'Diálogo del sembrador y otras extravagancias', Cecilio the elder adopts a surprisingly pessimistic attitude towards the elevated 'desorden' that has been let loose by the Federal Revolution. Indeed, when discussing with Pedro Miguel the course that Venezuela's history is in the process of taking, Cecilio the elder apocalyptically notes that '[y]o no veo sino muerte, fuego y escombros por todas partes [...] ¿Qué porvenir les estará reservado a ustedes los jóvenes?' (159). Moreover, as I will now move on to demonstrate, Cecilio the elder's socio-political theories also turn out to be unsuccessful in practice because he fails in his endeavour of instilling in Cecilio the younger his own appreciation of 'desorden', which he has unswervingly tried to foster through his eccentric tutorials.

That Cecilio the younger has a far stronger inclination for traditional modes of thought than for revolutionary doctrines is already suggested by the fact that the intellectual impulses of his early youth are directed exclusively towards bookish learning and poetry. Overall, his favourite books belong to the classics of the European canon, and include, for example, *Don Quixote*, the *Iliad*, and the works of Fray Luis de León. However, as Cecilio the younger grows up, he turns to the more active field of politics and dreams rather idealistically that he will one day be able to help those less privileged than he by becoming 'un hombre con las soluciones de los problemas de los otros hombres en sus manos abiertas para todos' (54). Yet this change of intellectual focus is not a sign of genuine personal development: as the narrator points out, 'de haber seguido las más íntimas inclinaciones de su alma [Cecilio el joven] habría quedado en poeta' (69). Instead, the change is caused to a large extent by the unstable socio-political situation of the Venezuelan nation, as well as by Cecilio the younger's desire to please his father, who obsessively wishes to fulfil his own parliamentary aspirations through his son. It is also important to note that Cecilio the younger is not able to 'depurar y completar la ciencia política que ambicionaba poseer' in his native country, but must head to the other side of the Atlantic (77). In fact, Fermín Alcorta's expectation that Cecilio the younger will use his knowledge of European political trends to rescue the Venezuelan nation from its troubles draws attention to the way in which his country continues to rely on imported socio-political models, even at a time when its national identity is being moulded.[39]

Cecilio the younger's adherence to originally imported and, what is more, often antiquated socio-political models, finds its most explicit expression in his understanding of matters of race and class. His understanding reflects in many respects Gallegos's own stated outlook. Though Gallegos emphasizes throughout *Pobre negro* the need to incorporate the black people into the Venezuelan nation-family, he simultaneously depicts them, on the one hand, as savage and lustful, and on the other hand, as ignorant children who are in desperate need of paternal guidance. Already in the novel's opening section, 'Tambor', the dancing blacks are represented as a group of sweating and ardent bodies, ecstatically twisting themselves to the monotonous rhythm of the tambour. This eroticized and animalized portrayal is further expanded in later sections such as 'Décimas y fulías' and 'Diablos y angelitos', both of which concentrate on the primitive ways in which black people celebrate and commemorate certain festivities and occasions. For instance, 'Diablos y angelitos' begins with a discussion of 'la fiesta de los diablos' where 'lo pagano [se mezcla] con lo piadoso' (162), and ends with a crude description of how, at the funeral of a little black boy, the mourners become intoxicated by '[a]guardiente' and '[una] [s]ensualidad enardecida por la presencia de la muerte' (167). It is, however, in 'Décimas y fulías' where Gallegos's surprisingly patronizing attitude towards black people finds a direct outlet in Cecilio the younger's observations and thoughts. The section is strikingly marked by a prevalent nostalgia for the bygone colonial times. This impression is already established by the fact that Cecilio the younger observes black people performing their 'décimas y fulías' from one of the 'viejos sillones frailunos, de respaldares de cordobán con las águilas de Carlos V', these 'sillones' functioning as evident relics of the colonial past (96). Slightly later on in the section, Cecilio the younger notes with delight that the scene he is contemplating recalls 'una escena de antiguos tiempos patriarcales y sencillos', when 'el señor y el siervo' could still peacefully listen to 'los rudos versos con una misma sonrisa de delectación' (100). As demonstrated in the section 'La revelación', Cecilio the younger fails to overcome his patronizing and paternalistic attitude towards the black people even when arguing for their emancipation. The section opens suggestively with a reminder of the peaceful, though firmly hierarchical, coexistence of 'el señor y el siervo', in which Cecilio the younger rejoiced during the performance of 'décimas and fulías' (110). Though Cecilio the younger tries at the beginning of the section to convince his father about the need to incorporate the black people into the *alma nacional*, the justifications with which he backs up his arguments are in themselves condescending. He suggests, for example, that it is the duty of the *criollos* to instil in the ignorant minds of the black people 'ideas que les formen hábitos provechosos', and further talks about the need to 'cultivar' the black race as 'una planta ya nuestra' (111). In other words, Cecilio the younger is suggesting that the *criollos* should strive to impose on the black people a specifically *criollo* mentality. Cecilio the younger's way of talking about the blacks as a 'planta' that needs to be 'cultiva[da]' evokes additionally Cecilio the elder's 'jardín' metaphor, as well as his warning about the dangers of trying to conserve the neat and ordered 'jardín postizo' of the colonial epoch (46). The insinuation that Cecilio the younger is inadvertently aspiring to maintain this 'jardín' is in accord with his constant regressions to conventional models of socio-political thought, which occur even when he strives to formulate progressive ideas.

In addition to his underlying attachment to the patriarchal order with its restrictive models of socio-political thought, Cecilio the younger's ability for productive and subversive action is further limited by Gallegos's authorial decision to inflict leprosy on him. This disease that rather ironically reduces the 'orderly' Cecilio the younger to the disorder of disfigurement has multiple, important narrative functions. On one level, Cecilio the younger's 'sangre dañada' (88) can be read as a sign that the *criollo* classes are in general degenerating, and in this sense his disease helps to make a case for the need for genetic rejuvenation through *mestizaje*. At the same time, leprosy also provides Gallegos with the means of paralysing Cecilio the younger, 'el de las esperanzas' (83), at a relatively early stage of *Pobre negro* (Chapter 2, 'Segunda Jornada'), accordingly disqualifying the one character who because of his youth, racial background, and education would most easily grow into the role of a legitimate hero and social reformer. By doing so, Gallegos is able to (re)direct the reader's *esperanzas* concerning social reforms towards the novel's more innovative reformers, namely, Luisana and Pedro Miguel. In fact, by trying to reject their traditional social positions these two characters already subvert the kind of patriarchal order to which Cecilio the younger is so attached. Cecilio the younger's subsequent death also solves a significant narrative problem. Had he still been alive at the end of *Pobre negro*, one might wonder how his trajectory could have been tied in with the novel's final message about the necessity of conciliatory, interracial romances. All in all, by compelling Cecilio the younger to 'aislarse del mundo' (90) and thus to retire from the scene of action, leprosy forces him to return to the sphere of theory. To be more precise, it is this involuntary exclusion that stimulates him to write a book about the socio-historical problems of Venezuela in order to help his *Patria* at least in some way. As I will now move on to demonstrate, what is specifically interesting about Cecilio the younger's book-within-the-book is that it is in many respects a microcosmic version of *Pobre negro*.

Already in terms of subject matter, Cecilio the younger's book echoes clearly that of *Pobre negro*. While *Pobre negro* explores the social, racial, and political problems of the Venezuelan nation and proposes interracial love affairs as a viable solution to these problems, Cecilio the younger's book correspondingly provides '[r]eflexiones sobre la estructura social y económica del país, con los males que de ella se derivaban y las posibles maneras de remediarlos' (124). Furthermore, at an earlier point, when Cecilio the younger is just about to start writing his book, he expresses his wish that 'sus escritos' will be able to cast some light 'sobre el nebuloso campo por donde se perdían los *caminos* de la joven Patria' (110, emphasis added). The reference to numerous 'caminos' is highly significant as it suggests that Cecilio the younger acknowledges the inherent heterogeneity of Venezuela, including the variety of paths along which the country's different sectors are heading towards the future. In addition, the allusion to these 'caminos' getting lost in 'el nebuloso campo' captures pointedly both the circumstance that these 'caminos' fail to lead to any specific destination, and the prevalent atmosphere of uncertainty and instability that reigns in Venezuela before and during the Federal Revolution. And in this sense the 'caminos' evoke the trajectories of the four central characters of *Pobre negro*, which, as I have shown, drive towards productive change but generally lead to dead ends. What is more, the fact that Cecilio the younger's book is the product of the cooperation between the novel's central characters also mirrors the way in which the plot of *Pobre negro* is woven out of the various trajectories of these characters. For instance, Cecilio the elder helps to make Cecilio the younger's otherwise rather factual and theoretical book more readable by providing him with anecdotes 'recogida[s] en la experiencia viva de sus andanzas' (124), and Luisana writes down Cecilio the younger's ideas when he can no longer 'manejar la pluma' (138). Meanwhile, Cecilio the younger tests his ideas on Pedro Miguel, whom he regards as the protagonist of the nation's current socio-political changes, by reading him sections of his book out loud.[40] It is, however, important to point out that the agency of each character as a literary cooperator is limited, as it is when these same characters are trying to act as social reformers. Illustratively, Luisana is only allowed to transcribe what Cecilio the younger dictates to her, while Cecilio the elder gives Cecilio the younger ideas but does not take up the pen. Pedro Miguel, on the other hand, functions merely as a student-like recipient of the ideas that Cecilio the younger judges to be 'más a [su] alcance' (154). On top of this, even Cecilio the younger's own literary endeavours are restricted by the circumstance that he becomes so ill that he can no longer write down his own ideas and he eventually dies leaving his 'libro [...] inconcluso' (148). In fact, the final and crucial feature that *Pobre negro* and Cecilio the younger's book have in common is that neither manages to provide a convincing or conclusive solution to the social, racial, and political problems of the Venezuelan nation. The shared inconclusiveness of the two books is artfully accentuated by the way in which the last mention of Cecilio the younger writing his book is to be found in the penultimate paragraph of 'Tercera Jornada', where attention is drawn to how his book '[estaba] por fin *cerca* de su término' (195, emphasis added). After this point *Pobre negro* also starts nearing its end, for the 'Cuarta Jornada' is the novel's final part. However, instead of preparing the ground for the novel's predetermined conciliatory romance, the fragmentary and appendix-like 'Cuarta Jornada' postpones the conclusion, and creates a general atmosphere of inconclusiveness and indecisiveness which undermines the plausibility of a solution based in heterosexual romance.

VI

The 'Cuarta Jornada' puts forward an extremely pessimistic interpretation of the Federal Revolution, and reveals a profound disillusionment with the creative and progressive power of 'desorden', which the revolution was supposed to epitomize. The fourth part of *Pobre negro* begins with a section entitled 'La furia', which as Ulrich Leo has pointed out, provides a 'vista de pájaro' of the futile destruction caused by the Federal Revolution, and thus functions as an introduction to the more particular descriptions of the effects that the revolution has on the lives of individuals.[41] The Federal Revolution is initially defined in 'La furia' as a war in which the forces of barbarism and disorder directly confront those allied to civilization and order:

> [Fue] el duelo a muerte entre la barbarie genuina en que continuaba la masa popular, con sus hombres, sus rencores y sus ambiciones, y la civilización de trasplante — códigos y constituciones aparentemente admirables — en que venía amparando sus intereses la clase dominadora. (197)

What is striking about this description of the Federal Revolution, in addition to the horticultural motif, is that neither of the warring sides is presented in a favourable light. Both fail to offer a desirable and constructive sociopolitical solution. Following the same line of thought, the narrator remains impartial towards the two sides throughout the 'Cuarta Jornada', while silently condemning the atrocities committed by both. For instance, the Federal officers prove to be just as capable of raping a young mother in front of her son's very eyes ('Aquella visión atroz') as the Government officers are of cold-heartedly leaving a protective mother surrounded by the corpses of her murdered children ('Venezuela'). As already explained in 'La furia', underneath the struggle between the two contradictory socio-political positions lies a bloodthirsty 'monstruo de la furia sin cabeza' (199) which, driven by hatred, destroys everything that falls in its path, without any clearly defined ideological aim. However, this lack of a coherent ideology is associated particularly with the Federal troops, who caricature the Federal Revolution as a war between 'el monte' and 'la ciudad' (198) and further become enthralled by slogans such as 'Dios y Federación', which blend political doctrines with 'lo religioso, primitivo y fetichista' (216–17). On the whole, the 'Cuarta Jornada' demonstrates that the Federal Revolution failed to inspire any genuine 'reivindicaciones sociales' (198) but merely managed to bring to the surface, and to deepen, the existing socioracial divisions of the Venezuelan nation.

After the introductory section, 'La furia', the four sections entitled respectively '¡Aquel silencio!', 'Aquella visión atroz', 'Fascinación', and 'Venezuela' also fail to contribute conspicuously to the development of the main storylines of *Pobre negro*.[42] These sections crucially focus on four previously unmentioned families, living in different parts of Venezuela, and on how they suffer under the Federal Revolution. While the past tense is generally employed throughout those sections that record events that are directly connected to the main storylines, '¡Aquel silencio!', 'Aquella visión atroz', and 'Fascinación', on the other hand, open in the present tense. For example, the setting of '¡Aquel silencio!' is established over the section's first few lines with a matter-of-factness that resembles that of scene directions: 'Un pueblo por donde no transita un alma, cerradas todas las puertas. Lo alumbra la luz siniestra de un sol sin brillo [...] Pesa sobre él un silencio trágico' (200). In its immediate effects, this use of tense and narrative technique collapses the temporal distance between the reader and the narrative events, hence implying that the reader is positioned in the midst of the action as an observer. However, these sections also actually put brakes on the principal action of *Pobre negro*. In other words, the intercalated stories retard the development of the main storylines, giving the impression that the narrative is losing its predetermined course. No doubt, the narrative's loss of a definite direction can be interpreted as a reflection of the way in which the Federal Revolution itself lacks a clear direction. Yet more importantly, the narrative disruption caused by these stories conveys a feeling of hesitancy, which is in accord with the novel's prevalent indecisiveness, and particularly with Gallegos's doubts concerning the heterosexual romance as a narrative and socio-racial solution.

The change in thematic focus that takes place in the 'Cuarta Jornada' is also extremely disruptive. In the earlier 'Jornadas', Gallegos explores the build-up to the Federal Revolution particularly with reference to the gradual social awakening and emancipation of the black people. For instance, the 'Primera Jornada' describes the increasing discontent of the black people, who start to develop a social consciousness thanks to Pedro Miguel's readings of radical publications; the 'Segunda Jornada' ends with the abolition of slavery; and in the 'Tercera Jornada' the black people are already starting to organize themselves for the imminent battles. The 'Cuarta Jornada' for its part devotes relatively little attention to how the black people experience the revolution. Instead, in the 'Cuarta Jornada' the consequences of the Federal Revolution are explored above all through the disintegration of the traditional family unit, which as Leo notes, functions as '[un] símbolo de la suerte de todo un pueblo devastado por la guerra civil'.[43] I will now move on to study in more detail how the disintegration of the family unit illustrates, on the one hand, the fratricidal nature of the revolution and its destructive effects, while, on the other hand, it marks the fall of the conventional, patriarchal order.

The fratricidal nature of the Federal Revolution finds one of its most pointed expressions in the section entitled 'La inútil sangre', which focuses on the highly personal battle that Pedro Miguel and Antonio de Céspedes fight against the backdrop of the wider military conflict. These two men, who are not only cousins of Luisana but also her suitors, are the personifications of the antithetical principles that clash in the course of the revolution. To be more precise, Pedro Miguel, who is now a celebrated leader of a Federalist faction, stands for 'desorden', change, and the subversion of existing hierarchies, while the Government officer Antonio de Céspedes tries to prevent change from taking place and wishes to maintain order by preserving existing socio-racial hierarchies. Already at the beginning of the Federal Revolution, Antonio refers to the Federal troops deprecatingly as '[f]acciones, montoneras, bisoñas, [y] bochinches de negros', and boasts confidently about the ease with which the Government troops 'restablecerán el orden' (179). Similarly, before the battle against Pedro Miguel's troops, Antonio looks down on Pedro Miguel's organizational skills, judging him incapable of tracing 'un plan coordinado' (237). Pedro Miguel in turn despises 'la disciplina militar' precisely because it evokes that extreme type of 'formalismo' which he associates with Antonio (218). Though in 'La inútil sangre' he initially succeeds in surprising Antonio's troops with his 'operación bien concebida', Pedro Miguel's military tactics in the end collapse into complete chaos as he stops seeing the provocatively insolent Antonio as 'el jefe enemigo' and becomes fully driven by his personal hatred for the man 'que un día le infirió [un] agravio injusto' (237–38). Indeed, Pedro Miguel is not only passionate about fighting Antonio because he is his rival in love, but also because he wishes to avenge the time the latter struck him across the face with a whip and thus painfully reminded him of his racial and social inferiority ('Día de acontecimientos', 52). No doubt, on a more general level, Pedro Miguel's desire for revenge can additionally be read as replicating the way in which the coloured masses, who have been exploited and humiliated since the times of the colony, seek vengeance on their exploiters, the *mantuanos*, during the Federal Revolution. However, the inherently fratricidal nature of the Federal Revolution manifests itself on a further level in the emergence of divisions among these very masses fighting for the Federation. As Pedro Miguel notes when trying to convince the hesitant *El Mapanare* of the need for immediate cooperation, some of the Federalist factions are 'tan enemigo[s] de nosotros, los guerrilleros independientes, como [...] de los oligarcas' (226–27). In fact, the rocky relationship between Pedro Miguel and his half-brother, *El Mapanare*, accentuates these divisions within the Federalist troops. Though both pretend to be 'correligionarios', Pedro Miguel is repelled by '[la] monstruosidad [...] que encerraba el alma de *El Mapanare*' (225), while *El Mapanare* is constantly lying in wait for the right moment to 'suplantar [a Pedro Miguel] en el ánimo de su tropa' (233). The rivalry between these two half-brothers, and the wider-scale antagonism that it stands for, reach their climax in the section 'El hombre de las circunstancias' when Pedro Miguel and his most loyal friend, Juan Coromoto, are fired on by the members of their own faction, who have adopted *El Mapanare* as their new leader.

The disintegration of the traditional family unit is, moreover, reflected in the sections '¡Aquel silencio!', 'Aquella visión atroz', 'Fascinación', and 'Venezuela' through the complete absence of father-figures in the war-torn *poblaciones* and *ranchos*. In '¡Aquel silencio!' the men have fled from the *población* in order to avoid forced conscription, while in other instances they are either dead like Manuela de Fuentes's husband ('Aquella visión atroz'), already fighting in the revolution as in the case of the older sons of the anonymous woman in 'Fascinación', or in hiding like the 'hombrecitos' of the 'balsera' (209). The only males left in the *poblaciones* are therefore old men and young boys, neither of whom can provide any significant protection against the ravaging military troops. Owing to the absence of men, the women are compelled to take on male occupations and to become the heads of their families. Manuela de Fuentes, for instance, courageously opens up her 'pulpería' for the approaching Federalist troops (202). Yet even so, the women are left at the mercy of the military officers, who with their licence to carry away adolescent sons, and to kill and rape indiscriminately, act as usurpers of the role of the father. In the end, the women discussed in these sections fail to protect their children, though each of them adopts a different attitude when trying to cope with the cruelties and demands of the military officers. For example, Manuela's boldness in 'Aquella visión atroz', or the protectiveness of the *balsera* in 'Venezuela', prove to be no more effective when it comes to sheltering their children than is the fatalistic resignation of the anonymous woman in 'Fascinación', who hands her 'muchacho [...] de trece años' over to the Federal troops (206). The cruel destiny faced by women and children during the revolution is, nonetheless, expressed most pointedly in 'Venezuela', the last of the short-story-like sections. The *balsera*, who at the end of this section stands on the raft surrounded by her dead children and dips 'de cuando en cuando la palanca [en el negro río], cual si buscase un rumbo' (211), can indeed be interpreted as a pessimistic allegorical figure of the Venezuelan nation that has increasingly lost its course during the revolution. What is also striking about the figure of the *balsera* is that it is now a woman, rather than the *mestizo* Pedro Miguel, who represents the fate of Venezuela. This circumstance clearly underlines the shift in focus from the fortunes of the black people to those of the women that has taken place over the preceding sections. Though the women in these sections fail in the end to protect their families, the complete absence of protective father-figures, and the courage with which women face the perilous situations, point to a movement away from the conventional patriarchal order. Significantly, a similar movement can also be discerned in the wider context of *Pobre negro*, as the Alcorta family disintegrates, leaving Luisana more and more in charge of herself. By the beginning of the 'Tercera Jornada' she has already lost her father, while later in the same 'Jornada', in the section titled 'La nueva Luisana', she acknowledges the need to 'prepararse para todo por los caminos del varón', because '[m]oriría Cecilio, volvería a marcharse el tío [y] la dejarían desamparada' (146). At the end of the 'Cuarta Jornada', Luisana finally loses both of the Cecilios. Cecilio the younger dies in 'Serenidad', and Cecilio the elder re-embarks on his endless wanderings in 'La capitana'. The episodic sections of the 'Cuarta Jornada' and the fact that Luisana gradually loses her father, brother, and uncle — that is, all the male family members who could assert their authority over her — once again capture the wavering attitude that Gallegos has towards the new, alternative social order which he is exploring in *Pobre negro*. The emphasis on the disintegration of the traditional family unit, and the elevation of the woman to a central position, gives rise to the confusing impression that the new order that is being promoted is actually one which should be constructed around the figure of the strong and emancipated woman rather than the *mestizo* man.

Regardless of the conflicting evidence, the model of the interracial, conciliatory romance still persists at the end of the 'Cuarta Jornada' as the necessary solution to Venezuela's socio-historical problems. In fact, the tension between the various narrative threads of *Pobre negro*, and the form-imposing frame of heterosexual romance finds a clever metaliterary expression in the sections 'El pacto' and 'La malla rota', which are significantly located at the dead centre of the 'Cuarta Jornada'. These two sections additionally bring to a temporary halt the stylistic and thematic experimentation that characterizes the first part of the 'Cuarta Jornada', and they mark the commencement of the return to the narrative thread that follows the development of Pedro Miguel and Luisana's romance — the thread having been dropped since 'Una declaración de amor' in 'Tercera Jornada'. 'El pacto' and 'La malla rota' explore in significant depth the fate of the previously energetic and radical Padre Mediavilla, who has now lost his wits and spends his days and nights 'cogien[do] [del aire] flotantes hilos sutilísimos, con las cuales iba tejiendo una malla ilusoria' (228). Indeed, Padre Mediavilla's endeavour of tying the numerous, disorderly dispersed 'hilos' into an orderly chain could be seen to stand for the way in which Gallegos unites the trajectories of the various characters of *Pobre negro*, as well as the disruptive narrative fragments, such as the anecdotes of the 'Cuarta Jornada', with the aid of the systematic narrative framework of heterosexual romance. Although at first glance the similarity of these actions can be put down to mere coincidence, the deliberate connection that exists between the two is revealed by the fact that Padre Mediavilla's endeavour of tying 'hilos' is directly associated with romantic (or sexual) unions between representatives of different racial groups. In 'La malla rota', Padre Mediavilla finds an imaginary 'hilo' on Pedro Miguel's shoulder, which he then ties with another one floating in the air, giving the sinister *El Mapanare* the chance to make an ironical comment about how the priest's act might mean that 'ya el cura [le] ha casa[d]o, quién sabe con quién, porque ansina mismo hace cuando me casa con mis blancas' (229). What is more, when Pedro Miguel realizes at the very end of the novel that '[y]a el destino de [Luisana] estaba unido al suyo', he remembers this 'escena del campamento de *El Mapanare*, atando el Padre Mediavilla dos hilos invisibles que flotaban en el aire' (252). In the meantime, however, Padre Mediavilla's method of contriving a chain out of the dispersed 'hilos' also captures Gallegos's underlying dissatisfaction with the framework of heterosexual romance, by figuratively pointing out some of the main deficiencies of this framework. Already Padre Mediavilla's manner of picking the imaginary 'hilos' out of the air with 'gestos de razón ausente' (224), which are further accompanied by '[u]n tic persistente [de los músculos faciales]' (228), can be viewed as a distorted reflection of the often rigidly mechanical process with which the divergent narrative threads of *Pobre negro* are joined together. Moreover, the way in which these '[h]ilos [...] venían desde el infinito [y llenaban] todo el espacio' (228) mimics the ultimate impossibility of containing fully all the contrasting and competing narrative threads and fragments within the bounds of the framework of heterosexual romance. In fact, although the fulfilment of the novel's predetermined romance is supposed to function as the final, form-imposing 'knot', it is, nevertheless, possible to discern, even at the very end, some loose ends and disparities, which cannot be accommodated neatly within the principal framework.

To begin with, it is worth noting that Gallegos fails to describe the fulfilment of the romance in 'La capitana', the novel's final section, in such a way that it would emerge convincingly as the basis of a genuinely less hierarchical social order. On various occasions in *Pobre negro*, Luisana and Pedro Miguel's relationship is indeed represented as a power struggle, where gender differences are further deepened and complicated by the racial and social backgrounds of the two protagonists. The section 'Una declaración de amor' captures exceptionally well the essence of this struggle, as it draws specific attention to the fact that both Luisana and Pedro Miguel are repelled by the very thought of occupying a social position which is inferior to the one occupied by the other. Provoked by Luisana's suggestions that he might not be man enough to thrive on the battleground, Pedro Miguel ends up defiantly asserting that '[le] advierto desde ahora que a mí no me embojotan las mujeres' (193). Luisana, in turn, gets upset by the way in which Pedro Miguel's words imply that men are naturally superior to women, and she replies vehemently that '[y] yo [te advierto] a ti que no vengo buscando amos que me tiranicen' (193). However, as I have suggested earlier on, when discussing the individual trajectories of Luisana and Pedro Miguel, it is Luisana who in the final section of *Pobre negro* wins the power struggle and obtains a superior hierarchical position by being named as 'la capitana'.

On top of this, a swift change in thematic focus takes place again in 'La capitana', immediately after the observation that the destinies of Luisana and Pedro Miguel are now tied together for good. What makes this change in focus particularly significant is that it clearly evokes the one which took place over the four episodic sections of Chapter 1 of the 'Cuarta Jornada'. Instead of providing anything close to a coherent account of the wider socio-racial implications of Luisana and Pedro Miguel's romantic union, *Pobre negro* in fact finishes with a lengthy description of the feeling of liberation experienced by Luisana, when leaving behind the war-torn mainland and heading towards Isla de Margarita:

> Algún día [...] debió de soñar ella con esto que ahora iba realizándose, pues, siendo imprevisto, no le caía extraño. [...] Atrás se quedaban por fin la hechura de aquel mundo de ideas y sentimientos de otros: la mujer sufrida y virtuosa, conforme a un concepto social [...] mientras que la capitana que ahora iba sobre el mar infinito y bajo el viento libre de nada, era criatura sino de su propia voluntad de encararse con la vida, sin miramientos que la limitasen. (253)

Without a doubt, this is the decisive moment when Luisana, to use Orlando Araujo's words, 'llega a perfilarse como verdadero protagonista y a desplazar a los restantes personajes, aun a Pedro Miguel'.[44] Although the emancipation of women is one of the most important themes of *Pobre negro*, and the 'Cuarta Jornada' highlights the new role made available to women during the Federal Revolution, the elevation of Luisana to a central position at the very threshold of the novel's end appears, nevertheless, somewhat abrupt. Besides, the optimism inherent in the discussion of Luisana's emancipation contrasts powerfully with the references to the purely negative consequences of the Federal Revolution, which are also abundant in 'La capitana'. For instance, in the early part of the section the narrator explains that the Federal Revolution has left the ground covered with 'cenizas regadas con sangre', and the hearts of the Venezuelans full of 'estragos irremediables' (249). Moreover, at a slightly later point, we are told that the convalescent and disillusioned Pedro Miguel views himself in a similarly pessimistic spirit as a mere 'desperdicio de la guerra' (251). In the light of the gloomy portrayal of the outcomes of the Federal Revolution, the rather sudden change of focus to Luisana's successful liberation can on the one hand be regarded as a compensatory tactic employed by Gallegos to diminish the prominence and impact of the unresolved social, and particularly, racial problems of the novel. The change of focus can, however, also be read as a sign that Gallegos is more confident about the benefits of the emancipation of women than about the advantages of giving coloured people increased agency; this interpretation is fully in accord with the overall depiction of the respective achievements of Luisana and Pedro Miguel. Finally, the image of Luisana and Pedro Miguel sailing 'sobre el mar infinito' (253), away from the troubled mainland of Venezuela, emphasizes the openness of the ending, which, despite its ultimately optimistic tone, pushes any true action and change outside the boundaries of the novel. While the portrayal of Luisana as a confident 'capitana', who has clearly retrieved the 'rumbo' that the *balsera* in the section 'Venezuela' was unsuccessfully trying to find (211), implies potential for development, one can only speculate what happens to Pedro Miguel in the end. On Isla de Margarita '[donde] habían emigrado ya casi todos los mantuanos de Barlovento' (251), he will undoubtedly be marked as the coloured man amongst the whites, with the additional drawback that he will now also be associated with those very Federalists from whom the *mantuanos* are trying to flee. In addition, if we follow this speculative line of thought further, we can deduce that over the generations his and Luisana's descendants will most likely mix with the island's *mantuanos*, therefore 'cleaning' out the trace of black blood still so apparent in Pedro Miguel. In fact, the conceivable consequences of Pedro Miguel's relocation to Isla de Margarita cannot but bear out the thesis that the incorporation of the black people into the nation-family, as Gallegos understands it in *Pobre negro*, implies necessarily the absorption of the 'inferior' black race by the white one. And this whitening process assures the continued hegemony of the white *criollos*.

Especially if considered in isolation, rather than in the wider context of Gallegos's novelistic production, *Pobre negro* does not seem to provide a viable model for a less hierarchical Venezuelan society, but instead restates to some extent a conservative interpretation of *mestizaje*. Yet I do not think that it is justifiable simply to dismiss *Pobre negro* as a novel that flirts with progressive narrative structures and ways of thought but eventually collapses into ambiguity, finally reverting back to the same models that it was trying to subvert. The crevices in the narrative framework of heterosexual romance, the attention drawn to the variety of paths to progress, as well as the emphasis on the specific issues of race and gender are all factors that suggest that Gallegos is moving in *Pobre negro* further away from his previously idealistic and relatively simplistic conception of the Venezuelan nation. Furthermore, the way in which women and black people become in *Pobre negro* the centre of narrative attention points clearly to the fact that Gallegos is in the process of rearranging his picture of the Venezuelan nation-family, which his earlier novels suggested should be constructed around the figure of the *criollo* patriarch. In the 'Cuarta Jornada' Gallegos even goes as far as to explore the possibility of devising a representative social agenda along the trajectory of an emancipated female character. Indeed, just as *Canaima* marked Gallegos's rejection of a smooth and linear understanding of progress, *Pobre negro* epitomizes the transitional phase that follows this pessimistic ideological turning point. Nevertheless, although *Pobre negro* does not offer a complete and well-formulated theory of the Venezuelan nation's relationship with progress, it does not dwell merely on the obstacles encountered by progress, but productively experiments with various different narrative and socio-political models that take into account the inherent heterogeneity and fragmentary nature of Venezuela. In so doing *Pobre negro* prepares in many respects the ground for more radical structural, stylistic, and ideological innovations. As an illustration, *Sobre la misma tierra*, Gallegos's next novel about Venezuela's socio-racial problems, takes the still hesitant reformulations that characterize *Pobre negro* decisively further. In fact, as I will demonstrate in the following chapter, *Sobre la misma tierra* abandons the systematic framework of conciliatory romance in favour of a tenuous narrative structure, which is woven out of various fragmentary love-plots that do not attain fulfilment. What is more, the subversive figures of the emancipated woman and the rebellious *mestizo* are strikingly fused together in Remota Montiel, the main character of *Sobre la misma tierra*, who successfully resists the traditional destiny of a woman by devoting her life to active social reform.

Notes to Chapter 2

1. Mónica Marinone, 'De pronto ... los otros (Sobre *Pobre negro*)', in *Escribir novelas, fundar naciones: Rómulo Gallegos y la experiencia venezolana* (Mérida: Libro de Arena, 1999), pp. 115–28 (pp. 118–19); Pedro Díaz Seijas, 'Sus tres últimas novelas venezolanas: *Pobre negro, El forastero* y *Sobre la misma tierra*', in *Rómulo Gallegos: multivisión*, ed. by Isaac J. Pardo and Oscar Sambrano Urdaneta (Caracas: Ediciones de la Presidencia de la República, 1986), pp. 227–55 (p. 230).
2. Antonio Scocozza, 'Rómulo Gallegos, labor literaria y compromiso político', in *Literatura y política en América Latina*, ed. by Rafael di Prisco and Antonio Scocozza (Caracas: La Casa de Bello, 1995), pp. 153–238 (pp. 196–97); Doug Yarrington, 'Populist Anxiety: Race and Social Change in the Thought of Rómulo Gallegos', *The Americas*, 56.1 (1999), 65–90 (pp. 80–83).
3. See Judith Ewell, *Venezuela: A Century of Change* (Stanford: Stanford University Press, 1984), pp. 74–75. When discussing the chaos that followed Gómez's death, Ewell points out, '[t]he violence that broke out [...] in the cities and oil camps was the most extensive that Venezuela had experienced in a quarter of a century' (74).
4. Rómulo Gallegos, 'Soy un hombre que desea el orden', in *Una posición en la vida*, ed. by Lowell Dunham (Los Teques: Ediciones del Gobierno del Estado Miranda, 1985), pp. 145–52. Subsequent page references to Gallegos's socio-political writings appear in parentheses in the text.
5. Juan Liscano, '*Pobre negro*', in *Rómulo Gallegos y su tiempo*, 2nd edn (Caracas: Monte Ávila, 1980), pp. 183–95 (p. 183).
6. In the words of an anonymous journalist writing in *Time Magazine* just a few days after Gómez's death, '[s]o many times in late years had the story [of Gómez's death] come down to Caracas that [when it actually happened] for hours no one would believe in it' ('Death of a Dictator', *Time Magazine*, 30 December, 1935 <http://www.time.com/time/magazine/article/0.9171,848393-1,00.html> [accessed 2 September 2008]).
7. The Federal Revolution has in general been poorly documented by historians. In my discussion of the Federal Revolution I draw mainly on Stephen F. Thompson, 'The Federal Revolution in Venezuela, 1858–1863' (unpublished doctoral thesis, University of Oxford, 1984). I am grateful to Malcolm Deas (St Antony's College, Oxford) for bringing this unpublished source to my attention.
8. Henry Cohen, 'The Question of Race in Rómulo Gallegos's *Pobre negro*', *Hispanófila*, 159 (2007), 41–46 (pp. 42–45).
9. Winthrop R. Wright, 'Positivism and National Image 1890–1935', in *Café con leche: Race, Class, and National Image in Venezuela* (Austin: University of Texas Press, 1990), pp. 69–96 (p. 77).
10. See Wright, 'Race and National Image in the Era of Popular Politics 1935–1958', in *Café con leche*, pp. 97–124 (pp. 97–103).
11. Ibid., p. 101.
12. Ibid., p. 102.
13. Ibid., pp. 103–24.
14. Historians disagree about the extent to which women were actually liberated by the social changes that followed the Federal Revolution. For instance, whilst Evelyn Cherpak, 'The Participation of Women in the Independence Movement in Gran Colombia, 1780–1830', in *Latin American Women: Historical Perspectives*, ed. by Asunción Lavrin (Westport, Conn.: Greenwood Press, 1978), pp. 119–234, optimistically suggests that the latter half of the nineteenth century saw the birth of feminism in Venezuela, Arlene J. Díaz, 'Contesting Gender Meanings from Below', in *Female*

Citizens, Patriarchs, and the Law in Venezuela, 1786-1904 (Lincoln, Nebr.: University of Nebraska Press, 2004), pp. 213-34, reveals that patriarchal values still persisted in the post-revolution era.
15. Elisabeth J. Friedman, 'The Paradoxical Rise and Fall of Women's Movement in the First Transition to Democracy (1935-1948)', in *Unfinished Transitions: Women and the Gendered Development of Democracy in Venezuela, 1936-1996* (University Park, Pa.: The Pennsylvania State University Press, 2000), pp. 53-100 (p. 53).
16. Ulrich Leo, '*Pobre negro*, como realidad novelística y como posibilidad histórica', in *Rómulo Gallegos: estudio sobre el arte de novelar* (Caracas: Biblioteca Popular Venezolana, 1954), pp. 131-55; and Orlando Araujo, '*Pobre negro*: novela del *mestizaje*', in *Lengua y creación en la obra de Rómulo Gallegos* (Buenos Aires: Nova, 1955), pp. 137-40, argue that by focusing predominantly on ethnographical and sociological concerns, Gallegos sacrifices the literariness of *Pobre negro*, and almost turns his novel into a long essay. Scocozza, on the other hand, draws attention in 'Rómulo Gallegos, labor literaria y compromiso político' to the way in which critics have unanimously agreed that *Pobre negro* marks the beginning of Gallegos's literary decline, which is to a large extent associated with his increased involvement in the field of politics from 1936 onwards (191-92).
17. Rómulo Gallegos, *Pobre negro* (Caracas: Ediciones Populares Venezolanas, 1964), p. 11. Subsequent page references appear in parentheses in the text.
18. Antonio Isea, 'La caracterización de lo racial-nacional en *Pobre negro* de Rómulo Gallegos', *Afro-Hispanic Review*, 20.2 (2001), 18-22 (p. 19).
19. Cherpak, pp. 119-234, and Díaz, 'A Nation for the Landowners', in *Female Citizens*, pp. 107-31, discuss at length women's role in early nineteenth-century Venezuela. Both pay specific attention to the fact that the end of the colonial epoch did not change women's position in Venezuelan society in any significant way. Though women had engaged actively in the struggles for independence, occasionally even taking on the dangerous duties of spies and soldiers, the return of peace marked the renewal of a profoundly patriarchal social order. The social and religious discourses of the post-independence era continued presenting women as the weaker sex, thus constantly reminding them that the duty of a woman was to be a good wife and mother. A woman's life was once again confined to the domestic sphere. She was by no means regarded as an acceptable participant in the nation's socio-political agenda.
20. As the narrator explains, Negro Malo has acquired his nickname because 'siempre [está] en humor de bromas y jugarretas', rather than 'por mala índole' (15). Yet one cannot help but wonder if Negro Malo's classification as 'malo' does not have at least something to do with the fact that instead of acting as an obedient slave, he constantly tries to subvert the inferior position that has been imposed on him by the white people.
21. Raúl Ramos Calles discusses at significant length the development of Ana Julia's psychosexual condition in the chapter '*Pobre negro*: una novela de inspiración psicoanalítica' of his book *Los personajes de Gallegos a través del psicoanálisis* (Caracas: Monte Ávila, 1984), pp. 187-90. He argues that the image of the gigantic black rapist 'deja huella imborrable en la mente de Ana Julia y hace su aparición en forma de síntomas neuróticas' (190). As he further adds, as time passes, this image of the threatening black man fuses together with Ana Julia's own libidinal urges and comes to represent 'su propia sexualidad reprimida' (190). In the 1949 essay, 'La pura mujer sobre la tierra' (396-425), Gallegos addresses directly the psychoanalytical readings to which Ramos Calles has subjected his novels. Whilst Gallegos clearly appreciates the fact that a renowned psychoanalyst has taken interest in his literary oeuvre, he disagrees with Ramos Calles that incestuous desire can be identified as the main source of the torment

of his characters. As Gallegos explains, the divided identities and existential crises that cause agony to the protagonists of his novels have their roots in 'el imperio de la violencia' and 'la iniquidad', which permeate the history of Venezuela (418). However, considering the circumstance that Gallegos worked as a teacher of psychology at the Escuela Normal de Hombres and the Liceo Caracas it can be assumed that he himself was also familiar with the recent developments in the field of psychology, including the psychoanalytical theories of Sigmund Freud.

22. Leo, p. 135.
23. Liscano, pp. 183–84.
24. Leo, p. 138.
25. The seven sections that concentrate on one of the novel's two interracial relationships are: 'Noche de embrujamientos', 'El salto más allá del límite', 'Las aleluyas de la enfermera', 'La nueva Luisana', 'Hágote capitán', 'Una declaración de amor', and 'La capitana'.
26. The love affair is only one important factor that prompts this development.
27. Hilda Marban, 'El segundo ciclo galleguiano', in *Rómulo Gallegos: el hombre y su obra* (Madrid: Playor, 1973), pp. 157–70 (p. 158), argues that 'la trama [de *Pobre negro*] se ciñe en torno a Pedro Miguel'; whilst Marinone, 'De pronto ... los otros', in *Escribir novelas, fundar naciones*, p. 122, claims that 'el relato se centra en la historia de Pedro Miguel Candelas'.
28. Richard L. Jackson, 'Into the Twentieth Century: The Discovery, Use, and Abuse of Black People and their Culture', in *The Black Image in Latin American Literature* (Albuquerque: University of New Mexico Press, 1976), pp. 36–59 (p. 54). Jackson discusses this notion of the 'superior' mulatto mainly with reference to Arturo Uslar Pietri's 1931 novel, *Las lanzas coloradas*.
29. Wright, 'Whitening the Population, 1850–1900', in *Café con leche*, pp. 43–68, associates the concept of 'whitening' with positivism, which became the leading philosophy amongst the Venezuelan elites in the late nineteenth century. The positivists equated the white race with civilization and progress, and thus justified their contention that the white elites possessed the prerogative to govern even if the majority of the country's population belonged to other racial groups. In order to 'cleanse' the Venezuelan population of the undesirable traits of the 'inferior' coloured races, the positivists encouraged the immigration of white Europeans into Venezuela. Overall, skin-colour still determined significantly one's social position in late nineteenth-century Venezuelan society. Most noticeably, the black minority continued to be entrapped in the same socio-economic position that it had occupied during colonial times. Whilst a full-blooded Negro seldom rose above the level of a labourer or street-vendor, *mestizos* on the other hand even held political posts. Accordingly, mixing with whites provided the blacks and *mestizos* a means through which to ensure that their descendants would rise in the nation's socio-political hierarchy. As Cohen has noted in his article 'The Question of Race', Gallegos was indeed strongly influenced by these positivist modes of thought despite the fact that he supported the opening of the national borders to the Afro-Caribbeans in the 1930s immigration debate, and generally argued for the need to acknowledge the black people as members of the Venezuelan nation-family. Cohen points out that Gallegos did not only study positivist social theory at university, but he wrote in the same newspapers and journals as the most prominent positivist thinkers of his time (50). For a detailed study of the centrality of positivism in Gallegos's writings, see Clemy Machado de Acedo, *La incidencia del positivismo en las ideas políticas de Rómulo Gallegos* (Baruta: Equinoccio, 1982).
30. Isea, p. 20.

31. Throughout the essay 'El verdadero triunfo' (49-52), Gallegos criticizes the inherently impatient disposition of the Venezuelans, and explains that this lack of patience is the reason why the Venezuelan people constantly opt for violent solutions. He further adds that the Venezuelans need to be civilized and educated before they can learn to solve problems through non-violent means.
32. Gallegos is torn between different instincts about women throughout his oeuvre. His attitude towards female sexuality is especially revealing in this sense. He finds exciting the fact that women are sexual, and as shown in the case of Luisana, he even goes momentarily as far as to present sexual emancipation as the first stage in a wider-scale liberation process. Yet in general Gallegos continues regarding female sexuality as something violent and primitive, thus depicting it as antithetical to progress and intelligence. Illustratively, Gallegos's most captivatingly sexual female character, Doña Bárbara, is presented as savage and backward, despite being an evidently emancipated woman. Meanwhile, in *Sobre la misma tierra* Gallegos downplays the sexuality of the highly independent and intelligent Remota Montiel by emphasizing the connection that exists between female sexuality and the yearning for motherhood. By constraining women's sexuality, Gallegos often ends up restating some aspects of the conservative stereotype of the subservient and virtuous woman, even though his genuine intention is to present a female character as an agent of social change.
33. Marinone, 'Cuando las mujeres vienen marchando (sobre *Reinaldo Solar*, *Doña Bárbara* y *Pobre negro*)', in *Escribir novelas, fundar naciones*, pp. 149-71 (p. 163).
34. I am indebted to Rafael Tomás Caldera (Universidad Simón Bolívar) for pointing out that the two Cecilios are based on actual historical personages. According to Caldera, the character of Cecilio the elder draws on the Venezuelan doctor, ethnographer, historian, and linguist Lisandro Alvarado (1858-1929), who during his journeys across the country collected the *Glosarios del bajo español en Venezuela* (1929). Alongside his fascination with the dialectical variations of the Spanish language and the everyday aspects of Venezuelan life, Alvarado is remembered as a first-class scholar also known for his book, *Historia de la revolución federal en Venezuela* (1909), and his posthumously published translation of Lucretius' epic poem *De Rerum Natura*. Cecilio the younger, on the other hand, is likely to have been based on the writer and poet Cecilio Acosta (1818-81), who also acted as the intellectual and moral mentor of Alvarado, who was his junior. Although Acosta's essays, such as the ones collected in the volume entitled *Caridad o frutos de la cooperación de todos al bien de todos* (1855), influenced a whole generation of Venezuelan and Latin American intellectuals, including José Martí, Acosta preferred to stay away from the spotlight and lived a highly secluded life. The fact that Gallegos inverts chronology in his fictional portrayal of the two Cecilios appears somewhat puzzling; it could possibly be read as yet another attempt to question accepted notions of socio-historical development.
35. See 'Soy un hombre que desea el orden' (145-52) for a comprehensive account of Gallegos's ideas about 'orden' and 'desorden'. Though Gallegos emphasizes in this speech his adherence to 'orden' he nonetheless acknowledges, exactly as he does in *Pobre negro*, that the kind of temporary 'desorden' (or 'decadencia') that characterizes any transitional period is full of productive potential, as it forms the basis of a new, less steeply hierarchical social order.
36. As Carlos Fuentes puts it in the chapter 'Espacio y tiempo del Nuevo Mundo' of his book *Valiente mundo nuevo: épica, utopía y mito en la novela hispanoamericana* (Mexico City: Fondo de Cultura Económica, 1994), pp. 50-71 (pp. 50-51), the original *conquistadores* soon found out that the nature of the New World is 'una naturaleza desproporcionada, excesiva, hiperbólica, inconmensurable', that is to say, 'una naturaleza que escapa de los límites del poder humano'.

37. See, for instance, Rómulo Gallegos, *Doña Bárbara*, ed. by Domingo Miliani, Letras Hispánicas, 5th edn (Madrid: Cátedra, 2004). In the chapter entitled 'Candelas y retoños' (315–22) the tradition of setting the pastures on fire is described in the following way:

    Ideas rudimentarias, profundamente arraigadas en el hombre de los campos venezolanos, e impotencia de los escasos pobladores de la llanura ante la enormidad de las tierras que reclaman sus esfuerzos, aconsejan el empleo del fuego, cuando ya se avecinan los primeros aguaceros del año, como único medio eficaz para que renazcan vigorosos los pastos agostados por la sequía y para destruir el gusano y los garrapatales arruinadores del ganado, y es costumbre, casi obligación de solidaridad, que todo llanero le pegue candela a los pajonales secos que encuentra a su paso, así pertenezcan a fincas ajenas. (316)

38. As Ewell, p. 8, explains, '[t]he conflagration known as the Federal Wars began in 1858 when liberals, conservatives, and local *caudillos* united to end the Monagas dynasty and to oust José Tadeo Monagas from office'.
39. Gallegos's attitude towards European-style education and cultural influence is altogether ambiguous. For instance, in the essay 'El factor educación' (58–81) Gallegos first identifies as harmful the way in which the Venezuelan educational system draws on models provided by foreign countries, because it means that the current educational system does not take into account the Venezuelan character. However, almost immediately afterwards, Gallegos goes on to explain how Venezuelans should look to the British educational system for a salubrious example. Similarly, in 'Necesidad de valores culturales' (82–109), Gallegos urges Latin American nations to resist being culturally 're-conquered' by Europe. Nevertheless, throughout the essay he argues that Latin Americans should not restrict themselves to *indigenismo*, which he regards as primitive, but should instead use creatively the knowledge that can be obtained from studying older and more advanced European cultures.
40. In his youth Cecilio the younger considers Pedro Miguel to be 'la criatura dramática de un plan que tenía que cumplirse, de una Idea que buscaba su Forma ('Día de acontecimientos', 54). Though in his adulthood Cecilio the younger rejects such overly romanticized ideas, he still continues regarding 'la existencia de Pedro Miguel como algo más significativo que la suya propia' ('Décimas y fulías', 97).
41. Leo, p. 144.
42. By 'main storylines' I mean the narrative trajectories of the four central characters of *Pobre negro*, as well as the formative plot that describes the relationships of the novel's two interracial couples.
43. Leo, p. 146.
44. Araujo, p. 139.

CHAPTER 3

~

Sobre la misma tierra: A New Socio-Political Agenda?

I

Unlike Gallegos's earlier novels, *Sobre la misma tierra* (1943) does not stage its search for a solution to Venezuela's socio-political problems in the past. On the contrary, the clear majority of the novel's narrative events take place in the late 1930s and early 1940s, when traditional social contradictions have become sharpened by the unequal distribution of the wealth of the country's oil industry.[1] Yet, as I already explained in Chapter 2 with reference to *Pobre negro*, this period also saw turbulent socio-historical change in Venezuela. The year 1935 marked the end of Juan Vicente Gómez's nearly thirty-year-long dictatorship, an event which, according to the Venezuelan critic Juan Liscano, impacted greatly on Gallegos as he composed *Sobre la misma tierra*.[2] While Gómez's demise was initially followed by socio-political instability, social order was restored relatively quickly by General Eleazar López Contreras, who became the President of Venezuela for the next five years. Although López Contreras did not thoroughly dismantle Gómez's autocratic legacy, new left-wing political parties began organizing themselves underground during his rule. Over time, López Contreras grew more lenient, and when his period of office drew to a close, he allowed the opposition party PDN to participate in the April 1941 elections.[3] The PDN candidate was none other than Rómulo Gallegos. Though merely symbolic, Gallegos's candidacy nevertheless represented yet another significant departure from the traditional, autocratic *caudillo* system. What is more, it turned out that the successful candidate, Isaías Medina Angarita, whom Contreras had handpicked as his successor, proved to be unexpectedly forward-thinking and tolerant. During Medina Angarita's presidency major steps were taken towards political freedom, as political parties, including the left-wing ones, were allowed to operate openly and press censorship was abolished. The historian Judith Ewell has specifically noted that '[t]he period from 1941 to 1945', when Medina Angarita was in power, 'saw more political discussion, organizing, and activity than had occurred at any time since the nineteenth century'.[4] Overall, the collapse of the old patriarchal order associated with Gómez's dictatorship, and the emergence of a significant number of new political parties, including Acción Democrática which Gallegos helped to establish in 1941, meant that the time for revising traditional social hierarchies had come. As Daniel H. Levine explains when discussing the politics of the post-Gómez years, 'the weakness[es] of old ties made many persons available for new forms of social organization', and consequently the successful parties were 'broadly based, with a wide range of appeals, reflecting the variety of groups on the move in Venezuela'.[5] During Medina Angarita's presidency, political parties came to function as a new organizational tool, capable of cutting across the social spectrum, thus bringing together workers, professionals, and intellectuals alike in one single sphere.

In view of the vast interpretative possibilities offered by the historical setting of *Sobre la misma tierra*, it is surprising that only a handful of critics have considered the novel worthy of study. Even so, critics such as Ulrich Leo, Juan Liscano, Pedro Díaz Seijas, and Antonio Scocozza have all noted that Gallegos adopts a new approach to Venezuela's socio-historical problems in *Sobre la misma tierra*, an approach which differs notably from the one he employed in his earlier novels.[6] While the critics put the change of approach down to increased optimism (or in the case of Leo, to pessimism), they merely gloss over the socio-political reasons behind this change and abstain from analysing its wider implications. Scocozza probably comes closest to justifying his assertions, when he notes that the novel's apparent optimism is generated by the 'nuevos gobiernos postgomecistas', but even he does not consider the impact of Gallegos's new outlook on his pivotal theories about nationhood and progress.[7] In the current chapter I will explore in depth the previously neglected, substantial revisions to which Gallegos subjected his ideas about the Venezuelan nation's relationship with progress, during the euphoria of the post-Gómez years. I wish to show that although *Sobre la misma tierra* does not address directly the distinct political events of late 1930s and early 1940s Venezuela, an atmosphere of radical socio-political change still pervades the novel, determining not only its subject matter and perspective but also its style. I will argue that rather than being unusually optimistic or pessimistic, as critics have claimed, Gallegos's approach to Venezuela's socio-political problems in *Sobre la misma tierra* is more realistic than ever before.

As a response to the socio-political changes that were taking place in post-Gómez Venezuela, Gallegos subjects the traditional nation-family to strict scrutiny in *Sobre la misma tierra*. Whereas in *Pobre negro* he merely flirted with the notion of a less hierarchical society by momentarily posing a woman and a *mestizo* man as potential social reformers, in *Sobre la misma tierra* he focuses on constructing a new social order on the ruins of patriarchy. Correspondingly,

Gallegos expresses his profound disillusionment with the conventional, *criollo* social reformer — the hero of his earlier novels such as *Doña Bárbara* and *Canaima* — by portraying the initially talented Demetrio Montiel as a treacherous good-for-nothing. And in order to further emphasize this move away from the traditional patriarchal system, which was still so central in *Pobre negro*, Gallegos daringly weaves the action of *Sobre la misma tierra* around a new type of social reformer, Demetrio's mixed-race daughter, Remota. In fact, while *Pobre negro*, with its careful experimentations, marks a transitional stage in Gallegos's socio-political thought, *Sobre la misma tierra* presents us with an innovative, yet strikingly realistic socio-political agenda, based on the outcomes of these experimentations. According to my interpretation, the widespread realization that change was now finally possible, as well as his own increased involvement in politics during the post-Gómez years, inspired Gallegos to trade the purely idealistic projects of his earlier fiction for achievable socio-political ends. This interpretation finds support in the fact that the correspondence between Gallegos's non-fiction and fiction is more pronounced in the works written in the early 1940s than during any other point of his literary career. As I will indicate frequently in my analysis of *Sobre la misma tierra*, material from speeches which Gallegos wrote for his symbolic 1941 presidential campaign, finds its way almost unaltered into the novel. Campaign speeches such as 'Ante su juicio yo concluyo y espero' and 'Constancia puesta en empeño de iluminación' overlap with *Sobre la misma tierra* in giving expression both to Gallegos's sceptical attitude towards the socio-economic progress initiated by the foreign-owned oil industry, and to his newly born preference for smaller-scale regional projects.[8] In point of fact, *Sobre la misma tierra* stands out as the first and only novel in Gallegos's *oeuvre* that does not simply question standard models of socio-political progress, but additionally assumes an openly critical attitude towards the very concepts of progress and modernization.

In *Sobre la misma tierra* Gallegos articulates his increasingly ambivalent attitude towards progress by tying progress intrinsically to the oil industry, which itself is a double-edged sword. On the one hand, the discovery of major oil fields in Venezuela in the 1920s triggered the modernization of the nation's economy, a process that would in the long run also produce significant developments in Venezuelan society. Most notably, the oil industry contributed to the changing distribution of population in Venezuela, as migration to cities and the petroleum areas grew, leaving many rural, formerly agricultural, areas almost deserted.[9] Meanwhile, already during Gómez's dictatorship awareness of the nation's abundant oil resources encouraged people to believe that Venezuela had the potential to grow into a strong, modern country, which could eventually shake off the manacles of the antiquated *caudillo* system. Yet the oil industry also became the emblem of the inherently corrupt nature of the Gómez regime. Upon the discovery of petroleum in Venezuela's subsoil, Gómez ruthlessly betrayed the Venezuelans by selling the rights of exploitation to foreign oil companies.[10] On the whole, in *Sobre la misma tierra* Gallegos focuses on the negative aspects of the oil industry, including Gómez's betrayal of Venezuela — an act which provides Gallegos with the means to denounce the old patriarchal system in still another effective way.[11] Consequently, throughout the novel Gallegos pays specific attention to the misery of the oil workers and the detrimental effects that North American neo-colonialism, a by-product of the foreign-owned oil industry, has had on Venezuelan society. Moreover, Gallegos further questions the efficacy of the socio-economic progress associated with the oil industry by placing part of the action of *Sobre la misma tierra* in the Guajira Peninsula, a region whose indigenous inhabitants continue living according to their age-old traditions, utterly oblivious to modern technology. As I will demonstrate in the current chapter, Gallegos also uses this neglected region, which has not enjoyed the benefits of socio-economic change, in a more general sense to single out the serious limitations of overly ambitious, nation-wide projects of social improvement.

As part of his new, more realistic socio-political agenda, Gallegos abandons conclusively the homogenizing and extensive models of progress so common to his earlier novels, and devotes his full attention to very specific regional and ethnic projects. Indeed, throughout *Sobre la misma tierra* Gallegos repeatedly recites the benefits of limited regional and ethnic projects, drawing the reader's attention to the fact that these projects collectively contribute to the general national well-being.[12] Along the same lines, Gallegos constantly underrates, and even openly ridicules, heterosexual love, which he has up to this point depicted as a standard solution to the nation's racial, social, and regional contradictions. On a cursory reading, *Sobre la misma tierra* seems simply to abandon the traditional framework of national romance in favour of a narrative structure more akin to a filmscript, characterized by short sections, frequent changes of scene, and lengthy pedagogical dialogues about Venezuela's socio-political problems. Considering the novel's fragmentary structure, it seems quite natural that critics such as Lowell Dunham and Ulrich Leo have come to the conclusion that Gallegos sacrifices style in *Sobre la misma tierra* in order to get his thesis across more bluntly.[13] However, by dismissing *Sobre la misma tierra* as stylistically inferior even to *Pobre negro*, these critics once again overlook the carefully constructed correlation that exists between the novel's thematic and structural developments. While a rigorous framework of romance is no longer employed to channel the narrative events towards the fulfilment of heterosexual passion and national consolidation, heterosexual love still remains a highly influential theme and an important framing device in *Sobre la misma tierra*. In this chapter, I will argue that Gallegos subverts the previously homogenizing framework of heterosexual romance by offering a narrative woven out of multiple, fragmentary love-plots which do not attain fulfilment. As I will illustrate, the novel's underlying framework of heterosexual romance constantly critiques and undermines itself, drawing our attention to its profound crevices and the ineffectiveness of the schematic socio-political solution that this particular framework has come to present. I will, nevertheless, also consider the reason why Gallegos does not fully dispense with the framework of romance, even though he constantly uses it in a negative way to dismantle itself. I will argue that the persistence of the framework of heterosexual romance, as well as the narrator's occasionally wavering attitude towards the novel's female social reformer, are both tokens of the fact that Gallegos is not altogether confident about the new socio-political agenda that he is promoting.

II

Apart from the alluring Doña Bárbara, for whom men were mere disposable objects, Remota is undoubtedly the most magnetic of Gallegos heroines, considering the way in which she effortlessly draws men to herself. While in *Pobre negro* Luisana's affections were torn between her two cousins, the conservative Antonio de Céspedes and the rebellious *mestizo* Pedro Miguel, Remota is courted in turn and desired by as many as six men. The male characters who show either a romantic or sexual interest in Remota can be divided into two main groups. The first consists of what I will subsequently refer to as her three principal suitors: the Indian warrior Jararayú, the *criollo* historian Ramiro Celis, and the North American oil exploiter Hardman. The ethnic backgrounds and professional occupations of each of these suitors represent the different sides of modern Venezuela, where primitive but heroic Indian traditions coexist and compete with *criollo* ideologies of regionalism and an increasingly powerful North American neo-colonialism. The function of these principal suitors is to epitomize alternative alliances and destinies, which Remota eventually rejects at least partly because of their exclusiveness. She is not ready to restrict her mission in life to that of a perpetuator of the 'estampa de Guajira heroica', preserved so markedly in the Indian warrior Jararayú, nor does she wish to become an accomplice in Ramiro Celis's regionalist nostalgia, or a 'parte integrante de [un] país extraño que [...] estaba pasándose una temporada en la suya' — the fate that would await her if she were to marry Hardman.[14] Whereas Remota's principal suitors are depicted as extremely likeable and their interest in Remota is based on genuine caring and respect, for Chuachuaima, Demetrio Montiel, and Adrián Gadea — the three other men in her life — she is an object of sexual greed. These three men are obvious *caudillo*-figures, that is, men who are capable of awakening both fear and admiration in the hearts of the

Venezuelan people, who willingly become seduced by what Gallegos in his essay 'Los poderes' has identified as 'personalismo' and 'la audacia del aventurero' (36–37). Indeed, the Indian Chuachuaima is 'el jefe de la casta epieyú' (40), while Demetrio Montiel is described by his adherents as an 'hombrón y medio' (204), and even the opponents of Adrían Gadea admit that he is 'poderoso [...] con todo su dinero y toda su influencia' (217). The presence of these men, who are relics of Venezuela's hierarchical and stagnant past, threatens Remota's fate both as a modern woman and as a social reformer. Consequently, Demetrio's suicide, Adrián Gadea's imprisonment, and Chuachuaima's obscure disappearance from the plot, can be read as necessary prerequisites, without which the success of Remota's plans of social reform cannot even be contemplated.

Remota's winsome charisma, which attracts two such different groups of men, does not have its roots in any female vanities but rather in the complexity and strength of her character. Although her aunts describe her as '[l]a majayura más bonita que [se] ha formado en Guajira' (42), when she is still an adolescent in *blanqueo*, Remota's first suitor, the Indian Jararayú, is seduced by Remota's talent to narrate engaging stories, not by her beauty. Also, the North American Hardman is initially attracted to Remota's intelligence and sense of humour, with which he becomes familiar during '[la] agradable conversación' (124) which the two begin on an aeroplane to Miami. And even the brutish Adrián Gadea is above all struck by the shrewdness and 'demostración de superioridad' (223) with which Remota urges him to return the money that he owes her deceased father, Demetrio Montiel. The local historian Ramiro Celis, whom Remota re-encounters on her return to Maracaibo, is, on the other hand, fascinated more specifically by her face, which without being 'propiamente bello' is nevertheless a 'rostro interesante [...] cautivador de las miradas que en él se detuvieran' (99). In fact, despite her intentions to trade femininity for pure practicality and intelligence in terms of both her behaviour and appearance, Remota's personality seems to radiate an unintended and innate sensuality — a sensuality that she has most likely inherited from her fiery mother, Cantaralia, 'la pelirroja, blanca, pero de facciones guajiras' (17). It is this combination of strength of character and innate sensuality that makes Remota so utterly irresistible to men and simultaneously a threat to the established social conventions. To quote a striking example, even her own father Demetrio Montiel struggles against incestuous yearnings during his only encounter with his then fifteen-year-old daughter in 'La temeraria travesía', and according to rumours he is thereafter always 'perdidamente enamorada de ella' (115). Along the same lines, the hypocritical Lastenia Cortasano can baselessly imagine Remota as a sexual predator, who visits Ramiro Celis in broad daylight, dressed primly in mourning ('La señora de enfrente'); and the very thought of a night with the firm but fearless Remota makes Adrián Gadea rub his hands in lascivious delight ('La mujer vendida'). However, in spite of the multiple offers of romantic alliances, the stubborn, independent, and forward-thinking Remota takes pride in boasting that she is completely 'insensible al amor' (147). Indeed, the numerous offers that she gets from potential lovers and suitors only emphasize the illusion of her own immunity to love. As I will now demonstrate, Remota's decision to reject each of her suitors ultimately has far less to do with their incompatibility, or even the different destinies that they represent, than with her headstrong decision to reject the very concept of heterosexual love.

Remota reveals her dislike for the institution of marriage in the section 'Era una tarde fea', where she tells her half-brother Marco Aurelio why she is repelled by the very thought of a husband: 'El matrimonio no está en mi destino [...] ¿Que [...] hay [maridos] buenos? ¡Sí, hombre! Incluso excelentes: pero siempre dueños. Amos considerados y afectuosos en el mejor de los casos' (147–48). By referring to husbands as 'dueños' and 'amos', Remota articulates the novel's more general view of marriage as a medium of financial exchange in which a woman becomes a mere commodity, or to put it even more crudely, a piece of merchandise. As is explained early on in the section 'El blanqueo', in the culture of the Guajiro Indians, 'cada mujer [que] pueda ofrecerse en matrimonio es una posibilidad de aumentar los rebaños del peculio doméstico' (32). Hence, the joy with which Remota's aunts Dorila and Palmira are ready to deliver the adolescent Remota into the hands of a wealthy older man, like Chuachuaima, and the stoicism with which the young Jararayú tries to gather enough 'reses y bestias', in order to meet '[el] precio que [...] le [han] puesto a Remota sus tías' (39). However, the idea of the woman as a commodity that can be exchanged for (or bought by) wealth is by no means limited to the Guajiros alone. Significantly, Hardman strives to make himself appear to be a good catch in the eyes of Remota by boasting how his promotion to 'jefe de la sección de perforadores' allows him to offer 'una vida mejor [...] a una mujer' (138–39). Even more strikingly, the lecherous Adrián Gadea expects literally to buy Remota's sexual favours first, and later her hand in marriage, with a cheque for 'doce mil bolívares' (224). Although Remota remains emotionally 'la mujer que de ningún dinero se vendería' (224) during her mock barter with Adrián Gadea, her ability to stage the barter without losing her composure implies that she knows how to exploit the underlying erotics of economic exchange to suit her own ends. But while Remota is ready to play along with the social expectations and discourses of existing sexual politics in order to obtain the money necessary for carrying out her projects of social reform in the Guajira, she regards love and marriage as inherently antithetical to her enterprise of social reform. Thus, seducing and pacifying the enemy or intruder through stratagems of affection does not form part of Remota's vision of socio-economic improvement. Remota's belief that heterosexual love and social reform are antithetical finds pointed expression again in 'Era una tarde fea', where she not only rejects the concept of marriage but also discusses her desire to devote her life to building a better future for the Guajiros. Remota declares forcefully that even though she will be ridiculed for being a spinster, she is not ready to 'enajenar [su] voluntad' by getting married, a declaration which Marco Aurelio interprets correctly as Remota's need to preserve her own will 'íntegra [...] para algo que bien valga la pena' (148). Later in 'Invitación sentimental', a section which precedes Remota's journey to reclaim the money owed by Adrián Gadea, she dismisses all arguments about what an excellent match Ramiro Celis would make, on the grounds that *she* is about to embark on '[una] empresa de hombre' (202). Suggestively, the fourth and fifth chapters of 'Tercera Parte', which prepare the ground for Remota's 'empresa de hombre' in Chapter 6, serve as a farewell to her three principal suitors. At first, the suitors are reintroduced into the narrative in the same order in which they originally appeared, starting with Jararayú in the section that bears his name, followed by Hardman in '*Keep it Quiet*', and finally, Ramiro Celis in 'Invitación sentimental'.[15] Inasmuch as each of the suitors exits the narrative for good after his brief reintroduction, the function of the reintroductions appears to be solely to clear the ground of any romantic obstacles that could stand in the way of the enterprise of social reform which Remota is about to initiate. By opposing heterosexual love and social reform on a larger scale as well, in terms of the organization of the narrative events — and not simply in Remota's mind — *Sobre la misma tierra* strikes a discordant note with Gallegos's earlier novels, in which romance and social improvement were presented as two analogical and interchangeable projects.

Already the section 'El canto del Keirachí', which introduces the character of Remota, lays out the two possible, contradictory destinies facing the novel's then still juvenile heroine. In this section the narrator notes Remota's sensitivity to the suffering of the Guajiro people, as she contemplates the sight of 'las caravanas de familias indígenas que diariamente atravesaban la árida llanura durante los recios veranos, rumbo a Maracaibo [...] para dedicarse allí a la mendicidad' (29). It is during these moments of melancholic contemplation that Remota's future as a social reformer begins to materialize, as is implied by the references to a 'misteriosa voz' of instigation, which she claims to hear much to the distress of her superstitious aunts, who incorrectly interpret the voice as the call of death (29).[16] During the same period of her childhood, Remota also establishes her potential as a leader-figure by becoming the head of a group of girls, whom she keeps mesmerized with her 'maravillosos cuentos' (30). Yet it is in the course of these story-telling sessions that Remota encounters Jararayú, whom the other boys soon start calling mockingly 'Keirachí', a reference to the lovesick hero of a Guajiro song, after his admiring gaze betrays his love for Remota. Following this revelation, Remota stops playing with the other children and withdraws into the seclusion of her aunts' house in order to spare herself the romantic attentions of Jararayú, thus establishing the repetitive pattern of romantic attraction and subsequent rejection that marks her whole story. However, Remota's way of responding to Jararayú gives us the first valuable insight into her character; in fact, throughout the novel the complexities and contradictions of Remota's personality are generally revealed through the manner in which she reacts to and interacts with her admirers. Hence, despite all the allusions to Remota's independence, she is to a large extent defined in opposition and with reference to her different suitors. It is certainly no coincidence that the character of Remota is introduced in a section entitled 'El canto del Keirachí', a section which carries the nickname of her first suitor. What is more, Gallegos also employs the same technique of introduction in the 'Segunda Parte' in the section entitled 'Hardman'. The grown-up Remota is reintroduced into the narrative in this section that highlights her independent disposition — amongst other things, she is 'la única mujer [...] en el avión' travelling to Miami (92) — a section which, nevertheless, is named after her North American suitor.

Furthermore, even though at the end of 'El canto del Keirachí' Remota seems to reject Jararayú and the very possibility of romance with a firmness uncharacteristic of her tender age, the subsequent section of Chapter 2 of 'Primera Parte', 'El blanqueo', reinstates immediately the theme of heterosexual romance. As is already implied by the section's title, the section describes the arrangements made for Remota's *blanqueo*, a Guajiro initiation ritual which prepares a young woman for 'las graves responsibilidades conyugales y maternales' (33). In fact, the remaining four sections of Chapter 2 concentrate on Remota's transformation into a marriageable woman, and the high expectations that her aunts have of a successful marriage.[17] On top of this, the penultimate section of Chapter 2 introduces the ideal type of suitor in the form of the wealthy and powerful Chuachuaima, who effortlessly buys Remota from her greedy aunts. Finally, after disappearing from the plot for the entirety of Chapter 3, Remota reappears in Chapter 4, in which she flees from her arranged marriage with Chuachuaima, only to become exposed to Demetrio's incestuous yearnings in the section 'La temeraria travesía'.[18] Thus, already within this limited narrative space consisting of three chapters, it is possible not only to perceive three unfulfilled heterosexual love plots corresponding to Remota's relationships with Jararayú, Chuachuaima, and Demetrio, but also the swiftness with which one love plot almost immediately gives way to another. This wealth of movement in the love plots, so foreign to Gallegos's earlier novels such as *Doña Bárbara*, *Canaima*, and *Pobre negro*, in which the main focus is always on one specific heterosexual relationship, is undoubtedly one of the most striking features of *Sobre la misma tierra*. Moreover, the tempo of the love plots accelerates further in the 'Segunda' and 'Tercera Parte', wherein Remota's three principal suitors, Jararayú, Hardman, and Ramiro Celis, acquire major roles. After being introduced into the narrative at the beginning of Chapter 2 of 'Segunda Parte', Hardman and Ramiro Celis take turns in becoming the centre of narrative attention in the Chapters 3 and 4, which explore the possibility of a romantic relationship between both of these men and Remota. Jararayú, on the other hand, is given a substantial role in the fourth chapter of 'Tercera Parte', which depicts Remota's return to Guajira. Overall, in the 'Segunda' and 'Tercera Parte' the narrative vacillates between Remota's encounters with her main suitors, before the three begin fusing together in Remota's nostalgic mind in the sections 'La temeraria empresa' and 'Noche de contradicciones' (Chapter 6, 'Tercera Parte'), two sections which dwell on the romantic life Remota is rejecting in favour of her *empresa de hombre*.

Although the actions of the various suitors and admirers influence the course of Remota's life, these admirers are not able to gain a 'life of their own'. They remain subordinate characters who never achieve an equal footing with the novel's heroine. In fact, the role of Jararayú, Ramiro Celis, and Hardman is almost entirely representative. These three principal suitors not only represent the contradictions of modern Venezuela, but they also collectively stand for the figure of the lover and suitor that Remota must learn to reject. Their reduction to lover-figures is emphasized by the essentially physical descriptions which accompany both Hardman's and Jarararayú's respective (re)introductions into the narrative:

> Un sujeto de formación no antigua todavía [...] de rostro aristado, sobre cuyas facciones no habría querido el artífice perder tiempo precioso en ternuras de suavizamientos, sino que lo echaría afuera apenas fraguada y soldada la armadura interior. Y para más completa y mejor apariencia de elaboración de altos hornos, tenía pupilas de acero taladrante. ('Hardman', 92)

> Rostro tallado en ángulos enérgicos, voluntarioso el perfil, erguido el cuello, anchos los hombros, bien modelado el torso, fornidos los brazos y las piernas al descubierto de la manta, el adornado y armado venía con todo su gallardía varonil transpirando gana de pelea. ('Jararayú', 185)

Both of the descriptions are presented as Remota's initial impressions of the two men. In a surprisingly sexualized way, her eye seems to catch the curves, shapes, and protrusions of Hardman's and Jararayú's facial and bodily features, with the care of a hand shaping a statue out of stone. Effectively, the notions that Hardman resembles an android and that Jararayú is just like '[un] Marte de bronce' (186) point clearly to an objectification of the male body, an objectification traditionally associated with the *female* body.[19] Yet while the male physique with its minuscule details appears inviting, the way in which it is carved out of hard substances ('acero' and 'bronce') makes it utterly impenetrable. The male body thus becomes for Remota something that can be appreciated from a distance but never intimately approached or possessed. Besides, the substitution of the vigorous and resilient flesh with lifeless and hard metals also plays along with the novel's almost obsessive interest in infertility, which I shall later discuss in detail. For now, I would like to point out that although the descriptions of Jararayú and Hardman seem on the one hand to reiterate the rejection of heterosexual love, the fact that these descriptions are based on Remota's careful observations of the male physique reveals that she might not be as 'insensible al amor' as she likes to imagine.

While Remota pulls back as soon as the threat of marriage (or physical consummation) draws too close, she is nevertheless to some extent attracted to each of her principal suitors. Her rejection of love therefore appears more of a choice than an innate characteristic of her nature. Already when seated next to Hardman on the plane to Miami, she flirtatiously joins his humorous game about '[la] inspección de los frenos de un tren, que tal vez se ha detenido en mi estación' (94) — this being Hardman's metaphor for a suitable lady that might have suddenly entered his life. Later, in Chapter 4 of 'Segunda Parte', Remota willingly accepts Hardman's invitation to take her on a ride across the petroleum extraction fields of Zulia, and she enjoys a day of unresolved sexual tension and witty conversations, which climaxes in Hardman's proposal. Even though Remota rejects Hardman, she spends her lonely trip across the Lago de Maracaibo justifying her choice to herself. She weighs both the benefits and downsides of the offer, concluding that while 'no era despreciable ni desde el punto de vista práctico, ni desde el puramente espiritual', she still does not wish to become 'un ser perteneciente a otro' (141). Generally speaking, Remota's need to justify her rejection of Hardman implies that although she sticks to her original decision, she seems momentarily to wonder if she made the right one. Despite the fact that out of all her suitors Remota seems most drawn to Hardman, who shares her sense of humour and concern for the people of Venezuela, she nonetheless also intentionally reawakens Ramiro Celis's and Jararayú's memories of the adolescent passion they had felt for her. For instance, when Ramiro Celis in 'Una lectura interrumpida' is unable to recognize her immediately, she coquettishly reminds him of how '[d]esde [la] azotea, hace dieciocho años, solía mirar un joven hacia el rincón del patio vecino [...] en el cual solía también estar una muchacha mirando, como hacia el cielo, pero en realidad hacia dicha azotea' (98). With a similar purpose in mind, Remota calls Jararayú by his nickname 'Keirachí', when thanking him for his offer to protect her from Chuachuaima's vengeful relatives, whose tribal pride has been shattered by the way in which she vanished on the night of her wedding (185). Remota's choice of using Jararayú's nickname, rather than his real name, is highly significant, since the nickname 'Keirachí' was originally employed by Jararayú's friends when teasing him about his infatuation with Remota.

Overall, Remota's unreasonable moves to rekindle romantic feelings that clearly belong to the past echo her obsession with what her life would have been like had she accepted the advances of any of her three principal suitors.

Remota's fixation on what might have been finds a further expression in her frustrated maternal feelings. Indeed, even when she tells Marco Aurelio in 'Era una tarde fea' that she does not wish to become anyone's wife, Remota admits that '[n]o carezco de sentimientos maternales e incluso me falta un hijo [...] [p]ero [...] mientras no me decida a declararme revolucionaria, para llegar al hijo hay que pasar por el matrimonio y soportar marido' (147–48). Moreover, in 'También allí', a section which records the consequences of Remota's emotional reencounter with Jararayú, we are told that Remota feels how 'de las fuentes profundas de la vida de sus entrañas le subía por momentos hasta el corazón un tierno deseo de hijo' (188). On this particular occasion, she even goes so far as to consider what it would have been like to mother Jararayú's children as a young woman. The description of the emotions that the encounter with Jararayú stirs in Remota is striking and surprising in at least two different but connected ways. On the one hand, the notion of tender maternity seems somewhat at odds with the desiring eye with which Remota devoured Jararayú's physique, with its '[torso] bien modelado' and '[brazos y piernas] fornidos' (185), only in the preceding section of *Sobre la misma tierra*. Yet in the meantime, the use of the expression 'las fuentes profundas de la vida de sus entrañas' — to describe maternal feelings — has a ticklishly erotic feeling to it. This is in fact one of the novel's many instances wherein erotic love is sublimated into a maternal one, a process which successfully undermines the importance of heterosexual desire *per se*, in still another, significant way, as I will show in the following section.

III

Remota herself is the product of 'apetitos sensuales irresponsables' (109) — that is, she is the result of a fleeting sexual encounter between her partly Indian mother, Cantaralia, and the *criollo* adventurer, Demetrio Montiel. The peculiarities of this encounter set the pattern for the way in which the sexual act is sublimated in *Sobre la misma tierra*. At first glance, Cantaralia and Demetrio's moment of passion, recorded in a section suggestively entitled 'El encuentro', appears purely erotic; after all, it depicts the joyful coming together of two highly sensual beings, both of whom seem to be driven by their primitive instincts. We are told that Demetrio 'envuelve [a Cantaralia] en contemplación sensual' (22), and she in turn surrenders to Demetrio without question following a short preliminary dialogue consisting of only a handful of phrases. Later there is even some speculation about whether she ever truly knew his name.[20] Yet 'El encuentro' places significant emphasis on the fact that, for Cantaralia, this random sexual encounter has a clearly defined purpose: to produce offspring. Indeed, throughout the section, Cantaralia's sexual desire is intrinsically linked to, and overshadowed by, her maternal feelings. When she sees Demetrio lying in a hammock, her first reaction is to become overwhelmed by happiness, as she senses that this is the man who will be able to help her to 'reali[zar] la madre que alentaba en su tumultuosa generosidad vital' (22). And slightly later on, she fails to maintain her carefree air in the presence of Demetrio, because as she sings, '[sus] palabras se [...] ahogan en la garganta [...] *incontenible la madre* que no quería frustrarse en ella' (23, emphasis added). Finally, the section's matter-of-fact closing line, 'Cantaralia la generosa [...] se disponía a concebir un hijo ante el lucero del alba' (23), provides a further affirmation of the secondary role that illicit sexual desire plays in relation to the yearning for motherhood. What Gallegos articulates here is an explanation of Cantaralia's libertine sexual behaviour with the excuse that she desperately wishes to fulfil the traditional destiny of a woman as a mother.

Even so, Gallegos evidently sees the need to set Remota apart from her free-spirited mother. This becomes clear when we compare the ways in which the two women, at their respective times, experience the isolation of the *blanqueo*, which is supposed to turn girls into women:

> Para reducirla al encierro del 'blanqueo' fué necesario construir una habitación especial, de donde no pudiera escaparse. Pero durante la reclusión [...] no fué posible lograr que aprendiera a manejar el telar ni a ejecutar, siquiera medianamente, las labores de mano a que debía aplicarse, pues se lo pasó cantando, a plena voz, cuanto se le venía a la mente. ('Cantaralia', 20)

> Eran ya tres años de reclusión, pero deseaba que aquello no terminase nunca. [Se] senta[b]a en la banqueta del telar, cuyo manejo ninguna otra majayura había aprendido tan pronto o con la aguja en la mano virtuosa para el tejido o ensartando las cuentas de colores para los brazaletes y los collares [...] [Pero] mientras sus manos se ocupaban en ello, el pensamiento se le reposaba en [...] una idea que no habría podido explicar en qué consistía. (Remota, in 'La Majayura', 37)

As can be seen from these two passages, Cantaralia's and Remota's experiences of the *blanqueo* are completely different: whereas Cantaralia feels entrapped and wastes her days singing spontaneously, without showing any aptitude for womanly pastimes, Remota enjoys the calmness of her solitude and excels in needlework. Interestingly, despite all the emphasis that the narrator places throughout the novel on the fact that Remota is stubborn and not particularly feminine, on this particular occasion she seems to be described as a rather subdued and conventional young Guajiro woman. However, the notion of Remota as a conventional woman is somewhat undermined by the reference to the 'idea que no habría podido explicar en que consistía', an idea which haunts Remota during the *blanqueo*. In point of fact, this idea seems to belong to the same category of unexplainable but significant phenomena as the 'misteriosa voz', which calls to the still juvenile Remota in 'El canto del Keirachí'. Assuming that, like the 'misteriosa voz', the perplexing 'idea' also alludes to Remota's future destiny as a social reformer, we are once again faced with an instance where Remota's two possible destinies are presented side by side. Yet here the two appear in such a close juxtaposition (Remota conceives the mysterious 'idea' *while* engaged in needlework) that the alternative future of social reform seems almost to fuse with the typical destiny of a woman. In fact, as I will illustrate in later sections which explore Remota's endeavours to build a better future for the Guajiros, Gallegos constantly manipulates and fuses together these two destinies so that the often threateningly independent Remota does not come across as a *marimacho*.

Whereas sexual desire is sublimated into a yearning for motherhood in *Sobre la misma tierra*, the potentially radical image of a female social reformer is similarly softened by the systematic comparisons made between Remota's projects of social reform and mothering. The most explicit example of the way in which the image of the female social reformer is softened can be found in the section entitled 'La Gran Madre', a pivotal section in which Remota establishes herself as a leader-figure in the eyes of the Guajiro community. The section opens with Remota musing about possible projects for socio-economic improvement, such as pumping water from underground springs — projects which begin to materialize in her mind as she contemplates the misery and drought that surrounds her:

> Iba de aquí para allá [...] con los brazos cogidos a la espalda, a la manera de los hombres que se pasean pensativos y eran pensamientos varoniles los que ocupaban su mente. [...] Sobre la oscura tierra sin fragancias de fronda se alzaban hacia el cielo encapotado, las negras pencas de los cardonales, como brazos de muchedumbre clamantes de la misericordia negada del agua [...] Una empresa para ser acometida por hombres de acción: toda la Guajira algún día erizada de torres laboriosas, propias y para el remedio de la propia necesidad apremiante [...] Una empresa de hombres donde desembocara su mujer frustrada por la orgánica desapetencia de amor. (172)

The very concept of social reform is here defined as an inherently manly business, as is suggested by the description of Remota's thoughts about this particular topic as 'pensamientos varoniles', and the way in which the project of building water towers is repeatedly affirmed as an enterprise that needs to be carried out by men. Moreover, the reference to how Remota's manner of walking begins to resemble that of 'hombres que pasean pensativos', as she becomes immersed in her thoughts about social reform, reinforces conventional gender stereotypes by depicting men as the ones who not only *act* but usually also *think*. On top of this, the projects of social reform are interpreted as an outlet for Remota's 'mujer frustrada', and as a substitute for 'amor'. By tracking her motivation for carrying out social reform back to two feelings (or negation of feelings) — that is, 'frustración' and 'amor' — Gallegos's narrator reiterates the presumption that women are above all driven by their emotions. The notion that projects of social reform provide an outlet for Remota's womanly desires works as yet another reminder of the way in which social reform is presented in *Sobre la misma tierra* as an alternative for love rather than a project that is analogical or interchangeable with heterosexual romance. At the same time, the allusion to how the 'mujer frustrada' in Remota can find fulfilment in helping her people also draws attention to the nurturing aspect of her role as a social reformer, an aspect which is elaborated in the later parts of 'La Gran Madre'. In the section's climactic scene, Remota saves a young Indian girl called Amaqui from the barbarous rituals of a witch doctor, who is trying to cure the girl of her sickness by spitting chewed tobacco on her while twisting convulsively and shaking the *maracas* (174). Although according to the primitive beliefs of the Guajiros, Remota's interruption of the ritual constitutes a dangerous act which could kill the sick girl, the witch doctor surprises everyone by placing the girl's fate in the hands of Remota, declaring, '[e]ntréguensela a la Gran Madre . . . Háganle lo que ella diga . . . La Gran Madre trae el remedio de todos los males' (176). Despite its superstitious origins, Remota adopts the epithet of 'la Gran Madre' willingly and thus becomes the leader and mother of the often childlike Guajiros, who look up to her and expect her to find solutions to their problems. Indeed, the section 'La Gran Madre' closes appropriately with an additional affirmation of Remota's newly gained role as a nurturing mother, as she ensures that the fragile Indian girl is given '[una] medicina reconfortante' and bathed (176).

In his essay 'La pura mujer sobre la tierra' (396–425), Gallegos makes it clear that Remota's role as nurturing mother was from the outset meant to be one of her most significant, defining features. He explains that, Remota, just like Luisana in *Pobre negro*, responds to his desire to expand on the flickering maternal feeling felt by Doña Bárbara in the chapter 'La estrella en la mira', and in so doing to 'encontra[r] [una] madre generosa, aun dentro de ese tipo de mujeres en quien lo femenil no es todo suavidad y dulzura' (420).[21] As Gallegos further goes on to note, he is convinced that this end was especially well accomplished in the character of Remota, who successfully finds '[empleo] más dilatado' for her 'necesidad de ternura maternal' (423). Yet Gallegos's vacillating attitude towards the exact role that women can (and should) occupy in social, political, or economic projects is not only limited to the portrayal of female heroines such as Remota Montiel and Luisana Alcorta, but also runs through his political writings. The most marked example can undoubtedly be found in the speech, 'Había aquí una lección por dar' (182–99), which Gallegos delivered in 1941 when running the first time for the presidency. In this particular speech, Gallegos lays out the benefits of democracy while also stressing the responsibility that each citizen holds with regard to the future of the Venezuelan nation. As part of the speech, Gallegos additionally announces his support for women's suffrage movements and addresses the female members of the audience in the following terms:

> Y aquí está la mujer venezolana en acto de presencia, no por dispuesta a desatender los cuidados del hogar ni la femineidad de su espíritu — dulce virtud y delicado ornato que nunca le falten [sic] — sino para imprimirle también calidad patriótica, que no le es ajena, sino por lo contrario inherente a sus atributos persuasivos y a la misión maternal por excelencia de darle hijos a la Patria [...] Como también por mostrarse digna de que a ella se le reconozcan los derechos que naturalmente posee, a participar [...] en la decisión de la suerte del país, porque no es cosa probada que haya más virtud ciudadana, más firmeza ni más abnegación en el hombre que en la mujer. Yo saludo en ella, aquí presente, al hombre mejor de mañana, por ella bien formado y con ella bien acompañado. (197)

Even while arguing for women's suffrage and involvement on the national scale, Gallegos nonetheless defines women's social role in extremely conventional terms. In his scheme, women's participation in national affairs should by no means be seen as a substitute for their domestic duties, or as an excuse to abandon their genteel, feminine manners. In fact, Gallegos believes that women can most effectively help Venezuela by extending their traditional role as mothers and wives to a national scale, that is to say, to 'darle hijos a la Patria'. Moreover, as indicated by the subsequent references to '[el] hombre mejor de mañana', who will be well brought up and attended to by the Venezuelan woman, what Gallegos is referring to here are essentially 'hijos' rather than '[hijas] de la Patria'.[22] Consequently, the only way in which the Venezuelan woman can effectively influence and assist the 'Patria', the ultimate male authority, is by proxy, through these 'hijos', be they actual sons or husbands or fathers. As Gallegos's speech makes clear, a woman's life and actions are constantly subordinated to male forces, which impose form and direction on her existence — a process which also maintains order in the society. In short, in this 1941 address Gallegos still presents the figure of a superior male — the fatherland and the husband — as the indispensable centre around which national life revolves.

Despite drawing an analogy between Remota's projects of social reform and the traditional duties of a woman, Gallegos nevertheless does delineate in *Sobre la misma tierra* — which appeared only two years after this campaign speech — a blueprint of a Venezuelan society where the superior male authority no longer stands as the unshakeable pillar sustaining order. As I will show later in this chapter, especially when discussing Demetrio's relationship with Remota, in

Sobre la misma tierra Gallegos discloses and condemns the sins committed by fathers, in whose hands history has for so long placed the fate of the Venezuelan nation and its peoples. In the Venezuela of *Sobre la misma tierra* father-figures are not trustworthy, as is seen in the case of Demetrio. Indeed, fathers like him first exploit and then readily prostitute their own children to undeserving intruders. Yet even so, with the fall of the father-figure the 'Patria' becomes a chaotic and unstable motherland, a world of crumbling family structures. I will argue that Gallegos uses the character of Remota to explore a possible way out of this often confusing and hostile chaos, making her the representative of a new social order, which will be less oppressive than the patriarchal one, without, however, appearing altogether radical.

IV

In the chapter 'Love *of* Country', Doris Sommer has argued that in populist novels, such as *Doña Bárbara*, in which patriotism appears 'more proprietary and less conciliatory', there exists a close connection between questions of land ownership, fatherhood, and the concept of 'Patria'.[23] According to the populist tradition, legitimate father-figures are indispensable custodians and masters of the often wayward (mother)land, which must be controlled, as well as protected from 'foreign or barbarous usurpers' (258). As Sommer clarifies, the very identity of the (mother)land depends on the father-figure, 'because the feminine *patria* literally means belonging to the father' (258). Meanwhile, the (mother)land provides the male powers with a terrain on which to affirm their patriarchal status, a docile and fertile body in which to sow their seeds. Even though *Sobre la misma tierra* does not end in the populist vein exemplified by *Doña Bárbara*, in which Santos Luzardo imposes order on the savage land of the *llanos*, Sommer's chapter is highly relevant when exploring the symbolical role played by the land in *Sobre la misma tierra*. In fact, the relentless instability of the Venezuelan nation is articulated in *Sobre la misma tierra* with the aid of a telluric metaphor: the image of the utterly uncontrollable and inherently feminine *arenal movedizo*. This quicksand that gradually swallows Remota's childhood home of Alitasía is established as a metaphor for the chaos of the Venezuelan nation by means of Marco Aurelio's comments in the section, 'Era una tarde fea'. As Marco Aurelio explains to Remota, the instability that characterizes Alitasía is a common feature of Venezuela: 'no son [los] médanos de Alitasía, especialmente. A todos en este país nos ocurre lo mismo. Nos asentamos sobre terreno inseguro y por momentos todo el país bambolea, amenazando hundirse' (146). Undoubtedly, Marco Aurelio's thesis that the Venezuelan nation lacks a solid foundation points to both the economic and the political situation that prevailed in Venezuela during the time Gallegos was writing his novel. With regard to the instability of the Venezuelan economy, it is worth quoting especially Gallegos's 1941 campaign speech, 'Ante su juicio yo concluyo y espero' (200–17). Here Gallegos not only condemns Venezuela's dependency on the foreign-owned oil industry, on the grounds that wealth derived from this type of industry is 'perecedera', but he further identifies the need to 'procurar [...] *base estable* y fecunda a [la] economía [venezolana]', by recourse to more traditional industries, such as agriculture (206, emphasis added). As for the political instability, as I noted in the introduction to this chapter, the post-Gómez years were marked by profound socio-political change, including the emergence of various new political parties, which overturned the antiquated political framework that had been solidly maintained by Gómez during his almost thirty-year-long dictatorship.

Apart from the references to the *arenal movedizo*, the instability of the Venezuelan land is additionally evoked in *Sobre la misma tierra* by the way in which the word *tierra* constantly shifts meaning. For instance, in the section 'Aquel Roseliano Figueras', Hardman welcomes the opportunity to 'asentar sobre la tierra misma [...] una agradable conversación que hemos dejado en el aire' (124). He thus uses the word 'tierra' to refer to the common ground under his and Remota's feet, as opposed to the air, where they literally began their still unresolved discussion. However, soon afterwards in 'Conversaciones a fondo', Hardman employs the word *tierra* in two additional ways. At first, he uses it to refer to a 'country' or 'homeland' when stating that he respects 'el sentimiento que cada tierra pone en el corazón de su gente' (131). In the same conversation with Remota he also uses the word 'tierra' as a synonym of 'el mundo', when announcing that each individual should be a good citizen of his or her 'país', so that when 'el día de las fronteras borradas' finally arrives she or he can become a 'buen ciudadano de la tierra entera' (131). At various points in the novel, *tierra* is further used to refer to a specific region, instead of an entire country, as is the case in the section entitled 'La vuelta a la tierra', which depicts Remota's return to the rural Guajira of her childhood. What is more, in this particular section, *tierra* is additionally closely linked with the concepts of 'paisaje' and 'terreno', as implied by the lengthy descriptions of the region's soil with its flora and fauna, descriptions which seem to be discordant with the novel's otherwise unornamental style (152–53).[24] Effectively, Remota's 'vuelta a la tierra' marks a more specific reconciliation with the soil and nature of the region, a process which is explored in more detail in the later sections of 'Tercera Parte', such as 'El duende del alba', which I will analyse below. On the whole, the impression that the word *tierra* resists a stable, monovalent definition contributes to the novel's questioning attitude *vis-à-vis* the concept of a nation as a solid and unified social construction, an attitude that primarily finds expression in the abundant references made to the socio-economic contradictions that coexist on Venezuelan soil. In fact, the slipperiness with which Gallegos plays with the word *tierra* goes as far as to cast doubt on the exact meaning that the word has in the novel's title, despite the title's suggestion of precise, identifiable sameness.

Although Gallegos uses the character of Remota to explore a way out of the chaos that has followed the fall of the patriarch, she is nevertheless closely associated with the land of her birth, the Guajira Peninsula. The peninsula is a shifting, unstable terrain, dominated by the *arenal movedizo*. Already the deictics of Remota's inherently spatial name echo the far-off location and the isolation of the Guajira Peninsula, pointedly captured by the *jefe civil* Olavera's description of it as '[una] region, que está realmente al margen de la nación venezolana' (164).[25] Located at the border of northern Colombia and northwestern Venezuela, far from the legislative centres of Venezuela, the people of Guajira continue living according to their tribal traditions and laws, ignored and forgotten by the rest of the nation. Moreover, as Olavera also explains, Colombia continues slowly absorbing Venezuelan Guajira through the flow of immigrants who cross the border attracted by the prospect of 'un nivel de vida más apetecible' (165), a process that reflects the way in which the *arenal movedizo* in turn gradually erases the village of Alitasía from the map by swallowing all vestiges of human occupation.[26] Yet while Guajira is for the rest of the Venezuelan nation nothing but '[u]na faja de tierra improductiva [con] unos pocos millares de indios desnutridos, semi-bárbaros' (165), Remota feels drawn to this arid and desolate land, even after spending all of her adult life, and part of her adolescence, in the prosperous and civilized United States. As she points out in a conversation with Marco Aurelio, no matter how settled she was in New York, the most significant, and indeed defining factor in her life is that she 'naci[ó] y creci[ó] en Alitasía, suelo de arenal movedizo' (146). Again on a later occasion, Remota justifies her return to Venezuela to her lawyer, Rogelio Viñas, by alluding to the incident of encountering a beetle on the roof of the Empire State Building, which made her realize how far away from her natural habitat she was herself. After the incident Remota feels that her homeland beckons her back. She claims that, in front of her very eyes, 'como en las pantallas cinematográficas, los rascacielos de New York se fundieron y se convirtieron en pencas de cardinal guajireño' (109). In fact, Remota's return to Guajira is not only described as a return to her origins, but as I noted briefly when discussing the multiple meanings of the word *tierra*, it also involves a spiritual reconciliation with the region's terrain and nature. This reconciliation is especially well recorded in the section 'El duende del alba', which focuses on Remota's impressions and actions on the first morning she spends in Guajira, after her eighteen-year-long absence. To begin with, when Remota wakes up, she becomes immediately engulfed by what the narrator refers to as 'uno de los sentimientos fundamentales de su raza: la compenetración con la naturaleza' (178). She then further fuses symbolically with the earth when pouring water over her naked body in the open air, 'al discreto oscurito del amanecer, *sobre la misma tierra*', before heading off to collect the scarce fruits of this barren earth — the 'datos maduros', which grow in 'el cardonal' (178–79, emphasis added). Yet considering the fact that Remota's plans of social reform are to a large extent concentrated around bringing water to Guajira, her close identification with the arid land seems somewhat contradictory. And the same can be said about the novel's underlying irony, which resides in the fact that Remota renounces her own reproductive destiny while crusading to make the barren lands of Guajira fertile. In the hope of casting some light on these confusing contradictions, I will now move on to analyse the implications of the barrenness of the land of the Guajira Peninsula and consider exactly how this barrenness relates to Remota's infertility. By so doing, I wish to illustrate how this essentially telluric barrenness initially underscores, but ultimately questions, the outcomes of the novel's renunciation of heterosexual romance.

In his discussion of the character of Remota, Juan Liscano has argued that she can be identified with 'la Madre Tierra en su aspecto benéfico, así como doña Bárbara encarnaba el aspecto destructivo de la Naturaleza'.[27] Although, as I explained earlier, Remota is indeed like a mother to her people and also closely associated with the land of her birth, unlike Liscano I do not regard Remota as the incarnation of the benevolent and fertile aspects of 'la Madre Tierra'. On the contrary, in addition to Remota's affinity with the barren land, I perceive an even more specific connection between the hostile *arenal movedizo* and her sexual repression. The image of the quicksand as an externalization of frustrated female sexuality has in fact been widely exploited in literature in works as varied as Wilkie Collins's *The Moonstone* (1868) and Nella Larsen's *Quicksand* (1928). In Collins's novel, the maidservant Rosanna drowns herself in the local quicksand because of her unrequited love for her master, from whom she is segregated due to the strict social hierarchies of nineteenth-century British society. Larsen's *Quicksand*, on the other hand, introduces us to a mixed-race heroine, Helga Crane, who is so terrified by the racist stereotype of the primitively sexual black woman that for a long time this fear prevents her from fulfilling her sexuality; in the end, however, her sexuality manages to take over her entire life. In *Sobre la misma tierra* the focal analogy between repressed female sexuality and the *arenal movedizo* is laid out in 'Era una tarde fea', where Remota and Marco Aurelio's discussion of Alitasía's *arenal movedizo* flows into Remota's declarations about how she has decided to renounce all heterosexual relationships (146–47). Apart from externalizing Remota's repressed sexuality, the *arenal movedizo* also captures the erotic frustration of her aunts, Dorila and Palmira, who spend their entire lives on this treacherous piece of land, 'sin que viniese hombre a tomarl[as] por mujer' (34). Whereas female sexual desire is consistently sublimated in *Sobre la misma tierra* into a yearning for motherhood, the *arenal movedizo* in turn gives a more specific expression to the dangers of a female body, which has not found fulfilment in maternity. Indeed, the physical dangers inherent in sexual repression and infertility are imprinted clearly on the shrivelled bodies of Remota's aunts, with their 'mejillas fláccidas' and 'mano[s] sarmentosa[s]' (167), bodies which seem to reflect back the arid landscape of sand and thistle. What is more, the *arenal movedizo* and repressed female sexuality are represented as two equally threatening and deceptive forces. Both are constantly quivering beneath a superficial calm that only conceals their overwhelming, untameable dangers. To cite one example, constructing Dorila and Palmira's new house on a hillock provides nothing but an ephemeral escape from the suffocating embrace of the *arenal movedizo*, which, as even Remota acknowledges, will in the end take over all of the land (188). Similarly, as seen with reference to Remota's often flirtatious behaviour in the company of men whom she nevertheless rejects as suitors, while female sexuality is a force that can be reined in, it can never be completely quashed. Thus, Remota's rejection of each of her suitors only promises a momentary victory over her sexual instincts, as the quicksand of her desires resurfaces with every new admirer, each of whom furnishes yet another potential temptation. In short, the metaphor of the *arenal movedizo* seems to suggest that for a woman, escaping the sexual and reproductive destiny imposed by nature can be far more dangerous than succumbing to this fate within the frameworks imposed by civilized society, where sexual desire finds an outlet in marriage and maternity. The potential tragedy awaiting single women is pointedly summarized by the character of Marco Aurelio, who to Remota's annoyance considers unmarried women, whether 'beata[s] rezandera[s] o intelectual[es] animadora[s] de centros de cultura feminina', as outright 'catástrofes biológicas' (148). While Marco Aurelio's sexist ideas should not be seen as direct reflections of those of Gallegos — who in the late 1940s openly supported 'centros de cultura feminina' — these ideas, alongside the metaphor of the *arenal movedizo*, nonetheless transmit Gallegos's underlying doubts about the viability of the alternative socio-political agenda, personified by his female social reformer.[28]

V

Yet to a significant extent, Remota's wayward, often unwomanly behaviour, as well as her barrenness, are not faults of her own but consequences of sins and crimes committed by others long before her adulthood. In order to understand the nature of these sins and how they determine the course of Remota's life, it is necessary to consider the inherent continuity between Demetrio's and

Remota's narrative trajectories in some detail. Although *Sobre la misma tierra* initially opens as the story of the scandalous squanderer Demetrio Montiel, as the novel proceeds, Remota becomes the main protagonist of the story. The existence of two characters, both of whom Gallegos by turns seems to present as main characters, has confused critics significantly, turning this particular problem into the pet topic of the otherwise scarce criticism on the novel. Pedro Díaz Seijas has voiced the general confusion felt at the time of the publication of *Sobre la misma tierra*, noting how contemporary critics

> opinaron que esta octava novela de Gallegos presentaba el caso extraño de dos protagonistas en un mismo sentido, sólo que la acción de uno, Demetrio Montiel quedaba interrumpida a la mitad del relato, por su desaparición física, continuando en sustitución suya, su hija Remota Montiel.[29]

Along the same lines, other critics including Orlando Araujo and Antonio Scocozza have schematically identified Demetrio as the main protagonist of 'Primera Parte' and Remota as that of 'Tercera Parte'.[30] These critics have further argued that the impersonal oil industry plays the central role in the 'Segunda Parte', a reading that sloppily overlooks the narrative attention devoted to Remota's relationships with Hardman and Ramiro Celis in this part of the novel. Out of all the critics who have written about *Sobre la misma tierra*, Liscano undoubtedly comes closest to understanding the true essence of the continuity between Demetrio's and Remota's trajectories, when he concludes that: 'En Remota Montiel, la misión social por cumplir viene siendo como el rescate de sí misma, en la superación de los complejos causados por el padre irresponsable y violento. Es Venezuela superando la violencia de su origen'.[31] If Remota's mission is indeed to overcome the destruction and pain caused by her father, the main function of the 'Primera Parte', which records the early stages of Demetrio's life, and even the function of the beginning of the 'Segunda Parte' with its focus on his involvement in the oil industry, appears to be mainly introductory. Accordingly, the sections which explore Demetrio's mischief and crimes gain their full significance only when studied in relation to Remota's story. In other words, these sections narrate the story of Demetrio's betrayal of the Venezuelan land and people, with the purpose of laying out the necessary preconditions for Remota's project of social improvement.[32] Besides, as the quoted passage further suggests, through her efforts of social reform Remota comes to represent Venezuela overcoming its violent origins, an observation which effectively groups Demetrio with the nation's original founding fathers, whose brutal conquest of the land is a generally acknowledged fact. However, in the light of the social issues addressed by *Sobre la misma tierra*, including the ones relating to the oil industry, and the historical context in which Gallegos wrote his novel, the character of Demetrio is likely to stand also for a far more recent patriarchal figure. His sometimes ruthless exploitation of the ignorant masses and willingness to sell the Venezuelan nation to North American oil exploiters evidently recall the actions of dictator Gómez, whose destructive heritage still casts its shadow on the post-*gomecista* Venezuela of the early 1940s. Taking all this into account, the innovative but carefully moderated character of Remota can easily be seen as the personification of the newly liberated Venezuelan nation, a nation suffering the birth pangs of democracy, while still burdened by the sins of the father(s), and yet confidently glancing ahead towards a better future. Consequently, Remota's independent behaviour, which borders on the unwomanly, as well as her renunciation of heterosexual love and motherhood, can be regarded as sacrifices that need to be made in order to find a way out of the destruction left behind by the unruly patriarchs. Even when it means momentarily undermining traditional family values, which Gallegos considers sacred, the main duty of Remota — and by extension that of the post-*gomecista* Venezuela — is to return something worthwhile to the people and land, which have been repeatedly raped and prostituted by the very father(s) who should have protected them.

The section 'Montiel Montiel de los Montieles', with which *Sobre la misma tierra* opens, already establishes the fact that Demetrio does not respect social convention or his own talents. In this section, the then still adolescent Demetrio shakes off his respectable family's titles –'[unos] tantos Montieles' (9) — by mixing with the 'plebe y hampa' (9), and turns disdainfully away from poetry as soon as he realizes that he has a natural inclination for it. The section thus sets the pattern for Demetrio's entire life: each time his business enterprises begin to prosper, he immediately abandons them. At one point he even intentionally throws away in one game of cards the fortune he has acquired by smuggling silk (50). In addition to this wastefulness, Demetrio's life is also characterized by a general lack of direction, which is cleverly epitomized by his favourite pastime of 'tirar faros', the activity of sailing aimlessly at night along rivers full of oxbows (52). Although, as Ángel Damboriena has noted, 'la vida de Demetrio Montiel [es] en todo momento una broma pesada', Demetrio is nonetheless loved and admired by the very people who fall prey to his mischief and crimes.[33] In fact, Venancio Navas, the helmsman of Demetrio's boat *La Arrepentida*, captures the more likeable side of Demetrio's personality well when he explains how his foreman always '[d]aba lo que lleva[ba] en los bolsillos cuando se encontraba con algún necesitado [...] porque a la hora de ser bueno, lo era hasta decir no más' (213). As Venancio's statement implies, Demetrio is not inherently evil but completely driven by his instincts and impulses. The character of Demetrio therefore presents what Damboriena accurately describes as 'una variedad peculiar de la barbarie'; that is to say, Demetrio carries out his reprehensible deeds 'con una absoluta irresponsabilidad [...] [sin] busca[r] absolutamente nada en la vida, fuera de satisfacer el impulso vital que a cada momento está pidiendo vía franca'.³⁴ It is left for the other characters of *Sobre la misma tierra* to make Demetrio aware of the life and potential he has wasted, in the section entitled '¡Si tú hubieras querido!', in which the unanimous voice of the Zulian masses berates him: 'Al Zulia le está haciendo falta un caudillo y tú lo habrías sido si lo hubieras querido' (90). However, squandering his leadership potential in impractical demonstrations of *hombría* instead of using it to benefit the masses, is just one of the many ways in which Demetrio betrays Zulia and its people. To cite another example, after getting bored with smuggling goods, Demetrio takes advantage of the extreme poverty of the Indians, who willingly exchange their family members 'a cambio de un barril de ron, una carga de panela, un saco de maíz [o] unas varas de cotonía' (50). He thereby starts a slave trade, selling Indians to the region's *haciendas*. Yet Demetrio's most deceitful betrayal of his (mother)land consists of selling large portions of land to foreign (mainly North American) oil exploiters, an act that makes him a collaborator in the North American neo-colonialist enterprise. During the early days of oil exploitation, Demetrio even tricks his friend and *compadre*, Roseliano Figueras, into selling his most fertile lands on the fictitious grounds that Roseliano has no rights over the 'subsuelo' underneath his plantations (80–83). In other words, Demetrio manipulates Roseliano into believing that the 'subsuelo' can be claimed by an oil company at any given moment. Later, the formerly prosperous Roseliano is reintroduced into the narrative as 'una de las víctimas del petróleo', living in poverty in '[una] casita humilde', without running water (124), a description which effectively gives a human face to this particular story of betrayal. As shown by the example of Roseliano Figueras, Demetrio just as readily betrays the people closest to him as he does the anonymous masses, a fact which attains potentially monstrous proportions in the case of his own flesh and blood.³⁵ Indeed, Demetrio's betrayal of family members, including his own children, echoes again the way in which on the national scale patriarchal figures have throughout Venezuelan history betrayed the very people who have relied on their fatherly protection and guidance.

To the same extent that Demetrio rejects social conventions, he also disrespects family ties, as becomes clear from the way in which as a youth he seduces María, his brother's fiancée, and leaves her pregnant with Marco Aurelio. Not only does Demetrio never acknowledge Marco Aurelio as his son, but he also pushes him onto the path of drunkenness and destruction by making fun of him on the day of his graduation, when he approaches his father 'para darle cuenta del buen uso que estaba haciendo de la vida' (144). Yet Demetrio's most serious violation of family conventions finds expression in the incestuous passion plot, which runs through the novel from the section 'La temeraria travesía' onwards. Too terrible to be articulated, the narrator almost never openly addresses the feverish desire felt by Demetrio for Remota, on the night he helped her to escape from her arranged marriage to Chuachuaima across the Lago de Maracaibo. But restricting direct references to incest to the mouths of insolent sailors who wonder, '¿[s]erá verdad que el caballo salvaje no se arrejunta con las hijas?'(65), and to rumour-mongers like Lastenia Cortasano who claims that Demetrio committed suicide because of his love for Remota (115), does not make the theme of incest any less unsettling. In fact, the night of Demetrio's incestuous intentions is repeatedly identified as a turning point in Remota's life. Suggestively, the section 'La temeraria travesía', which focuses on the events of this critical night, also records Remota's passage from the Guajira of her childhood to the 'mundo nuevo y raro' of urbanized Maracaibo (68) — an obvious moment of transition. There are, moreover, recurrent references in the novel to the fact that had Demetrio's incestuous impulse been acted on, it would have made Remota's life take a totally different course. Remota herself acknowledges this, as can be perceived from the urgency with which she thanks Venancio Navas in 'Conversaciones a fondo' for having intervened in her favour on the night when Demetrio was ready to defile the most basic law of morality. Similarly, Remota reiterates her gratitude to Venancio in 'Destellos de faro', the novel's concluding section, by declaring that '[s]i no hubiera sido por usted [...] nada de esto habría podido ocurrir' (234), a statement that certainly does not allude exclusively to Venancio's involvement in transporting the liberated Guajiro slaves towards an uncertain future. Indeed, the depth of Remota's gratitude is likely to have its roots in the fact that Venancio stopped the incestuous act from spoiling her as an adolescent, thus allowing her to grow into the strong, civilized, and morally righteous woman who has now begun her fight for social justice. In other words, Venancio's intervention enables Remota to escape the fate of Gallegos's most famous heroine, the once innocent Barbarita, who turns into a ruthless 'devoradora de hombres' after being raped by her own father and his crew on another *piragua* carrying contraband.[36] The alternative destiny that would have awaited Remota had she been raped by Demetrio is explored in *Sobre la misma tierra* with the help of the character of Marita, Remota's decadent double who, like Remota, has been loved and courted by Jararayú in her early womanhood. Raped by Demetrio while still but a girl in *blanqueo*, Marita marries Jararayú only in order to be cast out of his house almost immediately upon his realization that she is not a virgin. With her honour in ruins, Marita resorts to prostitution as a means to maintain herself and her family, thereafter living off 'lo que [le] dan los hombres en Maracaibo' (171). However, Marita's desolate fate is in no way extraordinary, as she explains to Remota: '[a] muchas les había pasado lo mismo. Demetrio Montiel siempre lograba meterse sin que lo vieran en las casas donde había majayuras en blanqueo' (189). In point of fact, this urge to rape specifically girls who are in *blanqueo* suggests a lingering incestuous undercurrent in Demetrio's sexual exploits. After all, Demetrio's incestuous desire for Remota was born at a time when Remota was herself a young woman who had just come out of *blanqueo*. It is as if raping young girls in *blanqueo* allows Demetrio to consummate his desire for Remota by proxy, with each of these multiple and repeated acts of sexual violence further accentuating the destructiveness of the desire, which acts as the original impetus for these acts. Moreover, even though Remota is not corrupted as an adolescent by a treacherous father (as Doña Bárbara was), there is still an underlying implication in *Sobre la misma tierra* that Demetrio's disturbing passion has had some sort of detrimental effect on the life of Remota. Considering the way in which the Bible presents barrenness as the punishment for the act of incest, it is plausible to assume that there exists an unspoken link between Demetrio's incestuous passion, Remota's fate as an infertile woman, and the barrenness of land of the Guajira Peninsula.[37]

VI

Yet Demetrio's violation of taboos relating to the family is just one of the many ways in which the notion of a traditional, protective family unit is dismantled in *Sobre la misma tierra*. To begin with, Remota never has what could be considered a stable family environment. On realizing that she is pregnant, Cantaralia moves in with her sisters, thus making sure that her child will 'formar[se] desde el principio dentro de la atmósfera de la familia materna, donde reside el espíritu del pueblo guajiro' (23). And, upon Cantaralia's untimely death, the responsibility of Remota's upbringing passes on to 'las tías taciturnas' (28), with the result that she reaches adolescence without a father-figure. Moreover, after fleeing to Maracaibo to avoid her arranged marriage with Chuachuaima, Remota is adopted by Demetrio's sister Selmira, and her German husband, Alejandro Weimar, who lives in a make-believe world where he is 'Alejandro el Grande' (72). Out of their yearning for a child of their own, Alejandro and Selmira impose on Remota the fictional, Germanized identity of Ludmila Weimar, '[una] Walkiria que nació en Maracaibo de quince años de edad' (104). It is only after the death of her adoptive parents that the world of make-believe in which Remota has been immersed begins to crumble, and she becomes driven by an acute urge to discover her true origins. Finally, all vestiges of illusion are swept away by Remota's encounter with her half-brother Marco Aurelio in the section 'Era una tarde fea', an encounter which forces her to face the brutal reality that she is but yet another of Demetrio's many bastards.[38] As these examples suggest, the family unit, as described in *Sobre la misma tierra*, is a constantly fluctuating entity which resists any generalizing definitions. Obviously, on the one hand, the collapse of the patriarchal family creates the necessary preconditions for Remota's autonomy; it is not likely that Remota could have grown into a female social reformer, under the restrictive gaze of a conventional father-figure. Yet this representation of the family unit — which in Gallegos's novels generally functions as a microcosm of the wider nation-family — as an unstable, unreliable, and fictional entity further reflects Gallegos's increasingly sceptical attitude towards the concept of a homogeneous Venezuelan nation. On the whole, Gallegos indicates effectively through his critique of the family unit that imposing any single, all-embracing social model on a country characterized by its striking contradictions, its rich variety of landscapes, cultures, ethnicities, and mindsets, is not a realistic option. Perfect national unity, be it on the level of social institutions or of projects for socio-political reform, can be nothing but a fiction. As we have already seen with reference to the novel's rejection of heterosexual romance, in *Sobre la misma tierra* Gallegos no longer seems convinced that the socio-political contradictions of Venezuela should simply be assimilated through homogenizing marriages. I will now move on to illustrate that one of the central dilemmas of *Sobre la misma tierra* is how to build a better future for the Venezuelan nation as a whole, without neutralizing the nation's social, ethnic, and regional differences.

As Gallegos notes in his 1941 campaign speech, 'Constancia puesta en empeño de iluminación'(218–37), regionalist feelings are not inconsistent with a wider-scale nationalism, '[p]orque no es cierto que al sentimiento total de la patria se puede llegar sin apoyo en el amor entrañable a la porción de ella donde uno nació y se formó' (219–20). The advantages of focused regional projects over highly ambitious national ones are articulated pointedly in *Sobre la misma tierra* by Olavera, the *jefe civil* of the village of Paraguaipoa, who functions as Gallegos's mouthpiece on the topic. On Remota's return to Guajira, Olavera brings her up to date with the region's misery, through a highly politicized discourse on how the lives of the Guajiro Indians continue to be regulated by the laws of the Venezuelan state, even though they receive none of the benefits on offer to other citizens of this state. Olavera thus attacks all-embracing, national legislations that do not take into account regional differences and even goes as far as to ask Remota if she does not agree that 'debiera existir una legislación especial para esta region, que está realmente al margen de la nación venezolana' (164). Yet Olavera does not suggest that the problems of Guajira should be solved by separating the region further from the rest of Venezuela. He believes, rather, that the region's socio-ethnic specificity should be acknowledged and respected within the general framework of the Venezuelan nation. As he also notes, solving the problems of Guajira would not be beneficial for the region alone, because although according to the general opinion, 'Guajira no vale la pena dentro del gran problema nacional, urgido de soluciones inmediatas de punta a punta del país', in reality Guajira is 'una de las puntas' (165). In short, Olavera's discourse highlights the fact that national improvement must always begin on an essentially regional level, with due attention to the needs of each individual region. His discourse accordingly presents us with the theoretical grounding necessary for justifying the viability of the relatively limited project of socio-economic improvement on which Remota is about to embark.

Remota's mixed-race background, which has been further muddled by her North American education and the years she lived in the make-believe world of the Weimars, should make her in principle a person who is acutely aware of the need to accommodate contrasting elements constructively. At first glance, she thus appears to be the type of social reformer who could potentially focus on specific social, cultural, or ethnic problems, without losing touch with how these problems relate to a larger framework — in this case, to the Venezuelan nation as a whole. Yet a more careful analysis of the character of Remota reveals that she is not at ease with the diverse ethno-cultural elements that constitute her own identity, a circumstance that constantly interferes with and delays her endeavours for social reform. In general, Remota's quest for improving the living conditions of the Guajiros overlaps, and intermingles, with her more personal quest to discover her genuine self.

On the most obvious level, Remota's divided identity finds a pronounced expression in the fact that she has two names. Even the narrator refers to her alternately as 'Remota Montiel' and 'Ludmila Weimar'. After being called 'Remota' for the entire 'Primera Parte', the novel's heroine returns, following her eighteen-year absence from Venezuela, at the beginning of the second chapter of 'Segunda Parte' as Ludmila Weimar, only to revert eventually to Remota. Already by the end of the section 'El violento contraste' in Chapter 4 of 'Segunda Parte', a section which explores the fate of the victims of the oil industry, Remota asks Hardman to call her Remota Montiel instead of Ludmila Weimar (131). The narrative voice follows Remota's lead in the subsequent section, 'Conversaciones a fondo', referring to the novel's heroine again as 'Remota', after having at first avoided mentioning her name for four pages (135). The final section of Chapter 4 of 'Segunda Parte', suggestively entitled 'Pensamientos de travesía', in turn stages a deliberate oscillation between 'Ludmila Weimar' and 'Remota Montiel', with the intention of granting primacy to the latter.[39] However, as Remota observes towards the end of this particular section, becoming Remota Montiel is not so very simple, because 'no era cosa de cambiarse solamente el nombre, sino de encararse totalmente con su realidad' (141).

In effect, the names 'Remota Montiel' and 'Ludmila Weimar' embody the two contradictory experiences that have shaped Remota's identity: her childhood in the isolated and backward Guajira region and her modern, international education in New York, a city which is referred to as 'el centro del mundo' (75). This division within Remota accordingly replicates the novel's generally stark juxtaposition of the world-view of the Guajiros and the mindset associated with capitalist modernity — a phenomenon which has been imported to Venezuela by the North American oil exploitation companies. A closer look at each of these contradictory realities facilitates a deeper understanding of the constant struggle that takes place within Remota, as she tries to accommodate her modern world-view and progressive plans with the backward, yet fascinating traditions of her native land.

The alternative, inherently magical, reality of the Guajiros is explored specifically in the numerous Guajira episodes of 'Primera Parte'. Sections such as 'El "Lloro" ', 'El blanqueo', and 'La profecía de Airapúa' give us ethnographical, sometimes even unnecessarily detailed, descriptions of the traditions, customs, rites, and superstitions of the Guajiros. Yet what is particularly striking about these Guajira episodes is the way in which myths, legends, and the supernatural constantly intermingle with everyday events. The account that Chuachuaima gives to Palmira and Dorila about recent events in the wider Guajira provides a vivid example of the blending of myth with reality:

> En Uitchanajai ya habían caído dos aguaceros y sus ganados estaban contentos; que por Castilletes se estaba hablando otra vez de las apariciones de la majayura rebelde, cuya fantasma habían visto varias personas bajar del monte y arrojarse al mar, en noches de luna; que al pasar por Kijot divisó los palos de la piragua fondeada cerca de la costa, seguramente la de *Diablo Contento* que estaría comprando indios por allí, que en los abrevaderos del caño de Poró-rimha vió mucho ganado gordo y muchas bestias. Y que, por cierto, al pasar por allí tropezó con un *guayú* viejo [...] que él se detuvo a saludarlo, pero no pudo entender lo que le respondió, pues parecía hablar un dialecto antiguo y más que persona viviente era como un indio de piedra, arrugado y renegrido y luego le dijeron que era un *jayaliyú* — casta de perro — de los tiempos de antes, del cual se había perdido la memoria, pues nadie lo reconocía y había comenzado a aparecerse por allí en esos mismos días. (40–41)

As this account illustrates, even an influential Guajiro like Chuachuaima, who expresses his superiority by using an 'indumentaria mixta de aborigen y criollo civilizado' (40), regards ghosts as such a natural part of everyday life that they can be discussed in the same key as the weather, fat cattle, or the *piragua* in which Demetrio conducts his slave trade. In addition to subverting the conventional borderlines between reality and the supernatural, the passage also skilfully compresses the past, the present, and the future into a single temporal sphere. While Chuiachuaima's intention is to focus on the present by narrating the current events of Guajira, the past constantly intrudes into his reportage through the references to 'la majayura rebelde' and the '*guayú* viejo [...] de los tiempos de antes' — both of whom are messengers from the past. What further complicates the temporal framework of Chuiachuaima's narration is that these messengers from the past anticipate future events that will take place in the remaining sections of 'Primera Parte'. Most noticeably, the allusion to the ghost of 'la majayura rebelde', which has been seen throwing itself into the sea 'en noches de luna', foreshadows Remota's own rebellious escape from her arranged marriage to Chuiachuaima on a night of 'luna llena' (42). At the same time, the mysterious old Indian who resembles 'un indio de piedra' and belongs to the 'casta del perro' prefigures the popular legend which holds that on the night of the wedding, the slave, Airapúa, metamorphosized into a dog and ran with Remota to the Ulípichi mountains, where the two then turned into stone statues.[40] In fact, the Guajiros happily explain away incomprehensible and unusual events, like that of a young girl disobeying the will of her elders, with reference to the supernatural. As we find out in 'Tercera Parte', the story of Remota turning into a stone has entered so deeply the collective imagination of the Guajiros that on her return to Guajira, the word quickly spreads that '¡La majayura de piedra ha bajado de Ulípichi!'(160). This fostering of legends, so common amongst the Guajiros, is further encouraged by the fact that active, historical time seems to have only limited access to Guajira and its environs. In 'Un espectáculo antiguo', the final section of 'Segunda Parte', the narrator refers to the rural areas that Remota passes through on her way to Guajira as constituting an 'olvidado rincón del mundo para el cual no [ha] corrido el tiempo' (156). Indeed, on her arrival in Guajira, Remota realizes that apart from an increase in poverty and misery, Guajira remains much like it was at the time of her childhood. To quote an example, Dorila and Palmira hold on to the age-old Guajiro etiquette and receive Remota with the same impersonal greeting, 'Anshi-Piá', with which they welcomed Chuachuaima almost twenty years before (40, 167). As Remota soon discovers, other Guajiro traditions also remain in place. Young girls, for instance, continue to be subjected to the tortures of the *blanqueo*, just as they were during her adolescence. Most strikingly, however, the Guajiros continue digging rustic wells and carrying water jars on their heads, as they have done for centuries, while in Maracaibo highly mechanized pumps extract petroleum from the subsoil (162–63). In short, the natives of Guajira, as well as the inhabitants of the neighbouring rural regions, seem to live in some kind of suspended present, utterly oblivious to historical change.

Apart from the last three sections of 'Segunda Parte', which follow Remota's journey towards Guajira, the reality of 'Segunda Parte' is a crude reality that strikes a discordant note with the magical mindset of the Guajira episodes. The action of 'Segunda Parte' takes place mainly in industrial and urban settings. Seventeen out of the twenty sections depict incidents which occur either in the newly built oil exploitation towns or in Maracaibo. In contrast to the unhurried atemporality of rural Guajira, the urban and industrial areas of Zulia seem to be saturated with historical time. Indicatively, already in the 'Primera Parte' the only substantial historical markers appear in the Maracaibo episodes of

Chapter 5, the final chapter of this part of the novel. As an example, in the section 'El cariñoso disparate', the narrator notes that '[l]as vacas gordas se paseaban por el mundo entero, pocos años después de la guerra que puso término a aquello de *Deutschland über alles*' (74) — an observation that allows us to deduce that the episodes occur in the aftermath of the First World War. Unlike most of the other sections of 'Primera Parte', these sections of Chapter 5 require some historical specificity because their key function is to provide an overview of what Maracaibo was like before it was invaded by North American oil companies. Meanwhile, almost all of the events of 'Segunda Parte', with their focus on socio-economic change and its human cost, take place within a carefully constructed temporal framework. The 'Segunda Parte' opens with the section 'El estupendo hallazgo', which depicts energetically the enthusiasm that followed the initial discovery of a major oil field in Zulia. This fictionalized rendition of the discovery of the well of *Barroso 2* on the outskirts of the town of Cabimas — an incident that turned Venezuela into a major oil producer — accordingly situates the action of Chapter 1 of 'Segunda Parte' in 1922.[41] In order to mimic the frenzy of the petroleum extraction enterprise and that of the Venezuelan people, who all want their share of the wealth promised by the oil industry, the narrative rhythm accelerates throughout Chapter 1. The gradually diminishing length of the sections, as well as the extensive use of exclamation marks, which do not only appear in the text but also in the titles of the sections ('¡Misericordia, petróleo!' and '¡Si tú hubieras querido!'), help to convey the marked swiftness of rhythm. Furthermore, this acceleration of narrative rhythm allows Gallegos to 'fast forward' the narrative up to the events of Chapter 2 of 'Segunda Parte', which occur approximately eighteen years later, during the Second World War, which provides the main historical marker of 'Segunda Parte'. The relevance that the geographically distant Second World War has for Venezuela is summarized pointedly in the section 'El violento contraste' by the statement, 'la guerra desatada sobre el mundo necesitaba el espíritu del aceite magnífico y tremendo' (130).[42] As this statement implies, the demand for oil by the Allied Forces put further pressure on the Venezuelan petroleum extraction enterprise, a circumstance that additionally turned Venezuela into an accomplice in the war effort of the Allies. The dominant reality of 'Segunda Parte' is thus the matter-of-fact reality of capitalist production. The individuals who form part of the machinery of the oil industry — be they common 'obreros', 'perforadores', or 'altos empleados de las compañías [petroleras]' (130) — are repeatedly required to be at a certain place at a certain time in order to ensure the continuation of what the narrator identifies from the very start as 'el trabajo [que] no puede interrumpirse en ninguno de los campos de la tremenda faena' (85). Henceforth, in the petroleum extraction fields the sirens can be heard frequently calling the workers to their shifts, while the days of the 'altos empleados' are divided into 'trabajo sedentario ante el escritorio' and moments of leisure in 'los verdes prados para el juego de *golf* y las canchas de tenis' (130). As both the centrality of historical markers and the meticulous breaking up of the working day indicate, the reality of capitalist modernity reproduced in 'Segunda Parte' is a reality characterized by an obsessive division and recording of time.

Remota, who has been protected from the crude reality of capitalist modernity in the make-believe world of the Weimars, cannot be associated with the negative aspects of capitalism, such as corruption and the exploitation of the individual. However, she has to some extent absorbed the mindset of a typically Western modernity, as can be seen from the way in which she contemplates its North American by-products. For instance, Remota is initially enthusiastic about the possibilities offered by the oil industry. The narrator relates that while gazing at the oil fields from Hardman's car, Remota 'se abandonaba [...] al influjo optimista de aquel poderoso esfuerzo industrial que estaba desarrollándose sobre una tierra cuyo porvenir próspero tenía que interesarle' (124). Moreover, when travelling through the newly colonized town of Cabimas, she is not as much surprised by the sight of '[los] cartelones de propaganda en inglés de productos de la industria norteamericana' (128) as by the apparent eccentricity of the town's name. In fact, she fails to relate the name to 'un árbol [venezolano] que abundaba mucho en [la] región', and at first assumes that 'Cabima' is 'una palabra importada también de Estados Unidos' (128). As illustrated in the section 'El escarabajo del rascacielo', Remota's conspicuously Westernized mindset dictates even the way in which her longing for her native Guajira finds an expression in New York. Following a conversation in which Alejandro Weimar tries to convince her unsuccessfully that she is '[un] ario puro' despite her 'cabellos guajiros', Remota has a strange dream in which people become progressively younger as they advance towards her along New York's Fifth Avenue (105–06). On her return to Maracaibo, when Remota explains to her lawyer Rogelio Viñas that she regarded the dream as an omen urging her to reconnect with her true origins, Viñas concludes that '[Remota se ha] aficionado demasiado a esa seudociencia de interpretación de sueños que ahora anda de boga' (107).[43] As Viñas's statement implies, Remota tries to justify her need to reconnect with her Guajiro origins by resorting to the psychoanalytical theories of Sigmund Freud, which are closely linked with the very concept and order of capitalist modernity.[44] Even more strikingly, it is later in this specific section that Remota explains how one day when she contemplated the city of New York from the rooftop of the Empire State Building, 'los rascacielos de New York se fundieron y se convirtieron en pencas de cardinal guajireño', just like 'en las pantallas cinematográficas' (109). Undoubtedly, there is some intentional irony in the fact that she first travels in her mind to Guajira with the help of the theories of Freud, and later visualizes her homeland beckoning her back with the aid of an artistic device which is completely alien to the inhabitants of the backward Guajira Peninsula.

Although, as I noted earlier, Remota considers herself, when standing on the Empire State Building, to be just as out of place as 'el escarabajo', '[u]n animalito del monte [...] sobre la hechura más admirable de la ciudad por excelencia' (109), on her return to Venezuela she soon discovers that neither does she feel completely at home with the Guajiros. Remota is already set apart from the semi-barbarous Guajiros in the section 'Escombros de una raza', which records her search for Dorila and Palmira in 'Tierra Negra, sabana de los aledaños de Maracaibo' (100), a squalid area which exists literally at the periphery of capitalist modernity. In this section, Remota has a lengthy conversation with a young Guajiro woman whom she questions about the fate of her aunts. As soon as the Guajiro woman's husband interrupts their conversation with 'una lenguarada en guajiro', Remota makes 'un gesto de apresar recuerdos' (102), before admitting that she is unable to understand what the husband is saying. It thus becomes clear that Remota has forgotten her native tongue almost entirely. What is more, neither the narrator nor the young Guajiro woman, who expects a handout in return for her help, seem to recognize Remota as a member of her tribe, a point which is lucidly captured in the following, short passage:

> — Dios te pague, simpática — díjole la india, cogiendo las monedas y disponiéndose ya a retirarse.
> Pero en esto vió que por el camino que conducía a la ciudad venían algunas mujeres de su raza y le dijo a Ludmila:
> — Ahí vienen indias viejas que pueden decirte lo que tú quieres saber. (102)

After having at first referred to the young Guajiro woman deprecatingly as 'la india', the narrator goes on to explain that though the original intention of this woman was to withdraw after receiving the money, she changes her mind on seeing the approaching group of 'mujeres de *su* raza' (emphasis added). The designation 'su raza' sets Remota conspicuously apart from the Guajiros, as it emphasizes the fact that the women in question should be grouped with 'la india' rather than with her. Any doubts concerning the referent of the pronoun 'su' are further dispelled in the following sentence by the way in which the young Guajiro herself identifies the women as 'indias viejas'. Finally, the difference between Remota and the ordinary Guajiros is underlined by the section's closing image of Remota returning to '[el] automóvil que más allá la esperaba', while the unresponsive old Indians stare at her with a mixture of indifference and bewilderment (104). Yet even after this emphatic image, the novel provides repeated reminders of the fact that Remota cannot be categorized in the same socio-cultural group as the Guajiros. For instance, we are told in the section 'La vuelta a la tierra' that although Remota constantly claims that the Guajiros are her people, the sight of the half-naked Guajiros stirs her 'delicadezas de mujer civilizada' (153). In short, despite her fixation with her Guajiro origins, Remota does not really belong to either of the two worlds juxtaposed in *Sobre la misma tierra*: she is as much of an outsider in backward Guajira as in the modern capitalist society epitomized by New York.

Even though the narrator identifies Remota closely with her native land, she nevertheless has to (re)familiarize herself systematically with this land, its people, and its customs on her return to Venezuela. Rather curiously, the duty of (re)introducing Remota to her native country falls initially to Hardman, a North American whose occupation as a driller connects him directly to the neo-colonial enterprise. Effectively, Hardman not only introduces Remota to the oil industry that has emerged in Zulia during her absence, but also to various defining aspects of the Zulian land and culture, which pre-date the oil industry. As seen with reference to Remota's confusion over the origins of the name of the town 'Cabimas', which she fails to link to the Venezuelan tree that bears the name, Hardman ends up giving Remota lessons on Zulian flora while further teaching her a regional vocabulary that she has forgotten. Similarly, when narrating the regional legend according to which a fortune-teller foresaw the discovery of petroleum in Zulia, Hardman has to remind Remota that *Cabeza de Plato Fino* is the appellative used by the indigenous people of Zulia to refer to 'el Padre Eterno' (134). Meanwhile, the early stages of Remota's return to Guajira are overseen by the paternal Rogelio Viñas, an educated *criollo* who gives Remota lessons on the potential as well as the deficiencies of the lands along the river Limón. He not only points out to Remota the '[r]estos de plantaciones fracasadas' (153), but further draws her attention to the '[t]ierras recién conquistadas al pantano' (155). By showing Remota these fertile lands, Viñas wishes to highlight the fact that '[s]eguramente podría hacerse lo mismo con el Gran Eneal, en beneficio de la Guajira' (155), referring to the area called Gran Eneal that Remota has inherited from her father. Viñas ultimately interprets to Remota both the customs and the actions of the indigenous people whom they encounter on their journey along the river. He gives the perplexed Remota an overview of the age-old principles of the subsistence economy of the Paraujano Indians, for instance, and also explains to her that the Guajiros 'entregados a una incesante actividad, sacudiendo paños y pañuelos' are simply '[e]spantándose los jejenes' (153).

Despite the vehemence with which Remota embraces her Guajiro roots and rejects her fictional identity as Ludmila Weimar, a constant battle between these two contradictory sides of her identity continues, even during the most crucial moments of her immersion into the Guajiro culture. In the section 'El duende del alba', which records Remota's 'compenetración con la naturaleza' as she washes herself in the open air, the novel's heroine still has to push aside the memory of Ludmila Weimar, a sophisticated woman who is 'acostumbrada [a] bañarse [...] en una bonita aunque pequeña sala de baño, con alto zócalo de baldosas de porcelana rosada' (178). And as late as the section 'Noche de contradicciones', which recounts Remota's journey upstream to Adrián Gadea's *hacienda* to reclaim the money he owes her deceased father, the sudden re-emergence of the prejudices of the Westernized Ludmila Weimar almost jeopardizes her firmness of purpose. Consequently, during her first night on *La Arrepentida* Remota rises twice from her bunk, determined to give orders to return immediately to Maracaibo and to renounce the risky journey on board a boat tainted with 'estigmas de delitos' and full of 'hombres desconocidos' (207). After reasoning that 'la ocurrencia del regreso bien podía ser de Ludmila Weimar todavía' (207), however, Remota successfully manages to banish her doubts and uncertainties and continues her journey with renewed confidence. Yet even though Remota is able to keep Ludmila Weimar in check in sections such as 'El duende del alba' and 'Noche de contradicciones', she still continues to view the life of the Guajiro Indians with the eyes of an outsider, as is shown pointedly in the section 'La ira en el amanecer'. In this section Remota becomes spellbound by the sight of a group of women and cattle gathered around a dried-up well:

> A Remota le pareció interesante el cuadro que se le ofrecía a la tierna contraluz de la mañana: las mujeres inmóviles, mantas, pañuelos y cántaros en un primer plano de la armoniosa composición estática; el ganado mugiente, los cuernos echados hacia los morrillos, los hocicos alzados; las copas de los caimitos atravesadas por rayos de sol. (182)

The perfect stasis of this composition, the careful positioning of each individual element within it, and the emphasis placed on lighting, bring to mind the type of tableaux painted in the nineteenth century to capture the regional and racial stereotypes of Latin America.[45] Meanwhile, the use of the word 'cuadro', the attention paid to the different components of the indigenous attire, as well as the fascination with the livestock gathered around the well, consciously remind us of the *cuadros de costumbres* that Gallegos exploits extensively in his earlier novels, such as *Doña Bárbara*.[46] Overall, the passage's close affinity with both the nineteenth-century tableaux and the *cuadros de costumbres* help us to identify Remota as a foreigner marvelling in and romanticizing a sight that for the Guajiros would have been extremely ordinary.

VII

On her return to Guajira, Remota makes significant efforts to adapt physically to her new environment. In 'El duende del alba' she displays signs of going altogether native as she dresses in the Guajiro attire that Marita has given her as a gift, while the section 'La voluntariosa' sees her skilfully mixing Guajiro and Western-style items of clothing, as she wears 'un pañuelo guajiro, a cuadros blancos sobre fondo negro' with '[un] impermeable' (210). Yet in the end, Remota's makeover from a modern Westernized woman into a Guajiro does not seem altogether successful if we consider the way in which in 'Sombras dolientes' she has to tell Adrián Gadea's slaves that '[s]oy guajira como ustedes', in order gain their trust (227). In other words, Remota's ethnicity is not a self-evident, visible fact but something she needs specifically to point out.[47] Nevertheless, as Remota acknowledges from early on, her indisputable difference from the Guajiros, whom she wishes to help and represent, does not necessarily have to stand in the way of her projects of socio-economic improvement. At the end of the section 'Un espectáculo antiguo', Remota pointedly justifies to Rogelio Viñas her decision to stay in Guajira by explaining that '[n]ecesito vivir donde yo no sea una mujer entre muchas; donde todo se espere de mí' (157). On the whole, Remota's status as an outsider in Guajira allows her to enjoy a degree of respect, as well as freedom, which would be unattainable in an ordinary, Western-type society, where she would be just like any other modern, educated woman. Not only is Remota admired for being a civilized woman, but she gains pseudo-mythical proportions in the eyes of the Guajiros, who by turns regard her as 'la majayura de piedra' (160), 'la Gran Madre' (176), and as 'el duende del alba' (181). What is more, this mythicization is by no means inconsistent with Remota's plans for modernizing Guajira, but actually aids these plans, as the Guajiros instinctively adopt her as the leader who will provide solutions to the region's numerous problems. Indeed, throughout the 'Tercera Parte' there is an evident implication that Remota is a messianic saviour-figure, who has returned to redeem the wasteland of Guajira and its inhabitants. For instance, already when passing through the neighbouring village of Paraguiapoa on her way to Alitasía, the villagers gather in the square in order to see 'pasar a aquel personaje casi legendario que era Remota Montiel' (164). Meanwhile, the village's *jefe civil*, Olavera, acknowledges effectively the connection between Remota's legendary status and her potential as a social reformer, when he states '[y]a esperaba yo que se pudiera poner confianza en el corazón de la Majayura de Piedra', as he thanks her for agreeing to support his socio-economic projects (166). Furthermore, on her arrival in Alitasía, Remota is met by yet another crowd of Guajiros, amongst whom she distributes 'buena parte de la abundante provisión de maíz y panela' originally intended for her aunts alone (170). After receiving their provisions, these Guajiros return to their huts, convinced that a saviour has finally arrived, happily spreading on their way home 'la noticia estupenda de la vuelta del tiempo bueno con el regreso de la majayura encantada' (170).

Besides distributing food to the starving Guajiros, Remota lights the torch of enlightenment and civilization in Guajira, which is depicted throughout the novel as a backward region where barbarism still reigns. Most notably, in the section 'La Gran Madre', Remota interrupts the witch doctor's exorcism of Amaqui by breaking away from the 'sombras taciturnas', a group of Guajiro women, who quietly listen to the witch doctor's moans, and by illuminating Amaqui's secluded room with a 'linterna eléctrica' (174–75). Intially, we are told that Remota 'se dirigió hacia la puerta [de Amaqui], ya con su linterna eléctrica encendida' (175), a statement which already reveals her purpose clearly enough. Yet even so, over the next few paragraphs additional, essentially redundant, details about Remota's handling of the torch are provided. Following the initial disturbance that her action causes amongst the superstitious Guajiros, Remota 'metía dentro de la habitación el haz de luz de su linterna' (175), and slightly later on, she gives the other women orders to remove the witch doctor from the room while directing the light of 'su linterna' on the repulsive old woman (175). In fact, the meticulous attention paid to Remota's handling of the torch emphasizes the symbolic importance of this act of banishing the shadows of barbarism with electric light, since the 'linterna eléctrica' is an obvious token of modern technology. The notion of Remota as a messenger of civilization, who brings hope to the Guajiros living in the shadows of barbarism, is further developed in Chapter 7, the final chapter of 'Tercera Parte'. Not only does Remota liberate from slavery a large number of Guajiros, suggestively referred to as 'sombras dolientes' (225), she also successfully sets free a group of 'hombres jóvenes' from 'la oscuridad del calabozo' (229), a torture chamber where these men are punished for having tried to escape Adrián Gadea's *hacienda*. The implication of these episodes of Chapter 7 is clearly that Remota rescues the Guajiro slaves both figuratively and literally from the shadows of barbaric despotism.

At first glance, all the positive symbolism that surrounds the character of Remota seems to suggest that despite the problems arising from her divided identity, her plans of social reform are bound to succeed. In addition to the positive symbolism, there are also some other significant factors in *Sobre la misma tierra* that help to create this particular impression. The fall of the figure of the *cacique*, dramatized by the arrest and ridiculing of Adrián Gadea at the end of 'El rescate', the novel's penultimate section in which the previously influential man is handled by the police officers 'como un delincuente vulgar' (233), contributes to such an impression. Essentially, Adrián Gadea's fall works as yet another reminder of the collapse of the old social hierarchies, and thus conveniently clears the ground for the innovative social order embodied by Remota. Moreover, even though Remota realistically notes at the beginning of 'La Gran Madre' that the socio-economic project that she is contemplating is 'superior a sus posibilidades inmediatas' (172), there are repeated allusions in the novel to the fact that progressive development can take place over generations.

Apart from Remota's decision to devote her life to redeeming the sins of her father, a comparison of the different types of *jefes civiles* that appear in the 'Primera' and 'Tercera Parte' reveals a similar development. As illustrated in the section 'Tirando faros', in the 'Primera Parte' the *jefes civiles* turn a blind eye to Demetrio Montiel's trading of Indian slaves and even jokingly ask him, '¿Cuánto marca su termómetro indiero, capitán?', when he passes through their ports of jurisdiction on *La Arrepentida* (51). Meanwhile, the *jefes civiles* of 'Tercera Parte' could not be more different from these predecessors. Olavera, the *jefe civil* of the village of Paraguaipoa, is so devoted to the well-being of his subjects, the majority of whom are Guajiros, that he finances the village's rudimentary hospital with 'la mayor parte de [su] sueldo' (165), while Antonio Marcial, the *jefe civil* of Santa Bárbara, is even praised by Ramón Contreras, the local patriot, in whose eyes all the earlier *jefes civiles* have been '[u]nos barbarotes' (216). Indeed, the novel reveals, Ramón Contreras is right in his judgement: on hearing about Remota's plan to bring an end to Adrián Gadea's tyranny over the lands surrounding Santa Bárbara, Antonio Marcial not only declares his full support, but keeps his promise by sending his men to arrest Gadea in the section 'El rescate', following Remota's call for reinforcements.

Yet despite all these optimistic signs, Remota's plans for social reform are seriously undermined by more practical concerns. As her lawyer Rogelio Viñas points out repeatedly, Remota's rights of ownership over El Gran Eneal, which her father bequeathed to her, are extremely dubious (108, 199). Considering the fact that turning the swampy lands of El Gran Eneal into pastures for the Guajiros' cattle is a key item on Remota's socio-economic agenda, her plans of social reform seem to rest on highly unstable foundations. Furthermore, as illustrated in the sections 'La vuelta a la tierra' and 'Un espectáculo antiguo', although swamps can be successfully converted into 'alegres praderas donde pac[e] ganado numeroso' (155), this is most often not the case. As Remota learns when contemplating the '[r]estos de plantaciones fracasadas' (153) and 'niños de aspecto enfermizo' (155), the swamp and the river are constantly waiting for the moment when they can fully reclaim the often unhealthy lands that humans believe they have conquered. Finally, Remota does not have the necessary financial means to carry out her projects of social reform in Guajira. Again the duty of divulging to Remota her lack of resources falls on Rogelio Viñas. He specifically emphasizes the fact that Demetrio's patrimony, 'que en un principio se supuso cuantiosa', turned out to be 'casi una miseria' (108). This circumstance by itself does not, however, demoralize Remota, who decides to finance her enterprises of socio-economic improvement with the money that various *hacendados* owe her, after having bought Guajiro slaves from Demetrio on credit. As Remota sees it, even though the money she will be dealing with is unquestionably 'dinero maldito' (207), this is 'uno de los casos en que el fin justifica los medios' (200). Consequently, in the section 'La mujer vendida' she manages to get hold of a cheque for 'doce mil bolívares', a cheque which Adrián Gadea signs not so much in order to pay his debts as in the hope of buying Remota's sexual favours (224–25). With the necessary money in her hands, however, Remota impulsively tears the cheque into pieces at the end of the section 'El rescate', following Adrián Gadea's crude reminder that 'doce mil bolívares' were 'el precio que le pagué por su cuerp[o]' (233). Ulrich Leo observes that this spontaneous action comes as a surprise, because Remota is usually depicted as 'tan sobria y dueña de sí misma'.[48] As Leo further explains, Gallegos also makes irrational narrative choices, which cut off Remota from the money she requires for the projects of social reform, at two earlier points in the novel:

> Dos veces en el curso del libro, se ha presentado la ocasión para Remota de heredar una fortuna, base para realizar sus planes de reforma. Su padre Demetrio Montiel, contrabandista, mercader de guajiros, usurero con el suelo patrio, habría podido morirse rico, sin restar en el mínimo grado eficacia poética o consecuencia psicológica a su muerte por suicidio [...] ya que tal suicidio no tiene nada que ver con cuestiones de dinero, sino que es expresión exclusiva del agotamiento moral de un hombre desilusionado de sí mismo [...] La otra posibilidad muy natural de facilitar a Remota los medios indispensables para su 'temeraria empresa', habría sido la de hacer fallecer acomodado en vez de pobre a su padre adoptivo [...] Alejandro Weimar [a quien] habíamos conocido como comerciante bien situado en Maracaibo.[49]

Leo considers these unjustifiable narrative choices, as well as the general lack of an explanation as to how Remota will finance her socio-economic projects, as mere sloppiness on Gallegos's part. Yet in my opinion, Gallegos's choice of compromising the potential success of Remota's plans for social reform, by putting practical and financial obstacles in her path, is but another sign of his wavering attitude towards the innovative socio-political agenda which he is projecting in *Sobre la misma tierra*. Essentially, Gallegos's attitude towards the possible success of Remota's plans recalls his standpoint with regard to the very image of the female social reformer, an image which, as we have seen, he constantly softens by linking social reform to mothering. In other words, throughout the novel, every radical step taken to depict a female social reformer who might genuinely succeed in her projects of socio-economic improvement is countered by the narrator's thinly masked scepticism.

The systematic interplay between ideological optimism and practical scepticism is nowhere as pronounced as in the novel's short, final section, 'Destellos de Faro'. The section's title encouragingly echoes the movement from darkness to light, from barbarism to civilization, which has already been recorded in the sections 'La Gran Madre' and 'Sombras dolientes'. Yet the narrator bluntly acknowledges the impractical nature of Remota's actions in the first paragraph of the concluding section by noting that transporting the liberated slaves back to Guajira means '[m]ás bocas para el hambre que reinaba en la Guajira, en vez de algún dinero para aplacarla' (233). Then almost immediately, the narrator notes that although the Guajiro slaves are 'desnutridos [y] macilentos', when they direct their gazes towards Remota there is nevertheless 'en sus rostros un despertar de humanidad recuperada, una emoción de gratitud y de esperanza' (233–34). The Guajiros accordingly seem convinced by the leadership potential of Remota, despite the fact that she has just committed a major tactical error by taking on the responsibility of a group of Guajiros whom she does not have the means to maintain. The hope inherent in the gazes of the Guajiros is in turn undermined in the next paragraph by the way in which Venancio Navas governs *La Arrepentida* by 'tirando faros por entre las vueltas riesgosas' (234). While this reference to 'tirar faros' could be interpreted as a mere sign of Navas's ability to steer Remota's *piragua* through dangerous waters, the expression gains wider implications when considered in the light of the fact that 'tirar faros' was identified as Demetrio Montiel's favourite pastime in 'Primera Parte'. To be more precise, in the 'Primera Parte' the activity of 'tirar faros' was used as a metaphor for the way in which Demetrio's life utterly lacked a clear direction. Taking all this into account, in the context of the novel's final section the reference to 'tirar faros' casts some doubt on the course that Remota's plans for social reform have taken, if the reference does not in fact already mean that her projects have lost their direction altogether. Regardless of these numerous signs of doubt, however, the section — and by extension the novel — ends with an optimistic image of Remota taking her place at the prow, where she is greeted by the constant flash of the lightning of the Faro de Catatumbo.[50] Indeed, as Gallegos reveals in a campaign speech he delivered in Maracaibo in 1941, for him 'el relámpago de Catatumbo' does not symbolize a 'tormenta amenazante, sino constancia puesta en empeño de iluminación' ('Constancia puesta en empeño de iluminación', 219). The concluding image of Remota sailing with her Guajiros towards the 'eternal' lightning thus suggests that while she might not yet have achieved her socio-economic aims, her perseverance and determination will pay off in the long run. As Díaz Seijas puts it, *Sobre la misma tierra* has essentially 'un final de película', because '[c]uando termina, parece comenzar la nueva vida de Remota Montiel'.[51] However, by projecting Remota's 'nueva vida' outside the boundaries of the novel, Gallegos avoids to some extent a conclusive evaluation of the strengths and shortcomings of the innovative and very specific socio-economic enterprise that he has been promoting throughout *Sobre la misma tierra*. Accordingly, as in *Canaima* and *Pobre negro*, so also in *Sobre la misma tierra* it is ultimately left for the reader to determine exactly what kind of future the protagonist is sailing towards.

Considering the fact that *Sobre la misma tierra* is Gallegos's last Venezuelan novel, we know that this is not a future that subsequent novels explore. Yet I do not think that the lack of definite closure makes *Sobre la misma tierra* an altogether disappointing novel. After all, *Sobre la misma tierra* provides a critical overview of the new order arising from the disorder generated by the collapse of *gomecismo*, whereas earlier novels such as *Pobre negro* merely speculated on the opportunities offered by a less hierarchical society. Written while the new order was actually in the process of finding its feet, *Sobre la misma tierra* portrays Venezuela's complicated relationship with progress through the prism of the socio-political uncertainties *and* possibilities that characterized the era. Using the *mestiza* Remota as a vehicle for change, the novel puts forward a regional and ethnic project which cannot solve Venezuela's problems at a blink of an eye but which is nonetheless likely to benefit the nation in the long run — the type of project that, as we have seen, Gallegos was also at the time promoting in his political speeches. Although Gallegos acknowledges that some traditional aspects of Venezuelan everyday life will be necessarily effaced by socio-economic change, he emphasizes throughout *Sobre la misma tierra* the need to exchange the imported models of development, which have been introduced to Venezuela by foreign oil exploitation companies, for ones that take into account the specifically Venezuelan socio-historical reality. Even more importantly, as illustrated in Remota's unconsummated love affairs that provide the backdrop for the novel's action, the era of conciliatory romances is now inevitably over. The *mestizo* character of Gallegos's earlier novels has in *Sobre la misma tierra* matured and turned into an active participant in national life. Overall, Gallegos strives to demonstrate in *Sobre la misma tierra* that the new Venezuela, which has emerged in the aftermath of the collapse of *gomecismo*, has finally moved beyond the original act of national consolidation. The Venezuelan nation has entered a new stage of socio-historical growth. Indeed, even though Gallegos might still cling onto the fragmentary remnants of the framework of heterosexual romance, and at points may long for a moderate heroine, there is no doubt that on the whole *Sobre la misma tierra* bears out the author's earlier ideological and formal experimentations. Gallegos thus concludes his fictional search for a solution to Venezuela's social, racial, political, and economic problems with a novel that effectively lays out at least the foundations of a new, more realistic socio-political agenda.

Notes to Chapter 3

1. The numerous references to the Second World War (1939–45) from Chapter 2 of 'Segunda Parte' onward locate over half of the events of *Sobre la misma tierra* in the years 1939–43.
2. Juan Liscano, 'Remota Montiel', in *Rómulo Gallegos y su tiempo*, 2nd edn (Caracas: Monte Ávila, 1980), pp. 197–204 (pp. 197–98). As Liscano notes, *Sobre la misma tierra* 'es

la primera obra que Gallegos concibe y escribe de un todo en una misma época, después de la muerte de Juan Vicente Gómez' (197).
3. The PDN was legalized and its name changed to Acción Democrática in September 1941.
4. Judith Ewell, *Venezuela: A Century of Change* (Stanford: Stanford University Press, 1984), p. 76.
5. Daniel H. Levine, *Conflict and Political Change in Venezuela* (Princeton: Princeton University Press, 1973), p. 18.
6. Ulrich Leo, 'Sobre la misma tierra: apuntes al estilo de la novela-película', in *Rómulo Gallegos: estudio sobre el arte de novelar* (Caracas: Biblioteca Popular Venezolana, 1954), pp. 183–261 (p. 249); Liscano, p. 161; Pedro Díaz Seijas, 'Sus tres últimas novelas venezolanas: Pobre negro, El forastero y Sobre la misma tierra', in *Rómulo Gallegos: multivisión*, ed. by Isaac J. Pardo and Oscar Sambrano Urdaneta (Caracas: Ediciones de la Presidencia de la República, 1986), pp. 227–55 (p. 252); and Antonio Scocozza, 'Rómulo Gallegos, labor literaria y compromiso político', in *Literatura y política en América Latina*, ed. by Rafael di Prisco and Antonio Scocozza (Caracas: La Casa de Bello, 1995), pp. 153–238 (p. 192).
7. Scocozza, p. 192.
8. Rómulo Gallegos, 'Ante su juicio yo concluyo y espero', pp. 200–17; and 'Constancia puesta en empeño de iluminación', pp. 218–37, in *Una posición en la vida*, ed. by Lowell Dunham (Los Teques: Ediciones del Gobierno del Estado Miranda, 1985). Subsequent page references to Gallegos's socio-political writings appear in parentheses in the text.
9. Ewell, p. 64, notes that the oil extraction town of Cabimas had only 1,940 inhabitants in 1920, but by 1936 its population had grown to 21,753.
10. For an excellent discussion of Gómez's betrayal of Venezuela, see Rómulo Betancourt, 'Castro y Gómez: despotismo, asfalto y petróleo', in *Venezuela, política y petróleo*, ed. by Irene de Valera, 6th edn (Caracas: Academía de Ciencias Políticas y Sociales, 2007), pp. 3–72.
11. Because the oil industry plays such an important role in *Sobre la misma tierra* there has been some speculation about whether the novel should be classified as a *novela del petróleo*. After contemplating this possibility, critics such as Liscano, p. 197; Orlando Araujo, 'Sobre la misma tierra: ¿Novela del petróleo?', in *Lengua y creación en la obra de Rómulo Gallegos* (Buenos Aires: Nova, 1955), pp. 147–52 (p. 149), Scocozza, p. 214; and Gustavo Luis Carrera, 'Breve historia del tema del petróleo en la novela venezolana', in *La novela del petróleo en Venezuela* (Caracas: Servicios Venezolanos de Publicidad, 1972), pp. 5–78 (p. 43), all come to the conclusion that *Sobre la misma tierra* is not a *novela del petróleo*. Again Scocozza justifies his point of view more clearly than any of the other critics when he states that

> [*Sobre la misma tierra*] no puede ser definida como la novela del petróleo porque efectivamente el 'preciso hallazgo' no es el personaje, [ni] el objeto principal de la novela. Es, podríamos decir, una nueva ocasión que pone de relieve el inédito drama del pueblo venezolano. (214)

For an exemplary Venezuelan *novela del petróleo*, see Ramón Díaz Sánchez's *Mene* (1936).
12. In this respect, Gallegos's handling of regional problems in *Sobre la misma tierra* differs significantly from the way in which he deals with similar issues in *Canaima*. Whilst Gallegos in *Canaima* portrays Venezuelan Guayana as a region that has been left behind in the race for socio-economic progress, he does not give any firm indication in this earlier novel as to how the solving of the region's problems could benefit the Venezuelan nation as a whole.

13. Lowell Dunham, 'Las últimas novelas', in *Rómulo Gallegos: vida y obra*, trans. by Gonzalo Barrios and Ricardo Montilla (Mexico City: Ediciones de Andrea, 1957), pp. 253–87 (p. 277); and Leo, p. 215.
14. Rómulo Gallegos, *Sobre la misma tierra* (Buenos Aires: Espasa-Calpe, 1944), pp. 187, 141. Subsequent page references appear in parentheses in the text.
15. Whilst Jararayú and Hardman become actual participants in the narrative events upon their reintroduction in 'Tercera Parte', we are reminded of Ramiro Célis and his romantic interest in Remota through a conversation that takes place between Rogelio Viñas and Remota in 'Invitación sentimental'.
16. The 'misteriosa voz' evokes '[las] voces clamantes en el desierto', which in *Canaima* urge Gabriel Ureña to turn his theories of socio-economic improvement into actions. See especially the section 'Las palabras mágicas', in Rómulo Gallegos, *Canaima*, ed. by Charles Minguet, Colección Archivos (Madrid: CSIC, 1991), pp. 43–47.
17. The remaining four sections of Chapter 2 of 'Primera Parte' are 'La profecía de Airapúa', 'La Majayura', 'Chuachuaima', and 'Diálogo sobre el médano'.
18. Chapter 3 of 'Primera Parte' records the mischief and misconduct of Demetrio Montiel.
19. For a detailed discussion of the objectification of the female body, see Simone de Beauvoir, 'The Formative Years', in *The Second Sex*, ed. and trans. by H. M. Parshley (London: Vintage 1997), pp. 295-444. Beauvoir argues that as a girl develops into a woman she becomes increasingly objectified by society:

    The young girl feels that her body is getting away, it is no longer the straightforward expression of her individuality; it becomes foreign to her; and at the same time she becomes for others a thing: on the street men follow her with their eyes and comment on her anatomy. She would like to be invisible; it frightens her to become flesh and to show flesh. (333)

20. Palmira speculates silently in the section 'El blanqueo', '¿Quién sería el padre de Remota? [...] ¿Por qué Cantaralia nunca pronunció su nombre? ¿Lo ignoraría realmente?' (34).
21. In the chapter 'La estrella en la mira', in *Doña Bárbara*, ed. by Domingo Miliani, Letras Hispánicas, 5th edn (Madrid: Cátedra, 2004), pp. 461–64, Doña Bárbara finds herself unable to shoot Marisela — who is talking lovingly to Santos Luzardo — because she is suddenly overcome by 'una emoción maternal, desconocida para su corazón' (464).
22. Gallegos's emphasis on the important role played by women as mothers of future generations of Venezuelans recalls surprisingly the policies of the Asociación Venezolana de Mujeres, a moderate women's organization that in the late 1930s and early 1940s worked to improve the Venezuelan woman's position without subverting existing gender stereotypes. Whereas the AVM members, who generally steered clear of politics, had no direct connection with Gallegos's party, Acción Democrática, many of the members of the far more radical Asociación Cultural Feminina were drawn to its ranks. For instance, Cecilia Núñez Sucre, the key figure behind ACF, was also one of the founders of AD. Although Gallegos's way of presenting Venezuelan women as mothers whilst arguing for women's suffrage does certainly reveal his own uncertainties regarding female emancipation, I believe that this particular approach to what at the time was still a controversial topic could additionally be seen as an intentional campaign technique, employed by Gallegos in order not to alienate the more traditional-minded voters. For an overview of the women's organizations which became active in the immediate post-Gómez period, see above, pp. 000-000. A more substantial account of women's social and political activity in the late 1930s and 1940s can be found in Elisabeth J. Friedman, 'The Paradoxical Rise and Fall of Women's Movement in the First Transition to Democracy (1936-1948)', in *Unfinished Transitions:*

Women and the Gendered Development of Democracy in Venezuela, 1936–1996 (University Park, Pa.: Pennsylvania State University Press, 2000), pp. 53–100.
23. Doris Sommer, 'Love of Country: Populism's Revised Romance in *La vorágine* and *Doña Bárbara*', in *Foundational Fictions: The National Romances of Latin America* (Berkeley: University of California Press, 1991), pp. 257–89 (pp. 257–58). Subsequent page references appear in parentheses in the text.
24. The section 'La vuelta a la tierra' opens with lavish landscape descriptions, which bring to mind the central role played by nature in Gallegos's *novelas de la tierra*, such as *Doña Bárbara* and *Canaima*. However, already in the third paragraph of the section, these descriptions are momentarily interrupted by the pragmatic statement, '[p]ero Remota no atiende al paisaje. A bordo de la barquilla va un grupo de indios guajiros' (152). The statement reminds us of the fact that the real subject matter of *Sobre la misma tierra* is not the 'paisaje' but the social and ethnic problems personified by the group of 'indios guajiros'. This said, Gallegos's narrator nonetheless expresses nostalgia for the authentic traditions and products of the Zulian earth in sections such as 'El escaño de los viejos' and 'El extraño caso'. These nostalgic sections strive to record a regional culture that is about to be wiped away by neo-colonial capitalism, which has been brought to Venezuela by the foreign-owned oil companies.
25. The notion that Remota's name denotes distance is further accentuated by the way in which the name originally appears in a song invented by Cantaralia, where the singer announces '[y]o vengo andando de *lejos* por conocerte, Remota' (22, emphasis added).
26. Ewell, p. 77, points out that Colombia and Venezuela finally agreed on the boundaries of the Guajira Peninsula in 1941. Gallegos mentions this boundary agreement in his speech 'Constancia puesta en empeño de iluminación' (218–37), a campaign speech delivered in Maracaibo in 1941. Whilst arguing for the need for Latin American solidarity at times of international conflicts, Gallegos draws his audience's attention to

> [el] acto realizado [...] en un punto de nuestra frontera con Colombia, donde se le puso término a un litigio enojoso y con abrazo cordial de ambas Repúblicas se simbolizó el estrechamiento de dos pueblos de un mismo origen, una porción común de historia y un mismo destino. (234)

27. Liscano, p. 203.
28. Gallegos's essay 'La pura mujer sobre la tierra' (396–425) was originally delivered as a lecture to a predominantly female audience at the Centro de la Cultura de la Mujer Cubana in 1949 (397).
29. Díaz Seijas, p. 249.
30. Araujo, pp. 147–49; and Scocozza, pp. 214–15. Dunham, p. 273, strikes a discordant note by claiming that Demetrio Montiel is the main protagonist of the entire novel.
31. Liscano, p. 203.
32. The sections 'Montiel Montiel de los Montieles', 'Diablo contento', and 'El estupendo hallazgo' provide some excellent examples of Demetrio's mischief and crimes.
33. Ángel Damboriena, 'La barbarie: los protagonistas', in *Rómulo Gallegos y la problemática venezolana* (Caracas: Universidad Católica Andrés Bello, 1960), pp. 243–87 (p. 272).
34. Ibid., p. 272.
35. When discussing the way in which Demetrio betrayed him, Roseliano Figueras clarifies the exact nature of his relationship with Demetrio by resignedly noting: 'habiendo sido yo siempre buen amigo suyo, además de compadre de sacramento, por un hijito que me bautizó, vino a echarme tierra en los ojos [...] pa que le vendiera un cocal' (126).
36. Although there is no direct description of Doña Bárbara's father raping her as an adolescent, there are various allusions in *Doña Bárbara* to the fact that this is what

happened. An excellent example can be found at the beginning of the chapter entitled 'La devoradora de hombres' (141–54), in which the fifteen-year-old Barbarita's shipmates are introduced in the following way: '[e]ran seis hombres a bordo, y al capitán lo llamaba "taita"; pero todos — excepto el viejo piloto Eustaquio — la brutalizaban con idénticas caricias: rudas manotadas, besos que sabían a aguardiente y a chimó' (141). As the description implies, unlike Eustaquio, her father the 'taita' is not excluded from administering these 'caricias'.

37. Leviticus 18. 24–30 enumerates the curses that will fall upon the land of the people who dare to defile God's command by participating in unlawful sexual practices, whilst Leviticus 20. 10–27 clarifies how individuals who have engaged in these types of practices should be punished. Barrenness is listed as the punishment for a number of incestuous activities, such as the nephew sleeping with his aunt or a brother seducing his sister-in-law.

38. Like Marita, whom I have already identified as Remota's decadent double, the character of Marco Aurelio also helps to remind us what Remota's life could have been like had things gone wrong for her. Unlike Remota, the dishevelled Marco Aurelio has not been able to rise above the obscure circumstances of his conception, and he consequently squanders his intelligence in drunken soliloquies. Yet it has not been Remota's strength of character alone that has made her a survivor; unlike Marco Aurelio who grew up in an orphanage, Remota has had various 'helpers' along her path, including her aunts and later the Weimars. Remota is also privileged in the sense that on his death Demetrio acknowledges her as his child, an 'honour' which Marco Aurelio does not share.

39. When Remota's name is finally mentioned towards the end of 'Conversaciones a fondo', it is repeated insistently over the remaining two pages of the section, thus accentuating the significance of the change that has taken place in the novel's heroine. It is also worth noting that the first mention of Remota's name — after her initial declaration that she is not Ludmila — concurs with the reintroduction of Venancio Navas into the narrative. Not only is Navas a person from Remota's past but also the man who in 'La temeraria travesía' secured her safe passage from the Guajira of her childhood to Maracaibo, where she was then transformed into Ludmila. Significantly, Venancio Navas's reintroduction into the narrative in 'Conversaciones a fondo' anticipates a reverse 'travesía', that is, the transformation of Ludmila back to Remota, a transformation that begins in all seriousness after the section 'Pensamientos de travesía'.

40. The similarities between the old Indian of Chuachuaima's account and Airapúa are not limited to their association with dogs and stones. In point of fact, whereas the Indian whom Chuachuaima encountered is depicted as 'renegrido', Airapúa's skin is described at an earlier occasion as 'muy oscuro, casi negro' (35). Moreover, whilst Chuachuaima is unable to understand what the old Indian tells him because 'parecía hablar un dialecto antiguo', we are told that in Airapúa's 'lengua parecían acusarse extrañas incrustaciones de alguna otra desconocida en toda la península' (35).

41. As Betancourt, p. 60, puts it, 'el 14 de diciembre de 1922, el pozo Barroso no. 2, ubicado en el estado de Zulia [...] revel[ó] al mundo la prodigiosa reserva de petróleo en el subsuelo venezolano'.

42. Ewell, p. 68, points out that during the Second World War, 'the recent advances in military technology and the increased strategic importance of oil rendered the long Venezuelan coastline particularly vulnerable to an attack by one of the great powers'.

43. Gallegos is here evidently referring to *The Interpretation of Dreams* (1899), one of Sigmund Freud's most famous works on psychoanalysis. As Thomas F. Glick notes in the chapter, 'Science and Society in Twentieth-Century Latin America', in *The Cambridge History of Latin America*, ed. by Leslie Bethell, 10 vols (Cambridge:

Cambridge University Press, 1994), VI.1, pp. 463–536 (p. 485), even though interest in psychoanalysis in Latin America dates back to 1915 and to the writings of the Peruvian Honorio Delgado, '"[o]rthodox" psychoanalytical groups [were established as late as] in the 1940s and 1950s'. Edward Shorter, *A History of Psychiatry: From the Era of the Asylum to the Age of Prozac* (New York: Wiley, 1997), p. 171, similarly observes that in North America, 'psychoanalysis began taking over the prestigious chairs and university departments' in the early 1940s. As Shorter clarifies, New York became the centre of the American psychoanalytical movement: it was the home of 'over a third of the analysts of the entire country' (171). It was, however, only after 1945 that psychoanalysis, and more specifically Freudianism, 'permeated American popular culture', as E. Ann Kaplan explains in 'Introduction: From Plato's Cave to Freud's Screen', in *Psychoanalysis and Cinema*, ed. by E. Ann Kaplan (New York: Routledge, 1990), pp. 1–23 (p. 10). Nonetheless, as Kaplan points out in the essay 'Motherhood and Representation: From Postwar Freudian Figurations to Postmodernism', also found in *Psychoanalysis and Cinema*, pp.128–42, it is possible to perceive also in slightly earlier films, such as *Now Voyager* (1942), a 'new Freudian awareness' (129). I am indebted to Peter Evans (Queen Mary, University of London) for bringing Kaplan's collection of essays to my attention.

44. Fredric Jameson, *The Political Unconscious: Narrative as a Socially Symbolic Act* (London: Methuen, 1981), p. 62, suggests that Freud's ideas about the unconscious and the psyche reflect the fragmentary nature of human experience in the alienating, carefully compartmentalized, capitalist society.

45. Joanne Rappaport discusses these type of tableaux at length in her article 'Fictive Foundations: National Romances and Subaltern Ethnicity in Latin America', *History Workshop*, 34 (1992), 119–31. Rappaport explains the background of such depictions as follows:

> In 1850 [...] the Colombian government [...] l[ed] a massive interdisciplinary expedition called the Comisión Corográfica, composed of cartographers, artists, botanists and writers, whose aim was to define the contours of the nascent republic through a detailed description of its boundaries, resources and inhabitants. In the days before photography was widely disseminated in rural areas, [the] expedition employed watercolourists to record the regional and ethnic diversity they came across in the course of their travels. The Comisión Corográfica watercolours [...] display a variety of ethnic groups, shown many times in tableaux portraying a variety of regional, occupational, and racial types. Rich in details depicting clothing, phenotype, and landscape, labelled with captions that define subjects by race or by occupation, the people who populate these watercolours are generally unoccupied in anything other than the business of representing categories of the Colombian citizenry. Mestizos, whites, mulattos and blacks (the few Indians are displayed separately) stare into space, never at one another: they are illustrative types, not characters; they inhabit tableaux, not narratives. (124–26)

46. For some excellent examples of *cuadros de costumbres*, see the chapters 'La doma', 'Los amansadores', and 'El rodeo', in *Doña Bárbara*.

47. It is possible for the reader to work out that Remota is only one-fourth Guajiro. Her mother Cantaralia, with her 'cabellos rojos', is mixed-race, the product of an affair that Remota's grandmother had with a red-haired Italian peddler.

48. Leo, p. 195.

49. Ibid., pp. 194–95.

50. In his *Letters on Natural Magic Addressed to Sir Walter Scott* (London: John Murray, 1832), the nineteenth-century Scottish physicist David Brewster defines the 'Faro de Catatumbo' as '[a] bright light [...] seen every night on a mountainous and inhabited spot of the banks of the river Catatumbo, near its junction with [Z]ulia' (330). He further specifies that this 'eternal' lightning 'is easily distinguished at a greater distance than *forty* leagues, and [...] navigators are guided by it as a lighthouse' (330, emphasis in original).
51. Díaz Seijas, p. 255.

CONCLUSION

The more feasible socio-political agenda offered in *Sobre la misma tierra* underlines the fact that Gallegos's fiction did eventually return something worthwhile to the Venezuelan reality that had functioned as its principal subject matter. However, as I have shown over the course of the three main chapters, Gallegos reached this deeper understanding of the Venezuelan nation's complicated relationship with socio-historical progress gradually. The initial idealism of *Doña Bárbara* first gave way to the pessimism of *Canaima*, and then to the careful ideological experimentation of *Pobre negro*. What is more, the socio-political writings that were produced during the same period as the later Venezuelan novels reveal a similar trajectory of development, although the author's ideas tend to find a relatively more subdued expression in these non-fictional pieces. In fact, it is justifiable to draw the conclusion that literature provided Gallegos with a stage on which to enact those socio-political ideas that he delineated in his non-fiction. On the whole, changes in the political atmosphere of Venezuela played an important part in determining how Gallegos presented questions relating to nationhood and progress in his fictional writings. As I explain in Chapter 1 with specific attention to the way in which a cyclical counterforce thwarts every attempt at reform in *Canaima*, Gallegos's momentarily defeatist attitude towards projects of socio-political progress had much do with the fact that he became disillusioned with the potential future of Venezuela in the early 1930s whilst in self-imposed exile. Written in the period immediately preceding and following the collapse of the Gómez regime, *Pobre negro*, on the other hand, marks a transitional phase in Gallegos's socio-political thought. As I demonstrate in Chapter 2, the author uses the opportunities furnished by the socio-political disorder associated with the end of *gomecismo* to experiment, albeit cautiously, with a variety of innovative paths to socio-political progress. Finally, in *Sobre la misma tierra*, which is written entirely after Gómez's death, Gallegos focuses on the emerging, significantly less hierarchical socio-political order that epitomized the beginning of the new political era. As I illustrate in Chapter 3, Gallegos's critical attitude towards some aspects of modernization and his evident preference for realistic, smaller-scale projects of reform can be attributed to the fact that he was now writing in a society where change was possible. By this stage socio-political progress was no longer an idealistic dream but a contemporary issue.

Moreover, whilst revising his ideas concerning socio-political progress,

Conclusion

Gallegos puts the very concept of the Venezuelan nation under further scrutiny. Whereas in *Doña Bárbara* he still offers an oversimplified vision of Venezuela, *Canaima*, *Pobre negro*, and *Sobre la misma tierra* dwell particularly on the inherently problematic nature of the Venezuelan nation. In contrast to *Doña Bárbara*, in which the *llanos* function as an allegory of the whole nation, *Canaima*, for one, emphasizes the regional specificity of Venezuelan Guayana. Using the region's isolated location as a point of departure, Gallegos expresses openly his doubts whether it is possible to apply any single, standard model of development to the diverse social and geographical sectors that make up the Venezuelan nation. With four main characters, including two *criollo* men, a woman, and a *mestizo*, who stand for the different types of people living within the boundaries of Venezuela, *Pobre negro* explores the fragmentary nature of the nation even more explicitly. The novel's focus on the fates of women and coloured individuals, two groups that have been traditionally marginalized, allows Gallegos to illustrate how the notion of a unified national life is nothing but a fiction. *Sobre la misma tierra* in turn draws a stark contrast between industrialized Maracaibo and the backward Guajira, both of which are located in the State of Zulia. Despite the fact that Gallegos does not pretend that the Guajira region can somehow represent Venezuela as a whole, he insists throughout the novel that region-specific projects can contribute to wider national well-being. Yet in the meantime, the divided identity of the novel's heroine Remota Montiel, who on one level represents the end-product of the process of *mestizaje* that Gallegos has so eagerly promoted in his novels, demonstrates that a perfect marriage between the conflicting socio-political elements that coexist on Venezuelan soil is impossible. Indeed, although Gallegos does not give up on the idea of *mestizaje* as the necessary starting point for national improvement, he seems eventually to arrive at the conclusion that the key to a better future does not lie in simply homogenizing Venezuela's heterogeneous society. All in all, over the course of *Canaima*, *Pobre negro*, and *Sobre la misma tierra* Gallegos comes to recognize increasingly the need to celebrate the racial, cultural, and regional diversity of Venezuela, even whilst accommodating it within the more general framework of the Venezuelan nation.

In fact, in his later Venezuelan novels, Gallegos makes significant attempts to visualize a less hierarchical Venezuelan society. As I have shown at various points in this study, he accomplishes this aim mainly by reshuffling the traditionally patriarchal family structure, which functions in his novels as a microcosm of the wider nation-family. At first glance, in *Canaima* Gallegos seems to remain relatively faithful to the patriarchal order that was re-established at the end of *Doña Bárbara*. He identifies Marcos Vargas, a *criollo*, as a potential social reformer, capable of leading the ordinary people towards a better future. What is more, the female protagonists of *Canaima* are not given equal footing with the novel's male hero: the Indian Aymara appears almost characterless, whilst the stubborn Aracelis is written off as a threat to both existing social conventions and Marcos's plans of reform. Nevertheless, Gallegos articulates his growing dissatisfaction with traditional, patriarchal leader-figures already in *Canaima*, by ultimately rendering Marcos unfit for productive action — a narrative choice that clears the ground for a new set of social reformers. Indeed, it is in *Pobre negro* that Gallegos begins seriously to rearrange his conception of the nation-family by identifying a *mestizo* (Pedro Miguel) and a woman (Luisana) as potential social reformers. The novel's male *criollo* characters, the two Cecilios, are in the meantime depicted as individuals who merely theorize about issues relating to socio-political progress. Yet Gallegos's lack of confidence in his new social reformers finds expression in the way in which he delimits Luisana's and Pedro Miguel's agency for action. Whereas Pedro Miguel is constantly torn between his two racial backgrounds and utterly incapable of conceiving any long-term plans, Luisana's actions are constrained by the stereotype of a respectable woman. Regardless of his indecisive attitude, Gallegos continues to examine the possibility of an alternative nation-family in *Sobre la misma tierra*, wherein he introduces a potential social reformer who is both female and of mixed race. Indeed, in his final Venezuelan novel, which presents traditional patriarchs as traitors of the Venezuelan nation, Gallegos uses the character of the *mestiza* Remota to explore a way out of the chaos that has followed the fall of patriarchy. Although evidently fascinated by the strong will and independent nature of his heroine, Gallegos does not seem altogether comfortable with the notion of a new, less hierarchical social order built around a female social reformer. He constantly tries to soften the character of Remota by drawing a close analogy between her endeavours of social reform and the duties associated with mothering.

Moreover, as I have demonstrated in the main chapters of this book, Gallegos's changing ideas with regard to issues of nationhood and socio-political progress are consistently reiterated by revisions that take place on the structural and temporal levels of his novels. These formal experimentations are nonetheless repeatedly kept in abeyance by the same hesitant logic that undermines Gallegos's attempts to restructure the nation-family. The carefully patched framework of national romance, which in *Doña Bárbara* successfully brings together the different racial and regional elements of Venezuela, begins to crumble in *Canaima*, in which the persuasiveness of Marcos's allegorical union with the Indian Aymara is compromised by the genuine passion he feels for the half-Italian Aracelis. The framework of heterosexual romance continues to lose its organizational power and socio-political significance in *Pobre negro*, where it becomes entangled with, if not at points almost entirely concealed by, the narrative trajectories of the individual characters. And finally, *Sobre la misma tierra*, with its multiple unfulfilled love plots, dismantles the remaining pillars of this traditional narrative paradigm. As I have repeatedly indicated, the gradual disintegration of the framework of romance highlights Gallegos's increasing disillusionment with regard to interracial love, and subsequent *mestizaje*, as standard solutions to Venezuela's great variety of social, racial, political, and regional problems. However, as I further noted in the conclusion to Chapter 3, Gallegos's decisive, final departure from this traditional narrative framework in *Sobre la misma tierra* is likely to have been instigated at least partly by the more concrete socio-political opportunities which materialized after Gómez's death. Yet Gallegos's persistent adherence to the framework of romance, even in these later Venezuelan novels which question the viability of a national solution based around heterosexual love and *mestizaje*, has important wider implications. To begin with, as I have shown in the three main chapters, the framework of heterosexual romance is open to thorough appropriation. In *Canaima*, *Pobre negro*, and *Sobre la misma tierra* Gallegos manipulates the framework of romance in such a way that he skilfully draws our attention to its crevices and limitations. The framework of these later Venezuelan novels literally deconstructs itself, underlining the unsuitability of a romantic resolution. Yet the remnants of the framework of heterosexual romance, with their nineteenth-century undertones, still serve as a reminder of the original act of national consolidation, which laid the very foundations of the Venezuelan nation, thus providing the necessary basis for the more advanced, future projects of socio-political improvement that Gallegos explores in his novels. Apart from the fact that the framework of heterosexual romance continues to fulfil a representative function in the later Venezuelan novels, its persistence can be additionally explained with reference to Gallegos's general inability to detach completely from the mindset associated with the conventional patriarchal society. Indeed, Gallegos's experimentations with alternative narrative paradigms — like his attempts to depict a less hierarchical Venezuelan society and efforts to formulate original socio-political agendas — are to a point hamstrung by the nostalgia he feels for the old-fashioned, often restrictive, values which he is endeavouring to subvert.

By combining thematic readings with structural analyses, I have illustrated in this work how national allegory dictates both the content and form of *Canaima*, *Pobre negro*, and *Sobre la misma tierra*. In so doing I have revealed that, although Gallegos's later Venezuelan novels might still to some extent be restrained by convention, they are nevertheless far more multilayered than has traditionally been acknowledged. Rather than being simple, uncouth socio-political commentaries, as some critics have claimed, these later novels in fact showcase the allegorical potential of narrative paradigms. In order to tease out in detail the correlation that exists between the thematic and more formal aspects of the chosen novels, I have intentionally limited my current study to three novels by Gallegos. My general aim has been to provide a critical review of the thematic and formal developments that take place over the course of *Canaima*, *Pobre negro*, and *Sobre la misma tierra*, these developments having been repeatedly overlooked by critics wishing to offer yet another interpretation of Gallegos's most famous novel, *Doña Bárbara*. However, I believe that a method combining close readings organized around national allegory and structural analysis could shed new light on Gallegos's literary production more generally, including his early novels and those dealing with the fate of Latin American nations other than Venezuela. A study along these lines would no doubt give us an even better understanding of Gallegos's overall trajectory as a writer and socio-political thinker. Moreover, it would fill the gap in existing, predominantly thematic criticism by defining Gallegos's growth as an author in terms of how his way of exploiting narrative form has changed over time. Even so, the present study of *Canaima*, *Pobre negro*, and *Sobre la misma tierra* functions as a pertinent starting point for a wider investigation of this sort. The works considered here are arguably the three novels that record the most significant points of articulation in Gallegos's literary and socio-political career. In these three novels, Gallegos gives in to a previously undeveloped urge for innovation, which, as we have seen, manifests itself through the increasing manipulation of narrative structure, and results in a series of ingenious allegories of the Venezuelan nation.

BIBLIOGRAPHY

I. Primary Source Material by Rómulo Gallegos

Fiction

Here is a listing of fictional works referred to in this book, with their original dates of publication.

GALLEGOS, RÓMULO, *Canaima* [1935], ed. by Charles Minguet, Colección Archivos (Madrid: CSIC, 1991). [This edition is additionally an invaluable research tool as it brings together various key essays on *Canaima*]
—— *Cuentos* [1910-22], *Obras completas*, 2 vols (Madrid: Aguilar, 1958), I, 1089-1353
—— *Doña Bárbara* [1929], ed. by Domingo Miliani, Letras Hispánicas, 5th edn (Madrid: Cátedra, 2004)
—— *El forastero* [1942], in *Obras completas*, 2 vols (Madrid: Aguilar, 1958), II, 645-868
—— *Pobre negro* [1937] (Caracas: Ediciones Populares Venezolanas, 1964)
—— *Reinaldo Solar* [1920], in *Obras completas*, 2 vols (Madrid: Aguilar, 1958), I, pp. 5-229. [The first edition of *Reinaldo Solar* was entitled *El último Solar*]
—— *Sobre la misma tierra* [1943] (Buenos Aires: Espasa-Calpe, 1944)
—— *La trepadora* [1925], in *Obras completas*, 2 vols (Madrid: Aguilar, 1958), I, 233-489

Non-fiction

Socio-political writings addressed in, or consulted in elaboration of, the present study. The following essays, articles, lectures, letters, and speeches are collected in *Una posición en la vida* [1954], ed. by Lowell Dunham (Los Teques: Ediciones del Gobierno del Estado de Miranda, 1985).

GALLEGOS, RÓMULO, 'La alianza hispanoamericana' [1909], pp. 40-44
—— 'Ante su juicio yo concluyo y espero' [1941], pp. 200-17
—— 'Las causas' [1909], pp. 15-22
—— 'Cómo conocí a Doña Bárbara' [1954], pp. 525-33
—— 'Los congresos' [1909], pp. 53-57
—— 'Constancia puesta en empeño de iluminación' [1941], pp. 218-37
—— 'El cuarto poder' [1909], pp. 45-48
—— 'Un ejemplo de todos los días para todos los días' [1941], pp. 162-81
—— 'El factor educación' [1909], pp. 58-81
—— 'Había aquí una lección por dar' [1941], pp. 182-99
—— 'Hombres y principios' [1909], pp. 5-14
—— 'Lección de fe' [1942], pp. 249-55

—— 'El mundo es del justo' [1941], pp. 153–61
—— 'Necesidad de valores culturales' [1912], pp. 82–109
—— 'Nos pusimos de pie, aquí y allá' [1941], pp. 238–48
—— 'Los poderes' [1909], pp. 36–39
—— 'Por los partidos [1909], pp. 31–35
—— 'La pura mujer sobre la tierra' [1949], pp. 396–425
—— 'Una renuncia' [1931], pp. 110–11
—— 'El respeto a la ley' [1909], pp. 27–30
—— 'Revista de instrucción pública' [1909], pp. 23–26
—— 'Soy un hombre que desea el orden' [1937], pp. 145–52
—— 'Las tierras de Dios' [1931], pp. 112–44
—— 'El verdadero triunfo' [1909], pp. 49–52

II. Secondary Sources

Criticism on Gallegos

The following is not intended as an exhaustive bibliography of critical material on Gallegos but is rather a list of works which are relevant to the study of *Canaima*, *Pobre negro*, and *Sobre la misma tierra*. Only those works on *Doña Bárbara* that in my opinion cast helpful light on Gallegos's later Venezuelan novels are cited below.

ALMOINA DE CARRERA, PILAR, '*Canaima*: arquetipos ideológicos y culturales', in *Canaima*, ed. by Charles Minguet, Colección Archivos (Madrid: CSIC, 1991), pp. 325–39

ALONSO, CARLOS J., ' "Otra sería mi historia": Allegorical Exhaustion in *Doña Bárbara*', *Modern Language Notes*, 2 (1989), 418–38

ARAUJO, ORLANDO, *Lengua y creación en la obra de Rómulo Gallegos* (Buenos Aires: Nova, 1955)

CARRERA, GUSTAVO LUIS, '*Canaima* y sus contextos', in *Canaima*, ed. by Charles Minguet, Colección Archivos (Madrid: CSIC, 1991), pp. 317–24

CARRERAS GÓNZALEZ, OLGA, 'Tres fechas, tres novelas y un tema: estudio comparativo de *La vorágine*, *Canaima* y *Los pasos perdidos*', *Explicación de Textos Literarios*, 2 (1974), 169–78

CASTANIEN, DONALD G., 'Introspective Techniques in *Doña Bárbara*', *Hispania*, 41.3 (1958), 282–88

COHEN, HENRY, 'The Question of Race in Rómulo Gallegos's *Pobre negro*', *Hispanófila*, 159 (2007), 41–46

CONSALVI, SIMÓN ALBERTO, *Auge y caída de Rómulo Gallegos* (Caracas: Monte Ávila, 1991)

—— *Rómulo Gallegos: el hombre y su escenario* (Caracas: Prensas Venezolanas de Editorial Arte, 1964)

—— *Rómulo Gallegos*, Biblioteca Biográfica Venezolana (Editora El Nacional: Banco del Caribe, 2006)

DAMBORIENA, ÁNGEL, *Rómulo Gallegos y la problemática venezolana* (Caracas: Universidad Católica Andrés Bello, 1960)

DELPRAT, FRANÇOIS, 'El realismo poético de Rómulo Gallegos: recepción crítica de *Canaima*', in *Canaima*, ed. by Charles Minguet, Colección Archivos (Madrid: CSIC, 1991), pp. 341–56

DESSAU, A., 'Realidad social, dimensión histórica y método artístico en *Doña Bárbara* de Rómulo Gallegos', in *Doña Bárbara ante la crítica*, ed. by Manuel Bermúdez (Caracas: Monte Ávila, 1991), pp. 129–43

DÍAZ SEIJAS, PEDRO, *Relectura de la novelística de Rómulo Gallegos* (Caracas: Ipasme, 1998)

—— *Rómulo Gallegos: realidad y símbolo* (Caracas: Centro del Libro Venezolano, 1965)

—— 'Sus tres últimas novelas venezolanas: *Pobre negro*, *El forastero* y *Sobre la misma tierra*', in *Rómulo Gallegos: multivisión*, ed. by Isaac J. Pardo and Oscar Sambrano Urdaneta (Caracas: Ediciones de la Presidencia de la República, 1986), pp. 227–55

DOUDOROFF, MICHAEL J., 'Introduction', in *Canaima*, ed. by Michael Doudoroff, trans. by Will Kirkland (Pittsburgh: University of Pittsburgh Press, 1996), pp. xi–xviii

DUNHAM, LOWELL, *Rómulo Gallegos: An Oklahoma Encounter and the Writing of the Last Novel* (Norman: University of Oklahoma Press, 1974)

—— *Rómulo Gallegos: vida y obra*, trans. by Gónzalo Barrios and Ricardo Montilla (Mexico City: Ediciones de Andrea, 1957)

FUENTES, CARLOS, 'Rómulo Gallegos: la naturaleza impersonal', in *Valiente mundo nuevo: épica, utopía y mito en la novela hispanoamericana* (Mexico City: Fondo de la Cultura Económica, 1990), pp. 97–121

GÓNZALEZ ECHEVARRÍA, ROBERTO, '*Doña Bárbara* Writes the Plain', in *The Voice of the Masters: Writing and Authority in Modern Latin American Literature* (Austin: University of Texas Press, 1985), pp. 33–63

HOWARD, HARRISON SABIN, *Rómulo Gallegos y la revolución burguesa en Venezuela*, ed. by Martin Sagrera, 2nd edn (Caracas: Monte Ávila, 1984)

ISEA, ANTONIO, 'La caracterización de lo racial-nacional en *Pobre negro* de Rómulo Gallegos', *Afro-Hispanic Review*, 20.2 (2001), 18–22

—— '*Pobre negro*, *Las lanzas coloradas* y *Cumboto*: tropismos del discurso de construcción nacional venezolana en siglo XX', *Revista de literatura hispanoamericana*, 48 (2004), 127–46

JOHNSON, ERNEST A., 'The Meaning of *civilización* and *barbarie* in *Doña Bárbara*', *Hispania*, 39.4 (1956), 246–61

JOZEF, BELLA, 'Lectura de *Doña Bárbara*: una nueva dimensión de lo regional', in *Doña Bárbara ante la crítica*, ed. by Manuel Bermúdez (Caracas: Monte Ávila, 1991), pp. 105–17

LEO, ULRICH, *Rómulo Gallegos: estudio sobre el arte de novelar* (Caracas: Biblioteca Popular Venezolana, 1954)

LISCANO, JUAN, *Rómulo Gallegos y su tiempo*, 2nd edn (Caracas: Monte Ávila, 1980)

—— 'Las tres novelas mayores: *Doña Bárbara*, *Cantaclaro* y *Canaima*', in *Rómulo Gallegos: multivisión*, ed. by Isaac J. Pardo and Oscar Sambrano Urdaneta (Caracas: Ediciones de la Presidencia de la República, 1986), pp. 195–225

LÓPEZ RUEDA, JOSÉ, *Rómulo Gallegos y España* (Caracas: Monte Ávila, 1986)

LLERENA, MARIO, 'Función del paisaje en la novela hispanoamericana', *Hispania*, 32.4 (1949), 499–504
MACHADO DE ACEDO, CLEMY, *La incidencia del positivismo en las ideas políticas de Rómulo Gallegos* (Baruta: Equinoccio, 1982)
MARBAN, HILDA, *Rómulo Gallegos: el hombre y su obra* (Madrid: Playor, 1973)
MARCONE, JORGE, 'Jungle Fever: Primitivism in Environmentalism: Rómulo Gallegos's *Canaima* and the Romance of the Jungle', in *Primitivism and Identity in Latin America: Essays on Art, Literature, and Culture*, ed. by Erik Camayd-Freixas and José Eduardo González (Tucson: The University of Arizona Press, 2000), pp. 157–72
MARINONE, MÓNICA, *Escribir novelas, fundar naciones: Rómulo Gallegos y la experiencia venezolana* (Mérida: Libro de Arena, 1999)
MARTÍNEZ, MARCO ANTONIO, *Temas galleguianas* (Caracas: Ministerio de Educación, 1975)
MASSIANI, FELIPE, *El hombre y la naturaleza venezolana en Rómulo Gallegos* (Caracas: Editorial Elite, 1943)
MEDINA, JOSÉ RAMÓN, *Rómulo Gallegos: ensayo biográfico* (Caracas: Editorial Arte, 1966)
MEGENNEY, WILLIAM W., 'Las influencias afronegroides en *Pobre negro* de Rómulo Gallegos', in *XIX congreso internacional de literatura iberoamericana* (Caracas: Ediciones del Centro de Estudios Latinomericanos Rómulo Gallegos, 1980), pp. 303–14
MICHALSKI, ANDRÉ S., '*Doña Bárbara*: un cuento hadas', *PMLA*, 85.5 (1970), 1015–22
MILIANI, DOMINGO, '*Canaima*, estructura mítica', in *Canaima ante la crítica*, ed. by Lyll Barceló Sifontes-Abreu (Caracas: Monte Ávila, 1995), pp. 69–91
MILLINGTON, MARK I., 'As if by Magic: The Power of Masculine Discourse in *Doña Bárbara*', in *New Hispanisms: Literature, Culture, Theory*, ed. by Mark I. Millington and Paul Julian Smith (Ottawa: Dovehouse, 1994), pp. 150–75
MORALES, ÁNGEL LUIS, 'El sentimiento de la naturaleza en Gallegos', in *Rómulo Gallegos ante la crítica*, ed. by Pedro Díaz Seijas (Caracas: Monte Ávila, 1980), pp. 85–165
MORÓN, GUILLERMO, *Homenaje a Rómulo Gallegos* (Caracas: Academia Nacional de Historia, 1984)
OSORIO, LUIS ENRIQUE, 'Entrevista con Rómulo Gallegos', in *Doña Bárbara ante la crítica*, ed. by Manuel Bermúdez (Caracas: Monte Ávila, 1991), pp. 11–12
OWRE, J. RIIS, 'The Fauna in the Works of Rómulo Gallegos', *Hispania*, 45.1 (1962), 52–56
PACHECO, CARLOS, 'Gallegos, la patria deseada y el parricidio', in *La patria y el parricidio: estudios y ensayos críticos sobre la historia y la escritura en la narrativa venezolana* (Mérida: Ediciones el otro, el mismo, 2001), pp. 77–97
—— 'Pensamiento sociopolítico en la novela galleguiana', in *Rómulo Gallegos: multivisión*, ed. by Isaac J. Pardo and Oscar Sambrano Urdaneta (Caracas: Ediciones de la Presidencia de la República, 1986), pp. 113–34
PENNINGTON, ERIC, 'Beyond Realism and Allegory: Myth and Psyche in *Doña Bárbara*', *Crítica Hispánica*, 9.1-2 (1987), 87–99
—— 'A Biblical Reinforcement in *Doña Bárbara*', *Crítica Hispánica*, 7.2 (1985), 129–32

PÉRUS, FRANÇOISE, 'Universalidad del regionalismo: *Canaima* de Rómulo Gallegos', in *Canaima*, ed. by Charles Minguet, Colección Archivos (Madrid: CSIC, 1991), pp. 417–72

PIPER, ANSON C., 'El yanqui en las novelas de Rómulo Gallegos', *Hispania*, 33.4 (1950), 338–41

PORRAS, MARÍA DEL CARMEN, 'Entre los peligros de la desmesura y las limitaciones de la normalidad: *Canaima* de Rómulo Gallegos', *ALPHA: revista de artes, letras y filosofía*, 18 (2002), 43–62

POTELET, JANINE, '*Canaima*, novela del indio caribe', in *Canaima*, ed. by Charles Minguet, Colección Archivos (Madrid: CSIC, 1991), pp. 377–416

PRIETO, LUIS B., 'Rómulo Gallegos, educador', in *XIX congreso internacional de literatura iberoamericana* (Caracas: Ediciones del Centro de Estudios Latinomericanos Rómulo Gallegos, 1980), pp. 39–46

RAMOS CALLES, RAÚL, *Los personajes de Gallegos a través del psicoanálisis* (Caracas: Monte Ávila, 1984)

RAMOS GUÉDEZ, JOSÉ MARCIAL, '*Pobre negro* y la guerra federal', in *El negro en la novela venezolana* (Caracas: Universidad Central de Venezuela, 1980), pp. 58–65

RODRÍGUEZ, MANUEL ALFREDO, 'La política en Venezuela (1884–1984)', in *Rómulo Gallegos: multivisión*, ed. by Isaac J. Pardo and Oscar Sambrano Urdaneta (Caracas: Ediciones de la Presidencia de la República, 1986), pp. 15–42

RODRÍGUEZ MONEGAL, EMIR, '*Doña Bárbara*: texto y contextos', in *Doña Bárbara ante la crítica*, ed. by Manuel Bermúdez (Caracas: Monte Ávila, 1991), pp. 119–28

RODRÍGUEZ SÁNCHEZ, JUAN GREGORIO, 'El "Pórtico" de *Canaima* como totalidad', in *XIX congreso internacional de literatura iberoamericana* (Caracas: Ediciones del Centro de Estudios Latinoamericanos Rómulo Gallegos, 1980), pp. 249–57

ROJAS GUARDÍA, ARMANDO '*Canaima* o la nostalgia de un héroe', in *Canaima ante la crítica*, ed. by Lyll Barceló Sifontes-Abreu (Caracas: Monte Ávila, 1995), pp. 149–68

ROSS, WALDO, 'Meditación sobre el mundo de Juan Solito', in *Canaima ante la crítica*, ed. by Lyll Barceló Sifontes-Abreu (Caracas: Monte Ávila, 1995), pp. 45–59

RUIZ, GUSTAVO ADOLFO, 'Ideas educativas', in *Rómulo Gallegos: multivisión*, ed. by Isaac J. Pardo and Oscar Sambrano Urdaneta (Caracas: Ediciones de la Presidencia de la República, 1986), pp. 97–112

SANOJA HERNÁNDEZ, JESÚS, 'Escenario y personajes en *Canaima*', in *Canaima ante la crítica*, ed. by Lyll Barceló Sifontes-Abreu (Caracas: Monte Ávila, 1995), pp. 103–11

SCHÄRER NUSSBERGER, MAYA, *Rómulo Gallegos: el mundo inconcluso* (Caracas: Monte Ávila, 1979)

SCOCOZZA, ANTONIO, 'Rómulo Gallegos, labor literaria y compromiso político', in *Literatura y política en América Latina*, ed. by Rafael di Prisco and Antonio Scocozza (Caracas: La Casa de Bello, 1995), pp. 153–238

SELMA VILA, JOSÉ, *Rómulo Gallegos* (Sevilla: Escuela de Estudios Hispano-Americanos de Sevilla, 1954)

SHAW, DONALD, *Doña Bárbara*, Critical Guides to Spanish Texts (London: Grant & Cutler, 1972)

―― 'Rómulo Gallegos', in *Encyclopedia of Latin American Literature*, ed. by Verity Smith (London: Fitzroy Dearborn, 1997), pp. 338–40

SKURSKI, JULIE, 'The Ambiguities of Authenticity in Latin America: *Doña Bárbara* and the Construction of National Identity', *Poetics Today*, 15.4 (1994), 605–42

SUBERO, EFRAÍN, 'Génesis de *Canaima*', in *Canaima*, ed. by Charles Minguet, Colección Archivos (Madrid: CSIC, 1991), pp. 309–16

WYLIE, LESLIE, 'Colonial Tropes and Postcolonial Tricks: Rewriting the Tropics in the "novela de la selva"', *The Modern Language Review*, 101.3 (2006), 728–42

―― *Colonial Tropes and Postcolonial Tricks: Rewriting the Tropics in the 'novela de la selva'* (Liverpool: Liverpool University Press, 2009)

YARRINGTON, DOUG, 'Populist Anxiety: Race and Social Change in the Thought of Rómulo Gallegos', *The Americas*, 56.1 (1999), 65–90

Other Works

The following works provide contextual — historical, political, cultural, and theoretical — information pertinent to the present study.

ACOSTA, CECILIO, 'Caridad', in *Obras*, 5 vols (Caracas: Empresa el Cojo, 1908), IV, 35–64

―― 'Reflexiones sobre la historia', in *Obras*, 5 vols (Caracas: Empresa el Cojo 1908), IV, 25–33

AHMAD, AIJAZ, 'Jameson's Rhetoric of Otherness and the "National Allegory"', *Social Text*, 17 (1987), 3–25

ALONSO, CARLOS J., 'The Burden of Modernity', in *The Places of History: Regionalism Revisited in Latin America*, ed. by Doris Sommer (Durham, NC: Duke University Press, 1999), pp. 94–103

―― *The Spanish American Regional Novel: Modernity and Autochthony* (Cambridge: Cambridge University Press, 1990)

ALVARADO, LISANDRO, *Glosarios del bajo español en Venezuela*, in *Obras completas*, ed. by Santiago Key-Ayala and Oscar Sambrano Urdaneta, 8 vols (Caracas: Ministerio de Educación, 1955), II–III

―― *Historia de la revolución federal en Venezuela*, in *Obras Completas*, ed. by José Moncada Moreno and Oscar Sambrano Urdaneta, 8 vols (Caracas: Ministerio de Educación, 1956), IV

ANDERSON, BENEDICT, *Imagined Communities: Reflections on the Origin and Spread of Nationalism*, rev. edn (London: Verso, 2006)

ARRINGTON, MELVIN S., 'Regionalism: Spanish America', in *The Encyclopedia of Latin American Literature*, ed. by Verity Smith (London: Fitzroy Dearborn, 1997), pp. 704–05

AZNAR, LUIS, 'Las transiciones desde el autoritarismo en Venezuela. El proyecto de Acción Democrática y sus efectos sobre el sistema sociopolítico', *Desarrollo Económico*, 30.117 (1990), 55–83

BAKHTIN, MIKHAIL, 'Forms of Time and of the Chronotope in the Novel', in *The Dialogic Imagination: Four Essays by M. M. Bakhtin*, ed. by Michael Holquist, trans. by Caryl Emerson and Michael Holquist (Austin: University of Texas Press, 1981), pp. 84–258

BEAUVOIR, SIMONE DE, *The Second Sex*, ed. and trans. by H. M. Parshley (London: Vintage 1997)
BENÍTEZ-ROJO, ANTONIO, 'José Joaquín Fernández de Lizardi and the Emergence of the Spanish American Novel as National Project', in *The Places of History: Regionalism Revised in Latin America*, ed. by Doris Sommer (Durham, NC: Duke University Press, 1999), pp. 199-213
BENJAMIN, WALTER, 'Allegory and Trauerspiel', in *The Origin of German Tragic Drama*, trans. by John Osborne (London: NLB, 1977), pp. 159-235
BETANCOURT, RÓMULO, *Venezuela, política y petróleo*, ed. by Irene de Valera, 6th edn (Caracas: Academía de Ciencias Políticas y Sociales, 2007)
BRENNAN, TIMOTHY, 'The National Longing for Form', in *Nation and Narration*, ed. by Homi K. Bhabha (London: Routledge, 1990), pp. 44-70
BREWSTER, DAVID, *Letters on Natural Magic Addressed to Sir Walter Scott* (London: John Murray, 1832)
CABALLERO, FERNÁN, *Un verano en Bornos: novela de costumbres* (Madrid: Mellado, 1858)
CALDERA, RAFAEL TOMÁS, *La respuesta de Gallegos: ensayos sobre nuestra situación cultural* (Caracas: Academia Nacional de Historia, 1980)
—— *Temas de sociología venezolana* (Caracas: Editorial Tiempo Nuevo, 1973)
CARPENTIER, ALEJO, *Los pasos perdidos*, ed. by Roberto González Echevarría (Madrid: Cátedra, 1985)
CARRERA, GUSTAVO LUIS, *La novela del petróleo en Venezuela* (Caracas: Servicios Venezolanas de Publicidad, 1972)
CHERPAK, EVELYN, 'The Participation of Women in the Independence Movement in Gran Colombia, 1780-1830', in *Latin American Women: Historical Perspectives*, ed. by Asunción Lavrin (Westport, Conn.: Greenwood Press, 1978), pp. 119-234
COLLINS, WILKIE, *The Moonstone*, ed. by Anthea Trodd (Oxford: Oxford University Press, 1982)
DAVIES, CATHERINE, 'On Englishmen, Women, Indians and Slaves: Modernity in the Nineteenth-Century Spanish-American Novel', *Bulletin of Spanish Studies*, 82.3-4 (2005), 313-33
'Death of a Dictator', *Time Magazine*, 30 December 1935 <http://www.time.com/time/magazine/article/0.9171,848393-1,00.html> [accessed 2 September 2008]
DÍAZ, ARLENE J., *Female Citizens, Patriarchs, and the Law in Venezuela, 1786-1904* (Lincoln, Nebr.: University of Nebraska Press, 2004)
DÍAZ SÁNCHEZ, RAMÓN, *Mene*, 2nd edn (Caracas: Editorial Elite, 1944)
DORCA, TONI, *Volverás a la región: el cronotopo idílico en la novela española del siglo XIX* (Madrid: Iberoamericana, 2004)
EWELL, JUDITH, *Venezuela: A Century of Change* (Stanford: Stanford University Press, 1984)
FIDDIAN, ROBIN, 'The Spanish "Chronomorph": Developing Structures in the Contemporary Novel', *Iberoromania*, 2 (1975), 137-48
FINEMAN, JOEL, 'The Structure of Allegorical Desire', in *Allegory and Representation*, ed. by Stephen Greenblatt (Baltimore: John Hopkins University Press, 1981), pp. 26-60
FRANCO, JEAN, 'The Nation as Imagined Community', in *Dangerous Liaisons: Gender, Nations, and Postcolonial Perspectives*, ed. by Anne McClintook, Aamir

Mufti, and Ella Shohat (Minneapolis: University of Minnesota Press, 1997), pp. 130–37

FRANK, JOSEPH, *The Widening Gyre* (New Brunswick: Rutgers University Press, 1963)

FRANK, ZEPHYR, 'The International Natural Rubber Market 1870–1930', <www.eh.net/encyclopedia/article/frank.international.rubber.market> [accessed 5 September 2010]

FREUD, SIGMUND, *The Interpretation of Dreams*, ed. and trans. by James Strachey (London: Penguin Books, 1991)

FRIEDMAN, ELISABETH J., *Unfinished Transitions: Women and the Gendered Development of Democracy in Venezuela, 1936–1996* (University Park, Pa.: Pennsylvania State University Press, 2000)

FUENTES, CARLOS, 'Espacio y tiempo del nuevo mundo', in *Valiente mundo nuevo: épica, utopía y mito en la novela hispanoamericana* (Mexico City: Fondo de Cultura Económica, 1994), pp. 50–71

—— *La nueva novela hispanoamericana* (Mexico City: Editorial Joaquín Mortiz, 1969)

GLICK, THOMAS F., 'Science and Society in Twentieth-Century Latin America', in *The Cambridge History of Latin America*, ed. by Leslie Bethell, 10 vols (Cambridge: Cambridge University Press, 1994), VI.1, 463–536

GÓMEZ DE AVELLANEDA, *Sab*, ed. by José Servera (Madrid: Cátedra, 1997)

The Holy Bible, New International Version (London: Hodder and Stoughton, 2000)

ISAAC, JORGE, *María*, ed. by Donald McGrady (Barcelona: Editorial Labor, 1970)

JACKSON, RICHARD L., *The Black Image in Latin American Literature* (Albuquerque: University of New Mexico Press, 1976)

JAMES, HENRY, *Roderick Hudson*, ed. by Geoffrey Moore (Harmondsworth: Penguin, 1986)

JAMESON, FREDRIC, *The Political Unconscious: Narrative as a Socially Symbolic Act* (London: Methuen, 1981)

—— 'Third-World Literature in the Era of Multinational Capitalism', *Social Text*, 15 (1986), 65–88

KAAPUR, GEETA, 'Globalisation and Culture', *Third Text*, 39 (1997), 21–38

KAPLAN, E. ANN, 'Introduction: From Plato's Cave to Freud's Screen', in *Psychoanalysis and Cinema*, ed. by E. Ann Kaplan (London: Routledge, 1990), pp. 1–23

—— 'Motherhood and Representation: From Postwar Freudian Figurations to Postmodernism', in *Psychoanalysis and Cinema*, ed. by E. Ann Kaplan (London: Routledge, 1990), pp. 128–42

KEEN, SUZANNE, *Narrative Form* (Basingstoke: Palgrave Macmillan, 2003)

KERMODE, FRANK, *The Sense of an Ending: Studies in the Theory of Fiction*, rev. edn (Oxford: Oxford University Press, 2000)

KESTNER, JOSEPH A., *The Spatiality of the Novel* (Detroit: Wayne State University Press, 1978)

LARSEN, NELLA, *Quicksand, and Passing*, ed. by Deborah E. McDowell (New Brunswick, NJ: Rutgers University Press, 1986)

LEBEAU, VICKY, *Lost Angels: Psychoanalysis and Film* (London: Routledge, 1995)

LEVINE, DANIEL H., *Conflict and Political Change in Venezuela* (Princeton: Princeton University Press, 1973)
LIEUWEN, EDWIN, *Venezuela*, 2nd edn (Oxford: Oxford University Press, 1965)
LOMBARDI, JOHN. V., *Venezuela: The Search for Order, the Dream of Progress* (Oxford: Oxford University Press, 1982)
LUCRETIUS, TITUS, *De rerum natura* ('De la naturaleza de las cosas'), trans. by Lisandro Alvarado (Caracas: Ávila Gráfica, 1950)
MAN, PAUL DE, 'The Rhetoric of Temporality', in *Blindness and Insight: Essays in the Rhetoric of Contemporary Criticism*, 2nd edn (London: Menthuen, 1983), pp. 187–228
MARIÁTEGUI, JOSÉ CARLOS, *Siete ensayos de la realidad peruana*, 19th edn (Lima: Amauta, 1971)
MÁRMOL, JOSÉ, *Amalia*, 5th edn (Madrid: Espasa-Calpe, 1978)
MENTON, SEYMOUR, 'In Search of a Nation: The Twentieth-Century Spanish American Novel', *Hispania*, 38.4 (1955), 432–42
MORSON, GARY SAUL, and CARYL EMERSON, *Mikhail Bakhtin: Creation of a Prosaics* (Stanford: Stanford University Press, 1990)
NAVARRETE ORTA, LUIS, 'El escritor ante el poder político en América Latina', in *Literatura y política en América Latina*, ed. by Rafael di Prisco and Antonio Scocozza (Caracas: Ediciones La Casa de Bello, 1995), pp. 33–47
PARRA, TERESA DE LA, *Las memorias de Mamá Blanca*, ed. by Velia Bosch (Nanterre: ALLCA XX, 1988)
PÉREZ GALDÓS, BENITO, *Doña Perfecta*, ed. by Rodolfo Cardona (Madrid: Cátedra, 1982)
RAMA, ÁNGEL, *Transculturación narrativa en América Latina* (Mexico City: Siglo Veintiuno Editores, 2004)
RAPPAPORT, JOANNE, 'Fictive Foundations: National Romances and Subaltern Ethnicity in Latin America', *History Workshop*, 34 (1992), 119–31
RENAN, ERNEST, 'What is a Nation?', trans. by Martin Thom, in *Nation and Narration*, ed. by Homi K. Bhabha (London: Routledge, 1990), pp. 8–22
RODRÍGUEZ, MANUEL ALFREDO, 'La política en Venezuela (1884–1984)', in *Rómulo Gallegos: multivisión*, ed. by Isaac J. Pardo and Oscar Sambrano Urdaneta (Caracas: Ediciones de la Presidencia de la República, 1986), pp. 15–41
SALERNO, ROGER A., *Landscapes of Abandonment: Capitalism, Modernity, and Estrangement* (Albany: State University of New York Press, 2003)
SARMIENTO, DOMINGO FAUSTINO, *Facundo, o civilización y barbarie: vida de Juan Facundo Quiroga*, ed. by Raimundo Lazo (Mexico City: Editorial Porrúa, 1966)
SARTRE, JEAN-PAUL, *La nausée* (Paris: Gallimard, 1980)
SHORTER, EDWARD, *A History of Psychiatry: From the Era of the Asylum to the Age of Prozac* (New York: Wiley, 1997)
SOMMER, DORIS, *Foundational Fictions: The National Romances of Latin America* (Berkeley: University of California Press, 1991)
—— 'The Places of History: Regionalism Revisited in Latin America', in *The Places of History: Regionalism Revisited in Latin America*, ed. by Doris Sommer (Durham, NC: Duke University Press, 1999), pp. 1–10
SPINKER, MICHAEL, 'The National Question: Said, Ahmad, Jameson', *Public Culture*, 6 (1993), 3–29

SPITTA, SILVIA, *Between Two Waters: Narratives of Transculturation in Latin America* (Houston TX: Rice University Press, 1995)
SULLIVAN, WILLIAM, 'Situación económica y política durante el periodo de Juan Vicente Gómez, 1908-1935', in *Política y economía en Venezuela 1810-1976*, ed. by Alfredo Boulton (Caracas: Edición de la Fundación John Boulton, 1976), pp. 247-71
SZEMAN, IMRE, 'Who's Afraid of National Allegory? Jameson, Literary Criticism, Globalization', *The South Atlantic Quarterly*, 100.3 (2001), 803-27
THOMPSON, STEPHEN F., 'The Federal Revolution in Venezuela, 1858-1863' (unpublished doctoral thesis, University of Oxford, 1984)
TROCONIS DE VERACOECHEA, ERMILA, *El proceso de inmigración en Venezuela* (Caracas: Academia Nacional de Historia, 1986)
USLAR PIETRI, ARTURO, *Las lanzas coloradas*, ed. by Domingo Miliani (Madrid: Cátedra, 1993)
VALERA, JUAN, *Pepita Jiménez* (Buenos Aires: Editorial Losada, 1939)
VARGAS LLOSA, MARIO, 'Primitives and Creators', *Times Literary Supplement*, 4 November 1968, 1287-88
VASCONCELOS, JOSÉ, *La raza cósmica: misión de la raza iberoamericana: Argentina y Brasil* (Buenos Aires: Espasa-Calpe, 1948)
WILLIAMSON, EDWIN, *The Penguin History of Latin America* (London: Penguin Books, 1992)
WRIGHT, WINTHROP R., *Café con leche: Race, Class, and National Image in Venezuela* (Austin: University of Texas Press, 1990)

INDEX

Acción Democrática 3–4, 28 nn. 9 & 11, 78, 79, 118, 158 n. 3, 159 n. 22
Ahmad, Aijaz 13, 29 n. 33
La Alborada 4, 7
allegory 1, 13, 14, 17, 18–19, 20, 21, 29 nn. 33, 35 & 41, 30 nn. 53 & 55, 34, 36, 37, 42, 85, 91, 107, 165, 166, 167, 168
Alonso, Carlos J. 19, 30 nn. 43 & 53
Anderson, Benedict 11, 12, 28 n. 24, 29 nn. 28 & 29
Araujo, Orlando 80, 113 n. 16, 116 n. 44, 138, 158 n. 11, 160 n. 30
Asociación Cultural Femenina (ACF) 79, 159 n. 22
Asociación Venezolana de Mujeres (AVM) 79, 159 n. 22

Bakhtin, Mikhail 12, 20, 23–27, 31 nn. 64, 65 & 66, 32 n 69, 52–53, 72–73 nn. 25 & 26
barbarism 7, 19, 28 n. 17, 103, 153, 155
Benjamin, Walter 14, 29 n. 41
Betancourt, Rómulo 3, 28 n. 16, 79, 158 n. 10, 161 n. 41
Biaggini, Ángel 3
Bolívar, Simón 3, 9, 48
Brennan, Timothy 11, 12, 28 n. 23, 29 n. 31

Carrera, Gustavo Luis 34, 36, 70 n. 4, 158 n. 11
Castro, Cipriano 2, 6, 9, 33, 70 n. 6, 71 n. 9, 158 n. 10
civilization 19, 65, 103, 114 n. 29, 153, 155
class 15, 79, 81, 91, 97, 100, 112 n. 9
 caudillo system 5, 6, 8, 9, 27 n. 4, 33, 34, 35–36, 63, 70 nn. 2 & 9, 116 n. 38, 117, 119, 121, 140
 criollo hierarchy 36, 41, 49, 55–56, 69, 70, 77, 83, 87, 88, 96, 101, 111, 119, 121, 128, 145, 150, 165–66
Cohen, Henry 78, 112 n. 8, 114 n. 29
El cojo ilustrado 7, 28 n. 13
Collins, Wilkie, *The Moonstone* 136
colonialism 11, 12, 13, 29 n. 33, 98, 100–01
corruption 35, 46, 148
cuadros de costumbres 151, 162 n. 46

Díaz Seijas, Pedro 75, 112 n. 1, 118, 138, 156, 158 n. 6, 160 n. 29, 163 n. 51
Dunham, Lowell 20, 27 n. 1, 28 n. 13, 31 n. 59, 70 n. 1, 112 n. 4, 120, 158 n. 8, 159 n. 13, 160 n. 30

educational system 4, 6, 35, 79, 116 n. 39,
Emerson, Caryl 24, 25, 31 nn. 64 & 67, 32 n. 69, 72 n. 25
Ewell, Judith 2, 27 n. 5, 28 nn. 10 & 11, 35, 70 nn. 6 & 8, 71 n. 9, 74 n. 41, 112 n. 3, 116 n. 38, 117, 158 nn. 4 & 9, 160 n. 26, 161 n. 42
Federal Revolution 75–76, 78, 81, 82, 87, 90, 92, 96, 99, 102, 103–06, 110, 112 nn. 7 & 14
First World War 147
Freud, Sigmund, *The Interpretation of Dreams* 114 n. 21, 148, 161 n. 43, 162 n. 44
Friedman, Elisabeth J. 79, 113 n. 15, 159 n. 22
Fuentes, Carlos 73 n. 29, 115 n. 36

Gallegos, Rómulo:
 novels:
  Canaima 1, 2, 8, 9, 15, 17, 20, 22, 27, 28 n. 12, 33–73, 76, 77, 79, 80, 111, 119, 125, 156, 158 n. 12, 159 n. 16, 160 n. 24, 164, 165–66, 167, 168
  Cantaclaro 71 n. 19, 80
  Doña Bárbara 3, 8, 9, 15–19, 22, 30 nn. 44, 51, 53 & 55, 33, 34, 46, 64, 71 nn. 10, 16 & 19, 72 n. 24, 73 n. 29 & 33, 79, 80, 93, 95, 115 nn. 32 & 33, 116 n. 37, 119, 121, 125, 131, 133, 136, 142, 151, 159 n. 21, 160 nn. 23, 24 & 36, 162 n. 46, 164, 165, 166, 168
  El forastero 27 n. 3, 112 n. 1, 158 n. 6
  Pobre negro 1, 2, 8, 10, 15, 17, 18, 19, 20, 22, 27, 28 n. 12, 30 nn. 56 & 58, 69, 70, 75–116, 117, 118, 119, 120, 121, 125, 131, 156, 157, 158 n. 6, 164, 165, 166, 167, 168
  Sobre la misma tierra 1, 2, 8, 10, 15, 17, 20, 22, 27, 30 nn. 56 & 58, 69, 70, 77, 111, 112 n. 1, 115 n. 32, 117–63, 164, 165, 166, 167, 168

La trepadora 8, 18, 22, 71 n. 10
El último Solar/Reinaldo Solar 8, 18, 28 n. 19, 115 n. 33
political career: 3, 4, 33
political exile: 3, 4, 8, 33, 34, 74 n. 41, 76, 164
socio-political writings:
'Ante su juicio yo concluyo y espero' 10, 19, 134, 158 n. 8
'Las causas' 4, 5, 28 n. 14, 70 n. 2, 77
'Los congresos' 6
'Constancia puesta en empeño de iluminación' 10, 119, 143, 156, 158 n.8, 160 n 26
'El factor educación' 6, 116 n. 39
'Había aquí una lección por dar' 10, 79, 131
'Hombres y principios' 6, 7
'Necesidad de valores culturales' 4, 6, 7, 28 nn. 13 & 15, 116 n. 39
'Los poderes' 5, 122
'Por los partidos' 6
'La pura mujer sobre la tierra' 1, 27 n. 1, 93, 113 n. 21, 131, 160 n. 28,
'Una renuncia' 8, 70 n. 1
'Soy un hombre que desea el orden' 10, 75, 76, 112 n. 4, 115 n. 35
'Las tierras de Dios' 8–9, 33, 36, 63
'El verdadero triunfo' 5, 6, 91, 115 n. 31
García Márquez, Gabriel 13
gender 4, 17, 70, 77, 79, 109, 111, 112 n. 14, 130, 159 n. 22
geographical location 5, 25, 35, 165
Gómez, Juan Vicente 2–3, 6, 8, 9, 28 n. 8, 33, 35, 70 nn. 8 & 9, 74 n. 41, 75, 76, 78, 79, 118–20, 134, 139, 158 n. 10, 164
gomecismo 7–8, 33, 34, 35, 75, 157, 164
Guajira Peninsula 120, 135–36, 142–50, 160 n. 26, 165
Guajiro Indians 123, 143, 151
  beliefs 131
  superstitions 145
  traditions 120–21, 135, 145–46, 160 n. 24
Guayana *see* Venezuelan Guayana

heterosexual romance 14–15, 17, 19, 20, 22, 26, 30 n. 52, 85, 103, 105, 108–09, 111, 121, 125, 131, 136, 143, 157, 166, 167
hombría 37, 39, 40, 46, 61, 64, 140

immigration 78, 114 n. 29
incest 113 n. 21, 122, 125, 140–42, 161 n. 37
indigenismo 116 n. 39
indigenous population 12, 17, 77, 120, 150–51
individualismo 9, 28 n. 20

Isea, Antonio 81, 87, 113 n. 18, 114 n. 30

Jackson, Richard 87, 114 n. 28
James, Henry 21
Jameson, Fredric 12–13, 14, 29 nn. 32, 33, 34 & 35, 162 n. 44

Kermode, Frank 21–24, 26, 31 nn. 60, 61, 62 & 63

land 4, 16, 65, 91, 98, 133–40, 142, 150
landscape 5, 49, 57, 137, 143, 160 n. 24
Larsen, Nella, *Quicksand* 136
Latin American:
  literature 14–17, 87, 114 n. 28, 168
  politics 7, 11–12, 14, 13, 14, 29 n. 28, 150 n. 26
Leo, Ulrich 20, 30 nn. 56, 57 & 58, 80, 84, 85, 103, 105, 113 n. 16, 114 nn. 22 & 24, 116 nn. 41 & 43, 118, 120, 155, 158 n. 6, 159 n. 13, 162 nn. 48 & 49
Liscano, Juan 49, 60, 71 n. 19, 72 n. 22, 73 n. 31, 76, 85, 112 n. 5, 114 n. 23, 117, 118, 136, 138, 157 n. 2, 158 nn. 6 & 11, 160 nn. 27 & 31
Lombardi, John V. 34, 70 nn. 5 & 9
López Contreras, Eleazar 3, 10, 117

Marban, Hilda 86, 114 n. 27
Mariátegui, José Carlos 36
Marinone, Mónica 19, 30 n. 49, 75, 86, 95, 112 n. 1, 114 n. 27, 115 n. 33
Medina Angarita, Isaías 3, 117
mestizaje 4, 6, 19, 36, 43–44, 69, 71 n.10, 77, 79–80, 82, 84–87, 101, 111, 113 n. 16, 165, 167
modernity 119- 22, 126, 144–45, 148–50, 152, 153
modernization 4, 8, 35, 119, 164
Monagas, José Tadeo 99, 116 n. 38
Morson, Gary Saul 24, 25, 31 n. 67, 32 n. 69
myth 12, 45, 145

narrative framework 18, 19, 69, 80, 108, 111, 167
narrative structure 14, 20, 23, 44, 49, 111, 120, 168
national romance 16–17, 29 n. 42, 41, 120, 166
nationhood 11–13, 15, 18–20, 69 70, 118, 164, 166
nation-building 12, 14
nation-family 15, 18, 36, 70, 77–78, 80, 87, 100, 110–11, 114 n. 29, 118, 143, 165, 166,
Navarrete Orta, Luis 13, 29 n. 38
neo-colonialism 120–21, 150, 160 n. 24
New York 8, 9, 33, 135, 144, 148, 150,
North America 15, 28 n. 20, 29 n. 33, 30 n. 43, 120, 139, 140, 144, 145, 147, 148
La novela de la tierra 16, 30 nn. 43 & 53, 73 n. 29
La novela del petróleo 158 n. 11

oil industry 2, 10, 117, 119–20, 134, 138, 144, 147–48, 150, 158 n. 11

Pacheco, Carlos 1, 27 nn. 2 & 3
Partido Democrático Nacional (PDN) *see* Acción Democrática
patriarchy 15–18, 118, 166, 36, 38, 70, 83, 97, 101, 102, 105, 107, 112–13 n. 14, 113 n. 19, 118–20, 133, 138, 140, 142, 165, 166, 167
Pérez Jiménez, Marcos 4
Perús, Françoise 36, 44, 45, 52, 60, 71 nn. 11 & 15, 72 n. 23, 73 n. 32, 74 n. 44
Potelet, Janine 36, 60, 71 n. 12, 73 nn. 31 & 36
progress 1, 2, 7, 14–16, 18, 20, 34–37, 47, 64, 67, 69, 75–77, 79, 86, 91, 97, 111, 114 n. 29, 115 n. 32, 118–20, 157, 158 n. 12, 164, 166
provincial towns 51–56, 61, 67, 72 n. 26
psychoanalysis 113 n. 21, 148, 161–62 n.43,

race 5, 15, 18–19, 30 n. 47, 36, 44, 69–70, 77, 81, 100, 101, 111, 112 nn. 8 & 9, 114 n. 29, 119, 136, 144, 166
   interracial romance 16, 19, 37, 44, 69, 80–87, 102, 107, 114 n. 25, 116 n. 42, 167
   racial politics 11, 12, 17, 18, 40, 78, 82, 84–85, 97, 98, 101, 102–05, 108, 109–11, 113 n. 18, 157, 167
Rappaport, Joanne 17, 30 n. 45, 162 n. 45,
regionalism 5, 10, 121
Renan, Ernest 11, 19, 28 n. 23, 29 n. 26
Rodríguez Sánchez, Juan Gregorio 60, 61, 73 n. 31
Rojas Guardía, Armando 49, 71 n. 19
rubber industry 35, 59, 60, 70 n. 7
rural regions 35, 119, 135, 146, 162 n. 45

Schärer Nussberger, Maya 44–45, 50, 60, 67, 71 nn. 15 & 20, 73 n. 31, 74 n. 42
Scocozza, Antonio 7, 20, 27 n. 3, 28 nn. 18 & 22, 31 n. 59, 75, 76, 112 n. 2, 113 n. 16, 118, 138, 158 nn. 6 & 7, 158 n. 11, 160 n. 30

Second World War 147, 157 n. 1, 161 n. 42
sexual politics 38, 42–43, 81–84, 86–87, 94, 108, 115 n. 32, 121–23, 127–30, 136–37, 141–42, 161 n. 37
Skurski, Julie 19, 30 nn. 51 & 52
Sommer, Doris 14–16, 17–21, 29 nn. 39, 40 & 42, 30 nn. 44 & 52, 133, 160 n. 23
space 23–25, 27, 31 nn. 63 & 66, 54, 61, 92, 125
   temporal-spatial matrix: 25–27, 49, 51–52, 66, 68, 72–73 n. 26
   see also time
Sullivan, William 35, 70 n. 8, 74 n. 41
Szeman, Imre 13, 29 n. 35

time 1, 2, 19, 20–27, 31 nn. 65 & 66, 37, 44–45, 48–49, 51–54, 55–56, 61–62, 63, 65, 68–69, 71 n. 17, 72 nn.25 & 26, 75, 76, 104, 145, 146, 148, 166, 168

Vargas Llosa, Mario 13
Venezuelan Guayana 34–35, 37, 41, 45–47, 52–58, 63–69, 70 n. 6, 71 n. 20, 74 n. 40, 158 n. 12, 165
Venezuelan history 74 nn. 40 & 44, 76, 81–82, 99, 133, 140
Venezuelan politics 33, 70–71 n. 9, 76, 96, 113 n. 16, 118–19
   social injustice 45–46, 59
   social reform 36, 47, 63–64, 69, 111, 122–24, 130–32, 138, 144, 154–56, 166
   socio-political problems 9, 29 n. 33, 34, 117–18, 120
Venezuelan War of Independence 48
violence 14, 35, 50, 57, 60, 65–66, 67, 74 nn. 40 & 41, 93, 112 n. 3, 142
women's emancipation 78–79, 95–96, 132, 159 n. 22
Wright, Winthrop R. 78, 112 nn. 9 & 10, 114 n. 29

Yarrington, Doug 18–19, 30 n. 47, 75, 112 n. 2

www.ingramcontent.com/pod-product-compliance
Lightning Source LLC
Chambersburg PA
CBHW071452150426
43191CB00008B/1326